To "First published February, 2019. Reprinted June, 2020. Printed in the USA.
Cover & layout design by Kim Littani.

This book has been developed independently of the IB and Themantic Education has no affiliation with the IB. All opinions expressed in this work are those of the author and of Themantic Education.

All images are used with license from bigstockphoto.com or from creative commons media, including wikicommons and pixabay.com. Any infringement is accidental and if informed of any breach, we will happily make amendments to future editions of this work.

For orders and new products, please visit our website: www.themantic-education.com

Facebook Group for Teachers: ThemEd's IB Psychology Teachers
Facebook Group for Students: ThemEd's IB Psychology Students
IB Psychology Blog: www.themantic-education.com/ibpsych
YouTube channel: Themantic Education

Got any feedback? While we've worked really hard to make this book as good as possible, we're aware that things can always improve. If you have any ideas, suggestions or questions about this book, please contact Travis at tdixon@themantic-education.com

Acknowledgements

Thank you to the ThemEd Team: Hannah and Ailiya for your help with logistics, Tara and Merrill for your tireless work in copyediting and proofreading, Kim for the excellent design work on all of our products, Evan for organizing all of our logistics and Jamie for managing the digital and online resources.

ISBN: 978-0-473-43173-0

Contents

How to Use This Book

This revision book accompanies our textbook, *IB Psychology: A Student's Guide*. It covers everything needed for the IB Psychology exam, including the Abnormal Psychology and Human Relationships options. Whereas the textbook is designed to be used on a daily basis and is written in a conversational and explanatory tone, this revision book includes only the essential details and facts needed to ace the exam. With this in mind, here are some tips on how to use this book:

1)   Support and Supplement

I recommend using this as a supporting text to read and revise after you have already had an attempt at learning this material in your daily lessons and with the help of the textbook and your teacher. Even though the content has been reduced to exactly what you need for the IB exams, there is still a lot of content. Therefore, it is important you are taking the time in your course and with your teacher's help to understand the content.

2)   Feel Free to Deviate

For nearly every topic in the IB Psychology course, the student's guide textbook, *IB Psychology: A Student's Guide,* offers multiple ways for you to answer each question. For example, there are three or four possible examples of localization of brain function that are covered in the textbook. For multiple reasons, I have included only one of those in this revision book. That is not to say that you can't use an example not included in this book. In fact, it can be to your advantage to design some of your own revision resources for other ways of addressing the exam questions because this will help your answer stand out from the rest. It would be difficult, if not impossible, for you to create all of your own revision materials in the detail provided in this book, so remember to pick your battles.

3)   Revise Regularly

Learning is the result of regular revision, so I would recommend having this book from the beginning of the course and using it to re-read and revise topics that you are covering in your regular classes. If you wait until right before the exams to try to cram all of this information into your brain, you probably won't succeed.

4)   Play to Your Strengths

If you're using our student's guide textbook, there are many ways to address some topics, especially those in the biological approach, as has been mentioned already. Therefore, it can be a good idea to try to learn as much as possible throughout the course (of course), but wait until you've covered all units in your course before figuring out which examples you want to use for each topic. This will also help you identify the overlaps between Paper One and Paper Two that you want to exploit.

A Note on the Text

This revision book relies primarily on the studies and concepts used in our textbook, *IB Psychology: A Student's Guide*. I was hesitant to add any new studies to this revision textbook. However, a few new studies have been added because of the changes to the IB Psychology curriculum that were made after the publication of our original textbook. All new studies have been chosen for their relevance and their simplicity, so this will not add extensively to your revision. You will be able to achieve top marks without learning any new studies, but they are included to give you more options and flexibility when preparing to write exam answers.

Good luck!

General Revision Tips

Paper One – Section A

- All possible topics in the core could be asked as a short answer question and you have to answer all SAQs. Therefore, prepare one central argument and one supporting study for every *topic* from all three *approaches*.

Paper One – Section B

- You only have to write one essay and you will have a choice on which approach you write your essay about (biological, cognitive or sociocultural). Therefore, choose one approach that you want to specialize in and prepare to write an essay for this approach in Section B (see the 3-2-1 approach below).

Paper Two

- There are three topics per option and one question will be from each topic in Paper Two. Therefore, you can adopt a 3-2-1 approach for the options as well (see below).
- For example, you might become an expert in explanations of disorders, followed by treatments and you can largely ignore the issues in diagnosis.

3-2-1 Approach

- Whenever you have choice in the exam questions you answer, you can adopt a 3-2-1 approach: become an expert in one topic choice, have a second one as a backup, and ignore the third.
- For example, you might prepare to write essays about any topic in the biological approach for Paper 1, have the cognitive approach as a backup, and largely ignore the sociocultural approach.

Paper Three

- Don't revise any more than is necessary – look at how many points are required for each question and be sure to prepare accordingly.
- For example, you get three marks for describing the research method used, which means you have to state the method (1 mark) and two characteristics of that method (2 marks). You do not need to evaluate the method, so revising this would be a waste of time for Paper 3.

Find Overlaps

- The same arguments and studies can be used in topics throughout the core and options. Therefore, study smarter and not harder by trying to find these overlaps. For example, you could revise the use of SSRIs as a treatment for PTSD as well as an example of how neurotransmission can affect behaviour.

3 Steps to Learn Anything

1. Find out what you need to know (use the key questions and the syllabus outlines to guide you).
2. Find your knowledge gaps (what you don't know).
3. Fill your knowledge gaps!

EXAM OVERVIEWS

Assessment	Time	Weighting	
		SL	HL
Internal Assessment (IA)	20hrs	25%	20%
Paper One	2hrs	50%	40%
Paper Two	1hr (SL) 2hrs (HL)	25%	20%
Paper Three (HL Only)	1hr	-	20%

Paper	Contents
Paper One **Core Approaches**	**Section A – Short Answer Responses (Total = 27 marks)** • Three short answer questions (9 marks each) • One from each approach (Biological, Cognitive, Sociocultural) • Answer *all* three questions **Section B – Essay (Total = 22 marks)** • Three essay questions • One from each approach (Biological, Cognitive, Sociocultural) • Answer *one* question • *HL: at least one question from the extension topics*
Paper Two **Options**	• 12 essay questions in total • Three from each option • One from each topic within each option **Standard Level (Total = 22 marks)** • Write an essay response to *one* question from *one* option **Higher Level (Total = 44 marks)** • Write *two* essay responses • One from two different options o E.g. One from the abnormal option and one from human relationships option.
Paper Three (HL ONLY) **Research Methodology**	**Question 1** • Three questions (3 marks each, 9 marks total) • Answer all three questions **Question 2** • One question about ethical considerations (6 marks) **Question 3** • One question (9 marks) **Total = 24 marks**

2 Biological Approach

Biological Approach to Understanding Human Behaviour

Topic	Content
The brain and behaviour	<ul><li>Techniques to study the brain in relation to behaviour</li><li>Localization</li><li>Neuroplasticity<ul><li>*Neural networks*</li><li>*Neural pruning*</li></ul></li><li>Neurotransmitters and their effect on behaviour<ul><li>*Synapse (excitatory and inhibitory)*</li><li>*Agonists and antagonist*</li><li>*Neurons*</li></ul></li></ul>
Hormones and pheromones and behaviour	<ul><li>Hormones</li><li>Pheromones</li></ul>
Genetics and behaviour	<ul><li>Genes and behaviour</li><li>Genetic similarities<ul><li>*Twin and kinship studies*</li></ul></li><li>Evolutionary explanations for behaviour</li></ul>
Ethical considerations and research methods	<ul><li>Students need to understand the use of research methods and relevant ethical considerations for each <u>topic</u>.</li></ul>

Terms it italics <u>may</u> be used in short-answer questions from May 2020 onwards.

Biological Approach to Understanding Human Behaviour

	Content	Key Questions	Key Studies
The brain and behaviour	**Techniques used to study the brain in relation to behaviour**	*How and why are one or more technological techniques used to study the brain in relation to human behaviour?*	• Passamonti et al., 2012 • Radke et al., 2015 • Plus others…
	Localization	*How have one or more examples of localization of brain function been determined?*	• Feinstein et al., 2011 • Ahs et al., 2009
	Neuroplasticity	*How can one or more examples of neuroplasticity be demonstrated in research?*	• Luby et al., 2013 • Sapolsky et al., 1990
	Neurotransmitters and their effect on behaviour	*How can one or more neurotransmitters affect human behaviour?*	• Moore et al., 2002 • Passamonti et al., 2012 • Pucilowski et al., 1985
Hormones & pheromones	**Hormones and behaviour**	*How can one or more hormones affect human behaviour?*	• Radke et al., 2015 • Albert et al., 1986 • Buchanan and Lovallo & Sapolsky (cortisol)
	Pheromones and behaviour	*How might pheromones affect human behaviour?*	• Cornwell et al., 2004 • Saxton et al., 2008
Genetics & behaviour	**Genes and behaviour**	*How can genes affect human behaviour?*	• Meyer-Lindenberg, 2008 • Caspi et al., 2002
	Genetic similarities	*How are genetic similarities in twin and kinship studies used to study genes and human behaviour?*	• Baker et al., 2007 • Grove et al., 1990 • Mason (1994)
	Evolutionary explanations for behaviour	*How can evolution explain one or more human behaviours?*	• Feinstein et al., 2011 • Ahs et al., 2009

All answers should be supported by evidence. Essay responses in Paper 1, Part B should include critical evaluation of the answer and the evidence. Students should also be prepared to discuss research methods and ethical considerations related to the relevant studies for the above <u>topics</u>.

Techniques to Study the Brain

Functional magnetic resonance imaging (fMRI)
How and why are technological techniques used to study the brain?

FMRIs are used in experimental research to see how chemical messengers can influence brain activity. This can provide deeper understanding of how those messengers can affect behaviour.

Key Details

- **Functional magnetic resonance imaging (fMRI)** machines measure the *activity (or function)* of areas of the brain when the participant is performing a task or cognitive process.
- They are often used in experimental research where the level of a chemical messenger is the IV (e.g. serotonin or testosterone levels).
- Participants receive a treatment (e.g. injection with a treatment or placebo) and then lay in the fMRI. They are then asked to perform a task (like viewing different types of faces). The task they perform is related to the behaviour being studied. For instance, viewing different types of emotional faces is designed to represent experiencing a social threat. Their brain activity is then measured while they are performing this task. By doing this, the researchers can see how chemical messengers can affect activity in certain parts of the brain during certain tasks, like perceiving a social threat.

- These studies provide greater insight into how chemical messengers like neurotransmitters (e.g. serotonin) and hormones (e.g. testosterone) may influence behaviour because of their influence on brain function (e.g. in areas such as the amygdala and prefrontal cortex).
- The use of fMRIs in this way could help to develop an understanding of origins of behaviours such as violence and symptoms of PTSD by showing us how chemical messengers associated with particular behaviours can also impact brain activity.

Key Studies

All of these studies investigate the effects of biological variables on brain activity (e.g. the PFC).

Serotonin's effects on the PFC and amygdala during social threat (Passamonti et al., 2012): The fMRI results in this study showed depleted serotonin reduced PFC activity when participants were viewing angry faces (i.e. facing a threat) and disrupted communication between the amygdala and the PFC. *(See page 18)*

Testosterone's effects on the amygdala (Radke et al., 2015): The results of this study showed that injecting testosterone increases activity in the amygdala when motivated to approach a threatening face. *(See page 20)*

SSRIs and PFC function (MacNamara et al., 2016): The fMRIs used in this study showed how SSRIs can improve PFC function when perceiving emotional stimuli (e.g. faces showing different emotions). *(See page 136)*

Exam Tips

- The guide says you can study "one or more technological techniques." It is advisable to focus on *technological techniques* as opposed to others (e.g. experimental methods, animal studies, post-mortem studies, etc.)
- Top marks will be given to answers that can explain *how* and *why* the technique is used, as well as showing this in example studies.
- To cut down on studies you have to remember, a good revision strategy is to prepare to use the same studies for techniques, research methods and ethical considerations.

- Localization of brain function studies: fMRIs can also be used to study localization of brain function. In these studies, participants are put in an fMRI and they are asked to perform certain cognitive tasks (or other types of tasks) while the machine measures their brain activity. From this, psychologists can see which parts of the brain are used when doing certain tasks, so they can conclude that the activated areas of the brain must have some function in the behaviours being performed.
- An example of this can be seen on studies involving **cognitive reappraisal** – the process of reinterpreting or reassessing an emotional stimulus to change the emotional impact it might have. An example of this would be thinking about something as being harmless so as to reduce the fear response. Studies like this have shown that the vmPFC is vital in this process and can also downregulate activity in the amygdala, which may explain how it reduces the stress response.
- Other examples include flashing emotional stimuli on the screen and seeing which part of the brain is activated. Studies like this have shown the function of the amygdala in unconscious perception of emotional stimuli.

Further Studies

Urry et al., 2012: In this study, 19 healthy participants were exposed to a range of emotional stimuli that were flashed on a screen while they were in an fMRI machine. They were asked to cognitively reappraise the stimuli by either increasing, decreasing or attending - they could "increase" by imagining the scene happening to someone they loved, "decrease" by imagining it wasn't real or "attend" by simply focusing on the details of the image. The results showed a negative correlation between vmPFC and amygdala activation – the higher the vmPFC activity, the lower the amygdala activation. This could explain the common finding of hypofunction and reduced volume in the vmPFC in patients with PTSD.

Ahs et al., 2009: The amygdala in the perception of fearful stimuli by Ahs et al. (2009): Female participants who identified as having a fear of snakes or spiders were placed in a brain imaging machine (PET) and were exposed to various images – some of snakes or spiders, others of neutral stimuli. The activation in their amygdala was higher when they were perceiving images of the stimuli they were afraid of (i.e. snakes or spiders) than when perceiving neutral images. This study shows the use of positron emission tomography (PET) which, like fMRI, measures brain activity during cognitive tasks. Participants are injected with a mild-dose of radiation and the areas of the brain that are active during a task light up on the screen. Ahs et al.'s use of PET can help us learn about how the amygdala is involved in emotion and perceiving threat.

Critical Thinking Considerations

- Participants have to lie completely still in an fMRI. How could this factor affect the generalizability of fMRI studies?
- Are results from fMRI studies inherently inhibited by a lack of validity? (You might want to consider mundane realism, ecological validity or construct validity)
- What are some other limitations of using fMRI? For example, what does an MRI tell us that an fMRI cannot?
- Are there ethical issues to consider with the use of fMRI?
- Technology is always evolving. How could brain imaging technology evolve in the future to increase its validity in the study of behaviour?

Localization of Brain Function

The amygdala and the stress response

How have one or more examples of localization of brain function been determined?

Particular parts of the brain are responsible for performing certain functions. This is a concept known as localization of brain function. One example is the function of the amygdala, which is to perceive threats and activate the stress response so we can experience fear. We know this from animal studies, fMRI studies and case studies.

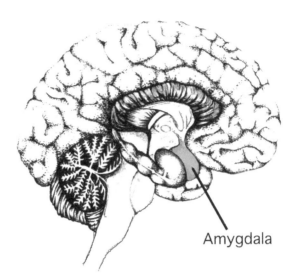

Amygdala

Key Details

- **Localization of brain function** means particular parts of the brain perform particular functions.
- The **amygdala** is a small almond-shaped part of the brain and is part of the limbic system, which is located within the temporal lobe (there is one amygdala on each side of the brain).
- The amygdala is called the emotional center of the brain because of its role in emotion and the stress response.
- One key function of the amygdala is that it perceives things that are threatening or dangerous and it activates our stress response. It does this by activating the HPA-axis, which results in the release of stress hormones (like cortisol and adrenaline) that help us experience the sensation of fear and trigger a fight or flight response.

Key Study

A case study of SM and the amygdala's function in fear (Feinstein et al. 2011): The aim of this study was to see if the amygdala plays a role in the experience of fear. SM is a patient with bilateral amygdala damage due to a genetic condition. This study followed prior studies that showed she had impairment in other fear-related behaviours, like fear conditioning and the ability to recognize fear in other people. The researchers tried to induce fear by taking her to a pet store (with snakes, spiders etc), a haunted house and showed her scary film clips to see if she would be afraid. They also gathered data on her life by using self-report questionnaires and interviews. The results of the study showed that none of these experiences caused her to feel afraid. For example, when she was in the pet store she wanted to touch and play with the large, dangerous snakes. When she was in the haunted house she was excited and did not show fear and in fact, she even accidentally scared one of the "monsters." SM's lack of emotional response to stimuli means she won't release cortisol to facilitate memory of emotional (e.g. fearful) situations. This could explain why she has repeatedly found herself in danger, including being in an abusive relationship for many years and being held at knifepoint - her lack of a fear response means she does not learn to avoid dangerous situations. From SM's case study, we can conclude that the amygdala is a key part of the brain that is responsible for our ability to experience fear.

Exam Tips

- SM is good for a SAQ. Add Ahs et al. for an essay.
- The examples in this topic could also be applied to evolutionary explanations of fear, as well as the use of technological techniques to study the brain.
- A common error is to describe a relevant study but not to clearly explain *how* it demonstrates the particular function of a part of the brain.
- Another good example that could be used for this topic is the vmPFC and its role in decision-making (Bechara et al.) and cognitive reappraisal (Urry et al.).

Extension: Evolutionary Explanation

- The function of the amygdala in perceiving threats, activating the stress response and inducing the emotion of fear is an evolutionary adaptation. This is because the amygdala's function of immediately and automatically activating the stress response in response to threat, including the release of stress hormones like adrenalin and cortisol, allows us to have the quick burst of alertness and energy we may need to escape from or confront our source of danger.

- Another interesting finding of the amygdala is that it can perceive threatening stimuli before we are consciously aware that we have seen it. This can be tested using an fMRI where images are flashed so quickly that the participant cannot consciously recall seeing any image, but the amygdala's activity increases as the image is presented.

Further Studies

The amygdala in the perception of fearful stimuli by Ahs et al. (2009): Female participants who identified as having a fear of snakes or spiders were placed in a brain imaging machine (PET) and were exposed to various images – some of snakes or spiders, others of neutral stimuli. The activation in their amygdala was higher when they were perceiving images of the stimuli they were afraid of (i.e. snakes or spiders) than when perceiving neutral images. This study provides evidence for the evolutionary explanation of the function of the amygdala in perceiving threats and activating the stress response because we can see that the activation was higher in things that the participants were afraid of (snakes or spiders). In a real-life encounter, the activation of the amygdala would activate the HPA axis (a.k.a. the stress response) and the women would get the burst of stress hormones that would prepare them to deal with the threat.

Critical Thinking Considerations

- The amygdala is not working by itself in the experience of fear – it relies on the interaction of complex neural networks. What other areas of the brain are responsible for experiencing fear? Hint: think about what happens *before* and *after* the amygdala perceives the threatening stimuli.
- How much we experience fear in response to danger is not just affected by the activity in the amygdala. How can our thoughts and/or other parts of the brain influence the stress response? (For help, read about cognitive reappraisal and the vmPFC in the Abnormal Psychology review materials, including Urry et al.'s study).
- Is everyone's amygdalae the same? Do you know of any factors that might affect the function of the amygdala in the fear response? It might be helpful to read Luby et al.'s study on stress and the brain below.
- Both studies above can explain how fear may be induced by the perception of external stimuli. Are they limited in demonstrating the role of the amygdala in experiencing other types of fear?
- What factors may influence the generalizability of the above studies? For example, are they limited in their population validity?
- What are the ethical issues related to SM's and Ahs et al.'s studies?

Neuroplasticity

Stress and the Hippocampus
How can one or more examples of neuroplasticity be demonstrated in research?

Our environment and experiences can change the function and structure of our brain. This is a phenomenon called neuroplasticity. Stress is one factor that can affect neuroplasticity in the hippocampus.

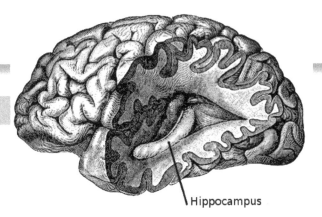

Hippocampus

Key Details

- **Neuroplasticity** is a term that is used to describe the brain's ability to change as a result of experience.
- It was a long-standing belief that our brain development was fixed from a young age. However, animal research (beginning in the 1960s) and modern studies using brain imaging technology have helped to show how the brain can change throughout our lives.
- Numerous studies have found correlations between poverty and brain development, particularly in the hippocampus, an area of the brain associated with learning and memory. This correlation could be explained by a lack of stimulation: our neurons connect to one another and create **neural networks** as we learn new things. If we are deprived of stimulation, then our brains are not developing the neural networks we need to learn and so some areas of the brain (like the hippocampus) might not develop fully.

- Parenting styles and stressful life events might also be mediating variables in the relationship between poverty and brain development. That is to say, poverty might affect parenting and stress which, in turn, affects the hippocampus. This could be because stress releases cortisol and prolonged release of cortisol in the brain has been shown to damage hippocampal neurons (see Sapolsky et al., 1990 in "Further Studies").

Key Study

Poverty and brain development by Luby et al., 2013: The aim of this study was to see if poverty was correlated with brain development and to see if there were mediating variables related to stress and parenting that could explain this relationship. The study was conducted on 145 children over a 10 year period. MRIs were used to measure correlations between poverty, stressful life events and parent-child interactions with hippocampal volume. Interviews and questionnaires were used to measure the children's stressful life events and income of parents was used to measure levels of poverty. The researchers measured the parent-child interactions by giving the child a small gift but telling them they must wait until their parent finishes completing a questionnaire. This is designed to stress the child and to test the patience of the parent. How the parent dealt with the nagging of the child was recorded by researchers standing behind a two-way mirror and interactions between child and parent were recorded. One result showed that the more positive the parent-child interactions were while kids were waiting for the gift, the higher (on average) the hippocampal volume. The results also showed a positive correlation between lower socioeconomic status and hippocampal and amygdala volume (poorer kids = smaller hippocampi and amygdalae). They also found that parenting and stressful life events were mediating variables in this relationship. That is to say, poverty increased stress levels and affected parenting which had an effect on the hippocampus. The study demonstrates neuroplasticity as it shows how childhood experiences can shape the development of important parts of the brain, like the hippocampus and the amygdala.

Exam Tips

- If asked about neuroplasticity in a SAQ, it is advisable to write about a human study (e.g. Luby et al.). However, if asked specifically about *neural pruning*, it is recommended that you include Wei et al. (see below) in your answer, even if only briefly.
- HL: Wei et al.'s study could be used for all topics in the Bio Extension.

Extension: Neural Networks and Neural Pruning

• Research has shown that chronic (long-lasting) stress might have adverse effects on the development of the hippocampus. This could affect the development of **neural networks** in the hippocampus by damaging the neurons and the synaptic connections they make.

• Animal studies have shown that prolonged release of the stress hormone, cortisol, damages neurons in the hippocampus (see Sapolsky et al., 1990 in "Further Studies").

• Stress might also affect the process of **neural pruning**. When we are young, our brains have trillions of neural connections. Some neural networks will be used heavily and will develop strong connections while those that are not needed will decay. This advantageous loss of synaptic connections is called neural pruning. This is an important process because it helps make our most-used neural networks stronger and more efficient.

Further Studies

Early life stress and neural pruning in the hippocampus in mice (Wei et al., 2011). The aim of this study was to see how early life stress in rats might affect the process of neural pruning. In their experiment, they exposed one group of mice to stress by briefly removing them from their litter when they were pups (under 30 days old). They compared these mice to a control group which were not removed. The results showed that the stressed pups had lower levels of an important protein (LBP) in their hippocampus. LBP helps with the neural pruning process by binding to the dendrites connected to unused synapses and helping to remove them. This pruning is an important process because it helps make our hippocampus more efficient. This study provides a possible explanation for why people exposed to early life stress might have cognitive difficulties later in life.

The effects of cortisol on the hippocampus (Sapolsky et al., 1990): The aim of this study was to see if cortisol would damage the hippocampus. One group of rhesus monkeys had a pellet of cortisol surgically inserted into their hippocampi. They were compared to a control group who had a cholesterol pellet inserted. After one year, the monkeys were euthanized and their brains were compared. The results showed the cortisol group had damage to their hippocampal neurons. This study shows how stress might affect neuroplasticity in the brain and may explain why people who experience long-term stress tend to have smaller hippocampi.

Critical Thinking Considerations

• What are the issues with external (and/or internal) validity of these studies? For example, why might it be difficult to generalize the animal studies to humans?

• What are the ethical considerations involved in these studies on the effects of stress on brain development?

• What are the possible applications of understanding how environmental factors such as poverty and stress might influence development of the hippocampus and other areas of the brain? For example, a common finding in people with PTSD is that they have low volume in their hippocampus. How might neuroplasticity explain this finding?

• Could there be a bidirectional explanation for hippocampal volume and poverty?

• Early-life stress has been correlated with cognitive problems in adulthood, such as troubles in learning and memory. How might the effects of stress on LBP explain this?

Neurotransmitters

Serotonin and aggression
How can one or more neurotransmitters affect human behaviour?

Changes in levels of neurotransmitters can influence behaviour. An example of this is the correlation found between serotonin and antisocial behaviour (e.g. aggression). This connection could be explained by looking at how serotonin levels affect activity in the PFC and amygdala.

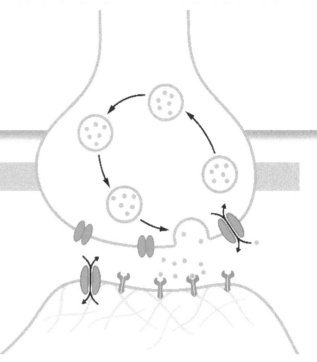

Key Details

- **Neurotransmitters** are chemical messengers that send messages along neural pathways. A variety of neurotransmitters have been identified and associated with different behaviours. One example is **serotonin**, which has been correlated with antisocial behaviour including aggression and violence. The evidence for this comes from human and animal studies.
- Neurotransmitters work by sending signals through the brain by binding to receptor sites on neurons and passing on impulses. A neurotransmitter may be **excitatory**, which means it allows the impulse to cross the **synapse**, or **inhibitory**, which means it prevents the impulse from crossing the synapse (IB Guide, p23). Serotonin is an inhibitory neurotransmitter.

- Neurotransmitters are affected by **agonsts** and **antagonists**. 'An agonist increases the effect of a neurotransmitter, while an antagonist reduces it' (IB Guide, p24).

Key Study

A meta-analysis of serotonin and antisocial behaviour (Moore et al., 2002): This study gathered the results from 20 other studies that investigated relationships between serotonin levels and antisocial behaviour. The results showed a significant overall negative correlation between serotonin levels and antisocial behaviour, with an effect size (ES) of -.45. This means that lower serotonin levels were associated with higher levels of antisocial behaviour. Another result from the study was that the relationship was strongest when age was accounted for. For example, the studies that had participants that were under 30 years old had an average effect size of -1.37, compared with an ES of -.31 for those over 30. This suggests that low levels of serotonin have the greatest effect on antisocial behaviour in young people. This meta-analysis provides strong evidence for the connection between low levels of serotonin and antisocial behaviour. However, it does not give us many reasons *why* this relationship exists.

Exam Tips

- The concepts and research in this topic are also relevant to the use of technology to study the brain (Passamonti et al. in "Further Studies" below) and animal research (HL Ext). There's another example that could be used in the Abnormal Psychology option (SSRIs and PTSD).
- Passamonti's study is the most effective at being able to support an explanation of *how* serotonin might affect aggression – aim to be able to write about this in an SAQ and essay.
- There's a chance that the following terms may be used in SAQs: *synapse (inhibitory/excitatory), agonist and antagonist.* It is not clear how they could be phrased in a question. My advice is to make sure you can explain how these terms relate to the neurotransmission process and then explain a link between serotonin and behaviour using one or more studies to support that explanation – trying to prepare studies that relate to all these terms would be overwhelming.

Extension: Serotonin and the Brain

- One reason why serotonin might influence antisocial behaviour is because it has an effect on important areas of the brain, like the prefrontal cortex.
- Serotonin (a.k.a. 5-HT) is synthesized from tryptophan, an amino acid found in foods like dairy products. Serotonin receptors are highly concentrated in the prefrontal cortex, an area of the brain that enables us to inhibit our impulsive decisions and actions. Dysfunction in this part of the brain could explain violence – if we lack an ability to think through actions and inhibit impulse, we may react violently to a threat or attack without thinking.

- The amygdala is another part of the brain that perceives threatening stimuli and activates the stress response. The PFC works to reduce activation of the amygdala, and thus reduce the stress response. Reduced function or damage in the prefrontal cortex has been correlated with violence and aggression in numerous studies (e.g. Grafman et al.'s report from the Vietnam Head Injury Study showed that war veterans with damage to the vmPFC were more aggressive than those with no damage or damage to other parts of the brain; you can read a full summary on our blog) and researchers hypothesize this link exists because of the PFC's role in regulating our impulsive behaviour.

Further Studies

Effects of injecting serotonin in the amygdala of rats (Pucilowski et al., 1985): For this experiment, the researchers injected rats with 20 micrograms of serotonin in their amygdala and then put them in a cage with another rat to measure the attack latency, which is the time it takes the rat to attack another rat when they're placed in the same cage. In order to make a comparison, they had another condition that involved putting a rat in a cage without any injection of serotonin. The results showed that the serotonin injection increased the time of the attack latency (meaning it reduced aggression).

Serotonin's effects on the brain (Passamonti et al. 2012): The aim of this study was to see what effect reduced serotonin has on the prefrontal cortex (PFC) when exposed to threat. 30 healthy participants participated in this repeated measures, double-blind, placebo-controlled true experiment. They had their levels of serotonin manipulated by either drinking a placebo drink (normal serotonin condition) or a drink that reduced their levels of tryptophan - a key amino

acid in the building of serotonin in the brain (this is the reduced serotonin condition). They were then placed in an fMRI machine and were shown a variety of different faces (angry, happy, sad, etc.) The results showed that participants who had their serotonin levels decreased had reduced function in their PFC when they were perceiving images of angry faces while in the fMRI. The results also showed a disruption in communication between the amygdala and the PFC. The reduced function in the PFC when exposed to angry faces (a threat) could explain serotonins link with aggression – people can't inhibit their impulsive reaction to the threat because the serotonin is affect the part of the brain that helps us to stop acting impulsively. Furthermore, the disruption between the PFC and the amygdala means that the PFC may not be able to reduce the activity and emotion generated in the amygdala. Because serotonin is an inhibitory neurotransmitter, it could be that low levels of serotonin results in disruptions to normal inhibitory processes in the amygdala. The study can be used to show why serotonin dysfunction has been linked with antisocial and aggressive behaviour.

Critical Thinking Considerations

- Besides serotonin, what other factors might affect aggression (e.g. social, cognitive or other biological factors)? What other factors might explain variations in serotonin levels? Are there other factors that might mediate or moderate the relationship between serotonin and aggression?
- What are the validity and/or reliability issues related to the above studies?
- Does not being able to measure serotonin levels in the brain influence the validity of the findings from the above studies?
- How might you explain the correlation between serotonin, antisocial behaviour and age found in Moore et al.'s study? Could the delayed development of the PFC be a factor?
- Are there ethical considerations associated with studying the effects of serotonin on behaviour?

Hormones

Testosterone and aggression
How can one or more hormones affect human behaviour?

Changes in hormone levels can influence human behaviour. This influence might be caused by an effect of the hormone on brain function, particularly the amygdala.

Key Details

- **Hormones** are chemical messengers released by glands in the endocrine system and transported around the body in our blood. Various hormones have been identified and associated with different behaviours. One hormone, testosterone, is associated with aggression.
- Animal experiments using castration and testosterone injections have shown that increasing testosterone causes increased aggression. Human studies have also found positive correlations between testosterone levels and aggression, including studies on violent criminals (meaning there is a link with having higher levels of testosterone and committing more violent crimes).

- **Testosterone** is a sex hormone produced in the testes (in males) and to a lesser extent in the ovaries (in females), so males naturally have higher levels of testosterone than females. This might explain why males are generally more aggressive than females.
- Aggressive behaviour could serve a vital function in maintaining high social status as it can assert social dominance. Testosterone could be key in this relationship between aggression and social dominance and status.

Key Studies

Castration and aggression in rats (Albert et al., 1986): Alpha males were identified from groups of rats. Testosterone levels were manipulated through castration and testosterone replacement. The results showed that when alpha male rats were castrated, they displayed decreased levels of aggression towards other rats placed in the same cage. When they had their testosterone replaced, their aggression returned to normal levels. This study shows a cause-and-effect relationship between testosterone levels and aggressive behaviour in rats. This is similar to some human studies that have also found correlations between social rank and testosterone levels.

Correlations between testosterone and aggression in violent criminals (Ehrenkranz et al., 1974): In this study, the researchers compared the average levels of testosterone for three groups of selected prisoners. One group had high levels of violence and aggressive behaviour, the second group were "socially dominant" and the third group were nonaggressive and nondominant prisoners. The results showed that the average testosterone levels were higher in the first two groups than in the third. This suggests that testosterone levels are also linked with aggressive behaviour and social dominance in human males.

Exam Tips

- Radke et al.'s study (below) provides the best opportunity for a detailed SAR about how testosterone affects behaviour. That being said, it is quite complicated. You can still score high marks by using Albert et al.'s study and Ehrenkranz et al.'s study in a SAR (and use all three for an essay).
- The effects of cortisol on memory is another good example that could be used for the hormones topic (see "Emotion and Cognition" in the cognitive approach).
- The examples in this topic can be used for evolutionary explanations of behaviour, the HL extensions, and origins of conflict.

Extension: Testosterone and the Brain

- Aggression can be broadly defined as a behaviour that is intended to harm or threaten another individual. It can be divided into different types. One type of aggression is "**impulsive-reactive aggression**." This is when someone reacts to a threat without thinking carefully about his or her actions.
- Function in the amygdala could be a mediating variable in the relationship between testosterone and aggression. That is to say, testosterone could increase activity in the amygdala, which increases the chances of reacting violently to threat.

- The amygdala is an area of the brain that activates the stress response when we perceive a threat. Testosterone increases the activity of the amygdala when we are motivated to deal with a threat and this increase in amygdala activity could increase emotional and physiological arousal and cause anger and aggression.
- While it's difficult to explain exactly *how* an increase in amygdala activity may cause aggression, the researchers cite animal studies that show activating the amygdala in animals can cause violent behaviour.

Further Studies

Testosterone's effects on the brain (Radke et al., 2015): The aim of this study was to see how an increase in testosterone may affect the amygdala when people are responding to a threat. 54 healthy female participants received injections of either testosterone or a placebo before viewing images of angry or happy faces. The participants were told to approach or avoid the face by moving a joystick to make the image bigger or smaller. This procedure in the experiment was designed to replicate what happens in real life when we approach or avoid a social situation, e.g. someone getting angry and threatening us. The results showed that the testosterone injection increased activity in the amygdala when the participants were approaching the angry face, but not when they were avoid it. This provides some evidence to suggest the amygdala facilitates aggressive reactions to social threat by increasing physiological and emotional arousal (key ingredients in aggression). That is to say, if someone has high testosterone, feel threatened and have a desire to confront the person threatening them, the testosterone may increase their amygdala activity which activates the "fight response."

Critical Thinking Considerations

- Radke et al.'s study explains impulsive, reactive aggression. Why might it not be able to explain other types of violence and aggression?
- What other factors might affect aggression and violence? Think about social, cultural, cognitive or other biological factors.
- Are there other moderating variables that might influence the relationship between testosterone and aggression? *Hint: the PFC.*
- How might cultural variables explain differences in levels of aggression shown across different groups of people? You can read more about the culture of honor and its link with testosterone in the sociocultural approach materials.
- Do the above studies have any validity or reliability issues? For example, why might it be difficult to generalize studies like Radke et al.'s from an fMRI to a real-life situation?
- Are there ethical issues associated with these studies?

Pheromones

Androstadienone and attraction
How might pheromones affect human behaviour?

Pheromones are chemicals that are released from one animal and affect the behaviour of another. Androstadienone is one chemical that may be acting as a pheromone and affecting attraction in humans. However, it's important to note that there is a strong debate about whether or not pheromones exist in humans.

Key Details

- **Pheromones** are chemical messengers that are secreted by one individual and are detected by another of the same species. They are usually detected by the olfactory system. Whereas hormones circulate within an individual, pheromones have an effect by travelling from one organism to another.
- Studies have shown that pheromones influence animal behaviour, especially behaviours relating to mating. For example, when female dogs are "in heat" they give off pheromones to attract a male.
- The **vomeronasal organ** (aka VNO or Jacobson's organ) is part of the olfactory system and this organ in animals is what detects pheromones. There is no evidence that the vomeronasal organ functions in humans, which is why there is uncertainty about whether or not pheromones can influence human behaviour.
- Studies in animals have shown that pheromones can influence behaviour even when the vomeronasal organ is blocked. This could mean that even though we have a lack of a functioning VNO in humans, our behaviour could still be affected by pheromones.
- **Androstadienone** is a chemical that is called a **putative pheromone** because it hasn't been proven to act as a pheromone in humans yet. Androstadienone is associated with attraction, is secreted under the arms of men and has been shown to have a stronger impact on females than males.

Key Study

Speed dating and androstadienone (Saxton et al., 2008): The aim of this study was to see if androstadienone would have an effect on how attractive females rated males during a speed dating event. During a speed dating event, 25 female participants were given one of three different types of cotton wool plugs in their noses. One was androstadienone with clove oil, another was just clove oil and one was water. They then participated in a speed dating event with 22 male participants. The results showed that in two out of the three tests, females exposed to androstadienone ranked the males as being more attractive than females in the other two groups. These results show that exposure to this pheromone might increase feelings of attraction. This study could provide evidence that androstadienone is acting as a pheromone because it is affecting the behaviour of the females.

Exam Tips

- Material from this topic can also be applied to the formation of relationships.
- The first example shows that androstadienone has an effect and the second example (below) provides possible explanations for *how* it has an effect.

- Androstadienone may work in a similar way to testosterone in that it attracts females by providing a signal of high mate quality.
- We have evolved to behave in ways that will enhance our chances of procreating with someone who will help us have healthy babies with strong genes. Androstadienone might signify an individual has strong genes.
- Similarly, pheromones may be working to signal that a potential mate has good genetic material that is compatible. MHC genes are a set of genes that affect the development of our immune system. To have offspring with strong immune systems, it is best to procreate with someone who has different MHC genes than our own. Yamazaki et al. (1976) showed this to be the case for male mice, who showed a preference for females with different MHC genes. Similar results were also obtained with fish. Human studies like Wedekind's (below) show that we actually prefer the smell of people who have different MHC genes than our own. Pheromones *could be* influencing this preference.

Further Studies

Androstadienone and face preferences by Cornwell et al. (2004): Participants were shown a series of faces that ranged in masculinity. After ranking the faces based on preference for a short or long-term relationship, the participants smelled vials that contained five different chemicals, one of these being androstadienone. The results showed a correlation between preference for masculine faces for a long-term relationship and preference for the smell of androstadienone. This suggests that this pheromone might work as an olfactory signal of good gene quality – if a male gives off high levels of androstadienone it might signify that he has strong genes.

MHC genes in the sweaty t-shirt study (Wedekind, 1995): In this study, 49 women and 44 men were selected for their variety of MHC gene types. The men were given a clean cotton t-shirt to wear for two days. After two days, the shirts were then put into identical boxes equipped with a smelling hole. The women volunteers smelled the shirts and rated them on a scale of 1-10 in terms of its intensity, pleasantness, and sexiness. There were three t-shirts that were similar MHC genes, and three that were from men with dissimilar MHC genes. Where possible, the timings of the smells were during the second week of the women's menstrual cycle (the most fertile stage). Overall, the women preferred the scents of t-shirts worn by men who had MHC genes that were different from their own. Interestingly, this was not the case if they were taking oral contraceptives (the pill).

The vomeronasal organ and pheromones in pigs (Dorries et al., 1997): This experiment aimed to see if the VNO is necessary in order for pheromones to have an effect. Previous studies had shown that exposing a female pig to androstenone causes the pig to adopt a mating readiness stance (i.e. she is ready to copulate with the male). They exposed two groups of pigs to androstenone, except one group had their VNO blocked and the other group didn't. The results showed that even when the VNO is blocked, the androstenone still has an effect. This suggests that even if the VNO does not function in humans, pheromones may still affect our behavior.

Critical Thinking Considerations

- What are the possible applications of understanding how androstadienone affects attraction? Are there ethical issues related to these applications?
- Are there other factors that might be influencing attraction? (see the 'Formation of Personal Relationships' topic in Human Relationships).
- Are there any ethical considerations in the above studies?

Genes and Behaviour

The MAOA ("Warrior") Gene and Aggression
How can genes affect human behaviour?

Expression of the MAOA gene could affect brain activity, which is why it might be linked with aggressive behaviour. However, genes alone cannot explain aggression and environmental factors are also important to consider.

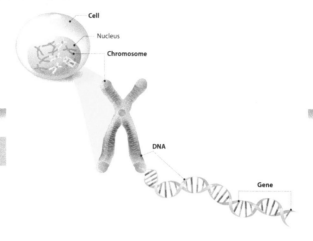

Key Details

- **Genes** are sequences of DNA that are found in chromosomes in cells. When a gene is expressed, it sends messages from the cells that trigger other reactions in the body, including neurotransmission activity in the brain. The effects of this gene expression on brain activity could be how genes can influence human behaviour.
- One specific gene that may affect behaviour is the **monoamine oxidase A (MAOA) gene**. It has been named "the warrior gene" by the media because of its correlations with aggressive behaviour.
- **Gene expression** of the MAOA gene produces an enzyme (monoamine oxidase A) that affects neurotransmission.

- Some variants of the MAOA gene have lower gene expression. These variants are collectively known as MAOA-L. The reduced expression could explain why studies have shown that people with the MAOA-L gene variation have differences in brain activity when perceiving emotional stimuli, especially in the PFC and amygdala. This could explain increases in **impulsive-reactive aggression** because the PFC might not be able to reduce the emotion and anger generated in the amygdala, and could fail to inhibit an impulsive reaction to a challenge or threat.

Key Study

MAOA gene variants and brain function by Meyer-Lindenberg et al. (2008): The aim of this study was to see how differences in the MAOA gene (high expression vs. low expression, MAOA-H vs. MAOA-L) affects brain volume (size) and activity when exposed to threat. 142 participants who had either the H or L variant took part in the study. They completed a number of tasks, including having MRIs to measure brain volume and fMRIs to measure brain activity when perceiving angry or fearful faces. The results showed that when exposed to emotional stimuli (angry or fearful faces) activity in the amygdala was significantly higher in MAOA-L participants and there was less activity in their orbitofrontal cortex (a part of the PFC) and their cingulate

cortex (a part of the brain that works with the PFC to reduce amygdala activity). In regards to volume, the results showed that MAOA-L participants had reduced grey-matter volume in their amygdalae as well as smaller volume in other parts called the cingulate gyrus and anterior cingulate cortex (both associated with emotion and behaviour control). These results suggest that the MAOA-L may be linked with aggressive behaviour because it increases activity in the amygdala, which increases emotional reactions to threatening stimuli and it reduces activity in the impulse-control regions of the brain. This means MAOA-L carriers may be prone to impulsive-reactive aggression.

Exam Tips

- For SAQs, the MAOA gene is excellent to write about as it allows for a deep explanation of *how* genes can affect behaviour (by looking at their effect on the brain). In an essay, you can also use the twin and adoption studies (below) to first show that genes do affect aggression and then the MAOA gene study to show *how*.
- The twin and adoption studies in the next section also can be used to show how behaviour is affected by genes (and the environment).
- Biological factors that influence aggression can also be applied as counter-arguments to social explanations of group conflicts (in the Human Relationships option).
- There are also animal studies in the HL Extension that are related to genes and aggression.

Extension

- Other studies have shown that people with the MAOA-L variation *and* have experienced trauma or abuse as a child are more prone to being aggressive and antisocial adults (compared with those who have the MAOA-L gene without adverse childhood experiences). This suggests it is not just genetics – it is the combination of genes and the environment.

Further Studies

Supporting study: Longitudinal study of MAOA-L variants, childhood abuse and antisocial behaviour ("The Dunedin Study") by Caspi et al. (2002): This study followed over 1,000 children in Dunedin, New Zealand over 25 years where researchers took measures every few years. They found that the MAOA-L gene moderated the effects of experiencing child abuse on adult aggression – that is to say, those participants with the MAOA-L gene variant and who were abused were more likely to be antisocial and aggressive adults. If participants experienced abuse as children, they were more likely to be antisocial, but the chances were almost 3 times as high for those with the MAOA-L variation compared with the MAOA-H gene.

See twin and adoption studies in the next topic for additional studies to use to explain links between genes and behaviour.

Critical Thinking Considerations

- Are there other variables that could be influencing aggression? For example, might social, cultural or other biological factors also be influential?
- Are there any validity or reliability issues in the above studies? For example, what are some issues with generalizing the findings from fMRI studies to real-life situations?
- Is there an area of uncertainty with the MAOA gene? We know the MAOA enzyme breaks down serotonin and other neurotransmitters in the synapse so they can be re-used, but why might that affect activity in particular parts of the brain?

Genetic Similarities

Twin and kinship studies

How are genetic similarities in twin and kinship studies used to study genes and behaviour?

The extent to which genetics influences behaviour can be studied by comparing behaviour variations and genetic similarities in twin studies. This can be used in studies on antisocial behaviour and aggression.

Key Details

- Twin and kinship studies are used to determine heritability – the extent to which variations in behaviour can be attributed to genetic factors. For example, 50% heritability for antisocial behaviour means that differences in antisocial behaviour are half (50%) due to genetics, and the other half due to the environment.
- Monozygotic (identical) twins have 100% of their DNA in common, whereas dizygotic (fraternal) twins have 50% of their DNA in common. Twin studies compare similarities in behaviour between monozygotic (MZ) and dizygotic (DZ) twins. Comparing similarities in behaviour between MZ and DZ twins allows researchers to see the extent to which these variations are based on genetics.
- To calculate heritability in twin studies, behaviours are measured in all participants. The average differences in behaviour between MZ twins are compared with averages in differences between DZ twins. Statistical tests are then carried out to produce the measure of heritability.
- Antisocial behaviour is a broad term that includes aggression and violence, but also other forms of undesirable behaviours, including drug use, truancy, delinquency, non-violent crimes, etc. Antisocial behaviour in children is a strong predictor for antisocial and aggressive behaviour in adults.

Key Studies

Twin study on antisocial behaviour (Baker et al., 2007): Over 1,000 MZ and DZ twins and triplets from diverse backgrounds in Southern California were studied. Antisocial behaviours included levels of aggression, psychopathic traits and disordered conduct (e.g. misbehaving). Multiple tests were used to measure levels of antisocial behaviour including self-report, teacher and caregiver questionnaires. The specific heritability scores for the different reporting methods were: caregiver report = 67%, child report = 42% and teacher report = 55%. Generally speaking, the results showed that heritability was around 50%, meaning that antisocial behaviour (including aggression) in children was about 50% genetics and 50% other factors.

Meta-analysis of twin and adoption studies (Mason, 1994): Baker et al.'s findings are supported by a meta-analysis of 12 twin and 3 adoption studies carried out between 1975 and 1994 that showed the same finding – 50% heritability for antisocial behaviour. However, the effects of genetics was stronger in extreme antisocial behaviour, suggesting these types of extremes are more genetically based and less influenced by environmental factors.

Exam Tips

- SAQs might ask specifically about twin and kinship studies, so you should be prepared to write about this.
- Since there is not much to write about Baker et al.'s study, using Mason and/or Grove et al.'s in addition to this could be a good strategy for an SAQ (depending on the question).
- The studies in this topic can also be used in SAQs and essays on genes and behaviour.
- When writing about "research methods," it is important to note that the IB does not consider twin, kinship and adoption studies to be research methods. Instead, these are examples of "correlational studies" because they are testing the strength of the relationship between genes and behaviour (they are seeing how strongly they are correlated).
- If a question asks about "genetic similarities" without mentioning twin and adoption studies, Meyer-Lindenberg's study could be used to explain how people with similarities in specific genes can be studied.

Extension: Adoption Studies

- Kinship studies are studies that use various family members of different genetic relatedness to compare similarities in behaviour.
- Adoption studies compare twins that have been raised together or apart. Using separated MZ twins, psychologists can study heritability because genetics is a controlled variable (they have 100% of their genes in common) and so differences in behaviour can be attributed to environmental factors.

Further Studies

Adoption study on identical twins and antisocial behaviour (Grove et al., 1990): In this study, 32 sets of identical twins were studied. These twins had been separated shortly after birth and were adopted into different families. From this study, the researchers calculated that the heritability of antisocial behaviour in children was 41% and in adults was 28%. This suggests that genetics and environment are contributing factors towards antisocial behaviour. It also suggests that as we get older, the environment might be more of a factor and the influence of genes reduces.

This code will take you to our blog post that has more information about twin and kinship studies on antisocial and aggressive behaviour.

Critical Thinking Considerations

- How does the use of triangulation strengthen the findings of Baker et al.'s study?
- How can twin and adoption studies be used to show that behaviours (like aggression and antisocial behaviour) can be a combination of environmental *and* genetic factors?
- What other factors (besides genetics) could influence antisocial behaviour? Think about social, cultural, cognitive and/or other biological factors.
- Does the variance in heritability calculated in Baker et al.'s study highlight limitations in this correlational methodology? What are some of the other limitations of the methodologies used in these studies? For example, why might studies that identify specific genes be of more value?
- What are the ethical considerations involved in these type of genetics studies?

Evolution and fear
How can evolution explain behaviour?

Evolution can explain the effects of emotion (and cortisol release) on memory because this could help us to survive by allowing us to find food and/or keeping us safe from harm.

Key Details

- An **evolutionary explanation of behaviour** means that the behaviour exists because it helps an individual to pass on their genes by helping them to survive, procreate and/or produce healthy children.
- One behaviour that can be explained from an evolutionary perspective is fear. The amygdala's ability to perceive threats and to generate emotions like fear is essential for our survival. When the amygdala perceives a threat or something dangerous, it activates the HPA axis, which releases stress hormones such as cortisol and adrenaline. This helps us prepare the body for the "fight or flight" response. Preparing the body to deal with danger in this way will help individuals to keep safe and avoid danger.

- In this way, having a healthy fear response is essential to survival (and therefore essential for passing on our genes because if we do not survive we cannot procreate). If our amygdala had not produced the emotion of fear, we might have found ourselves in danger. The case study of SM shows the importance of the amygdala in generating a healthy fear response.

Key Study

A case study of SM and the amygdala's function in fear (Feinstein et al. 2011): The aim of this study was to see if the amygdala plays a role in the experience of fear. SM is a patient with bilateral amygdala damage due to a genetic condition. This study followed prior studies that showed she had impairment in other fear-related behaviours, like fear conditioning and the ability to recognize fear in other people. The researchers tried to induce fear by taking her to a pet store (with snakes, spiders etc), a haunted house and showed her scary film clips to see if she would be afraid. They also gathered data on her life by using self-report questionnaires and interviews. The results of the study showed that none of these experienced caused her to feel afraid. For example, when she was in the pet store she wanted to touch and play with the large, dangerous snakes. When she was in the haunted house she was excited and did

not show fear and in fact, she even accidentally scared one of the "monsters." SM's lack of emotional response to stimuli means she won't release cortisol to facilitate memory of emotional (e.g. fearful) situations. This could explain why she has repeatedly found herself in danger, including being in an abusive relationship for many years and being held at knifepoint - her lack of a fear response means she does not learn to avoid dangerous situations. From SM's case study, we can see that the function of the amygdala in creating a fear response is a healthy evolutionary adaptation. Her case also provides some evidence that a healthy stress response to consolidate emotional memory can help to keep us safe from harm. This could be one reason why our amygdala responds to fearful situations by activating the release of cortisol.

Exam Tips

- The material in this topic is also good for showing how hormones can affect behaviour, localization of brain function, as well as in the cognitive approach to show how emotion can affect cognition.
- When giving an evolutionary explanation of behaviour, it is essential you can clearly explain how that behaviour helps an individual pass on their genes, either by helping it to survive, procreate or have children with healthy genes who are likely to survive.
- This QR code will take you to a video explanation of this topic and the relevant studies.

- When we feel negative emotions (e.g. fear), our stress response is activated and **cortisol** is released. The release of cortisol has been shown to have an effect on **memory consolidation** – the transferring of short-term memory to long-term memory.
- Enhanced memory for positive emotions could help survival, like if we can remember where to find or how to access food. If we were searching for a fresh water supply or food, the ability to remember where we found this would have been a big advantage to our early ancestors.

- In terms of fearful memories, remembering where we had encounters with dangerous animals or events could help us survive as we would be able to remember where and how to avoid them in the future.
- Evolution explains the biological factors that facilitate the behaviour, like the release of cortisol when we are experiencing high levels of emotion.

Further Studies

Cortisol secretion and emotional memory consolidation by Buchanan and Lovallo (2001): 48 participants (24m and 24f) were randomly allocated to receive 20mg of cortisol or a placebo. They were then shown 60 pictures on a TV monitor and told to focus on the images (they were not told it was memory test). The pictures were either "arousing pleasant," "arousing unpleasant" or "non-arousing neutral." Exactly one week later, they came back to the lab and completed a memory test where they had to describe the images to two scorers (who were "blind" to their condition). The results showed that when recalling the images, the cortisol condition recalled more images than the placebo group. Across all participants, the arousing images were recalled significantly more than the non-arousing slides. From these results, we can see that an increase in cortisol (both through the drug and the arousing images) can improve memory of emotional material, which could

be an evolutionary adaptation that would increase the chances of us passing on our genes to our offspring (because it helps us to survive).

The amygdala in the perception of fearful stimuli by Ahs. et al. (2009): This study showed that activation of the amygdala is higher when participants were perceiving images of the stimuli they were afraid of (i.e. snakes or spiders) than when perceiving neutral images. This study provides evidence for the evolutionary explanation of the function of the amygdala in perceiving threats and activating the stress response since we can see that the activation was higher in those images (snakes or spiders) that the participants were afraid of. In a real-life encounter, the activation of the amygdala would activate the HPA axis (a.k.a. the stress response) and the women would get the burst of stress hormones that would prepare them to fight or flee.

Critical Thinking Considerations

- Fear can be explained from an evolutionary (and biological) approach. However, this ignores the role of social and cognitive factors in fear. How can our experience of fear be influenced by the environment (hint: fear conditioning)? In addition, how can our experience of fear be regulated by our internal cognitive processes? Read more about cognitive reappraisal and Urry et al's study in the Abnormal option.
- Excess cortisol over long periods of time has been shown to have a *detrimental* effect on memory through its effect on the hippocampus. Could this also be explained from an evolutionary perspective?
- Is evolution influencing behaviour, or is behaviour influencing evolution?
- SM's amygdala damage comes from a genetic disorder. Could this affect generalizability?

True experiments

How and why are true experiments used in the biological approach?

True experiments (a.k.a. laboratory experiments) *are used when the researchers manipulate an independent variable and create different conditions. Then, as much as possible, they control for all extraneous variables and measure the effects of the independent variable (IV) on the dependent variable (DV). By carefully controlling the extraneous variables, the researchers can maximize the chances that any differences in the DV can be explained by the IV. This allows for conclusions about causality to be made.*

Key Details

*   **True experiments in the biological approach to understanding behaviour**: In this approach, the focus is on the study of relationships between biological variables and behaviour. For this reason, many **true experiments** investigate how biological variables can influence behaviour. In order to do this, experiments are used by having a biological variable as the **independent variable** and the behaviour as the **dependent variable**. In some cases, the dependent variable is activity in the brain, which can be used to explain links between biological factors and behaviour. Many of these studies also use brain imaging technology (like fMRIs), with the dependent variable being brain activity.

Key Studies

The brain and behaviour: In these studies, biological factors such as chemical messengers (including neurotransmitters like serotonin and hormones such as testosterone) are manipulated in laboratory settings and their effects on the brain are measured using fMRI. In these studies, brain activity is the DV. This is helpful when animal experiments have shown causal relationships between biology and behaviour and human subjects are used to understand how brain function might explain this relationship (e.g. testosterone and aggression).

Radke et al., 2015; Passamonti et al., 2012

Hormones and pheromones and behaviour: *See above explanation.* In addition, animal studies allow researchers to manipulate hormones and directly measure their effects on behaviours that could not be studied (ethically) on humans. A good example of this is aggression.

Radke et al., 2015; Albert et al., 1986

Genes and behaviour: *See the animal extensions for more information about how genes can be manipulated in laboratories using genetic knockout techniques.* SL students are encouraged to write correlational studies for genes and behaviour (e.g. twin and kinship studies).

Critical Thinking Considerations

*   Are true experiments inherently limited in generalizability because of their artificial environments?
*   How can correlational studies inform true experiments? Hint: where might a researcher get the idea to manipulate serotonin to measure aggression?
*   What are the ethical considerations associated with true experiments?

Informed consent in true experiments

How and why are ethical guidelines considered in the biological approach?

*At the heart of **ethics** in psychological research is considering the impact the research might have on others, especially the participants. Informed consent is one consideration that can reduce some of the stress and other negative effects of participating in a study. **Informed consent** means you get an agreement from participants that they want to be in the study (consent) and that they are basing this decision on information you have given them (informed).*

Key Details

- In true experiments in the biological approach, **informed consent** is an important consideration because researchers must carefully consider how much information to reveal to participants and when. In true experiments that investigate the biological effects on behaviour, biological factors are often manipulated in some way so the researchers can compare conditions. In order to do this, researchers alter the physiology of participants. If participants are not informed of the possible effects they may experience, this could cause stress and emotional harm. Therefore, in order to ensure a study is ethical, informed consent must first be obtained.

Key Studies

The brain and behaviour: In studies where levels of chemical messengers are manipulated and their effects on the brain are measured, informed consent is an important consideration because researchers often use a blind design and placebos for control conditions. This helps researchers to isolate the biological change (e.g. serotonin or testosterone levels) as the only variable affecting the dependent variable. However, ingesting a substance that alters physiology in a way that is hypothesized to affect the brain is something that participants might find unpleasant. Therefore, researchers need to consider how much information to include in their informed consent forms so as to have a balance between looking after the psychological well-being of participants whilst not jeopardizing the validity of the study through expectancy effects.

Radke et al., 2015; Passamonti et al., 2012

Hormones and pheromones and behaviour: *See above explanation.* In addition, animal studies on the effects of hormones on behaviour also have their own sets of ethical considerations – see the HL extension material

for more information about this.

Radke et al., 2015; Albert et al., 1986

Genes and behaviour: Studies on genetics often focus on sensitive topics like antisocial behaviour. When studying such behaviours (e.g. child abuse and violence), researchers need to consider how this might impact their participants. Since genetics is something that we cannot control, it is especially sensitive. For studies on the MAOA gene, participants need to undergo genetic testing to identify if they have the MAOA-L gene variation or not. Since this is correlated with antisocial behaviour, it might have a negative psychological effect to learn you have this particular type of gene. Researchers need to consider this when constructing their informed consent forms.

Caspi et al., 2002; Meyer-Lindenberg, 2008

(Note: these are natural experiments, not true experiments, but the explanation remains the same. See also ethics on animal experiments for better examples, pp77-78.)

Critical Thinking Considerations

- How might informed consent affect the validity of a study?
- Should researchers reveal everything in their informed consent forms?
- Are there other ethical considerations relevant to true experiments at the biological approach?

Research Method #2

Correlational studies
How and why are correlational studies used in the biological approach?

Correlational studies measure how strongly two (or more) variables are related. Unlike experimental methods that include a direction of causality (IV→DV), correlational studies have co-variables.

Strong Positive Correlation   Strong Negative Correlation

Key Details

• **Correlational studies in the biological approach to understanding behaviour**: In this approach, correlational studies are used to assess the strength of relationships between biological factors and behaviour. Researchers gather data by first measuring the behaviour in some way. For example, questionnaires, surveys and interviews can be used to measure levels of aggression and/or antisocial behaviour. The co-variables also have to be calculated, and they include things like genetics, hormone and neurotransmitter levels. How strongly the behaviour is correlated with a biological factor is then calculated. The correlation co-efficient gives us a value of how strongly the variables are correlated, with 1.0 being a perfect positive correlation and -1.0 a perfect negative correlation (0.0 is no correlation). A 0.4 (or -0.4) correlation is considered moderate and anything around 0.7 or higher is considered strong.

Key Studies

The brain and behaviour: Neurological factors like serotonin have been correlated with behaviours like antisocial behaviour. Correlational studies are also used to see how environmental variables are correlated with brain volume and activity. This is commonly the case in studies that look at how environmental factors can affect the brain (e.g. studies on neuroplasticity). For example, neglect, stress, poverty, and parenting are all factors that have been correlated with brain development.
Luby et al., 2013; Karl et al. (2006)

Hormones and pheromones and behaviour: Hormones like testosterone have been correlated with behaviours like antisocial behaviour and aggression.
Ehrenkrantz et al. 1974

Genes and behaviour: The IB considers twin and adoption studies as being correlational. This may be because they measure heritability, which is a measure of how strongly genes are correlated with behaviours. Read more in the topic *"Genetic similarities"* for how and why correlations in twin and kinship studies are used to understand connections between genes and behaviour.
Baker et al., 2007; Grove et al., 1990; Caspi et al. (2002);

Critical Thinking Considerations

• Correlation does not mean causation. This is the fundamental limitation of correlational studies. One way of making this point is by explaining examples of how other variables might affect the two being correlated in a study. Can you think of examples of this for any of the above?
• Another way of critiquing correlational studies is by showing how bidirectional ambiguity may be an issue in the study. Is it variable A affecting B or vice-versa? Can you explain any examples of bidirectional ambiguity in the above studies?

Exam Tips

• It is important to note that you might be asked about research methods used at the biological approach in general or in relation to one or more of the three specific topics.
• Preparing to use correlational studies to critique the use of true experiments (and vice-versa) is an effective strategy if you're planning on writing an essay for the biological approach. This will enable you to have an effective evaluation or discussion, use a range of studies and show depth of understanding.

Ethical Consideration #2

Anonymity in Correlational Studies
How and why are ethical guidelines considered in the biological approach?

Anonymity in psychological studies means that the names of participants are not revealed when recording and/or publishing results of studies. This is an especially important consideration when the topics being studied are sensitive.

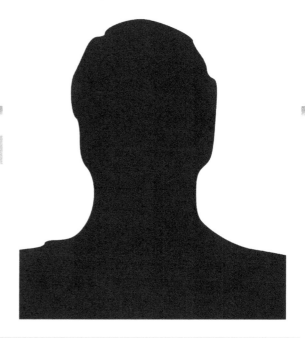

Key Details

- In studies at the biological approach, the behaviours being investigated are often highly sensitive, including antisocial behaviour, aggression, violence, neglect, stress, etc. For this reason, anonymity is important because participants probably would not want others to know about their results in these studies. Informed consent forms should promise anonymity and, if there are exceptions, it should be made clear to the participants before they consent to join the study.

Key Studies

The brain and behaviour: Because we know the importance of brain activity and volume in connection with behaviour, this is an incredibly sensitive topic. Therefore, anonymity is an essential consideration in any study that measures participants' brain activity and/or volume. Similarly, studies that correlate stress, parenting-styles and socioeconomic status also require anonymity, as people may not want others to know these personal details.

Luby et al., 2013; Moore et al. 2002

Hormones and behaviour: Because testosterone has been correlated with aggression and antisocial behaviour, participants might not want others to know their results.

Ehrenkrantz et al. 1974

Genes and behaviour: Studies on genetics often focus on sensitive topics, like antisocial behaviour. When studying such behaviours (e.g. child abuse and violence), anonymity becomes an important consideration because participants would not want their sensitive details shared with others unless they are given anonymity. For studies on the MAOA gene, participants may also not want others to know which variation they have since this has been correlated with antisocial behaviour.

Baker et al., 2007; Grove et al., 1990; Caspi et al. (2002);

Critical Thinking Considerations

- Are there any limitations in giving anonymity to participants? Can you think of any circumstances or reasons why not giving 100% anonymity might be beneficial? For example, what if severe cases of neglect or abuse are discovered during a study – should researchers break any agreements guaranteeing anonymity or should they stick to this guideline?

Exam Tips

- SAQs are most likely to ask about one research method and/or ethical consideration. Essay questions should allow you to write about one or more.
- An explanation of ethical considerations is most effective when it is linked to common research methodology used to study a particular topic, hence the layout of these review materials. However, you can still write about anonymity in true experiments and/or informed consent in correlational studies.

3 Cognitive Approach

Cognitive Approach to Understanding Human Behaviour

Topic	Content
Cognitive processing	• Models of memory 　• *Multi-store model* 　• *Working memory model* • Schema theory 　• *Cognitive schema* • Thinking and decision making 　• *Rational (controlled)* 　• *Intuitive thinking (automatic)*
Reliability of cognitive processing	• Reconstructive memory • Biases in thinking and decision making
Emotion and cognition	• The influence of emotion on cognitive processes
Ethical considerations and research methods	• Students need to understand the use of research methods and relevant ethical considerations for each topic.

Terms it italics may be used in short-answer questions from May 2020 onwards.

Cognitive Approach to Understanding Human Behaviour

	Content	Key Questions	Key Studies
Cognitive processing	**Models of memory** • *Multi-store model* • *Working memory model*	*How does the multi-store model explain memory formation?* *How does the working memory model explain short-term memory?*	MSM • Peterson and Peterson (1959) • Milner and Scoville (1957) • Glanzer and Cunitz (1966) WMM • Robbins et al. (1996) • Klingberg et al. (2005) • Cain et al. (2016)
	Schema theory	*How does our mind use cognitive schemas to make sense of the world?*	• Bransford and Johnson (1972) • Stone et al. (1997) • Cohen et al. (1981)
	Thinking and decision making	*What is one model or theory of thinking and decision making?*	• Kahneman and Tversky (1974) • Bechara et al. (2000) • Roth (1979)
Reliability of cognitive processes	**Reconstructive memory**	*How does the misinformation effect demonstrate the reconstructive nature of memory?*	• Loftus and Palmer (1974) • Shaw and Porter (2015) • Loftus and Pickrell (1995)
	Biases in thinking and decision making	*How can one or more biases in thinking and decision making be demonstrated in studies?*	• Stone et al. (1997) • Cohen et al. (1981) • Kahneman and Tversky (1974)
Emotion and cognition	**The influence of emotion on cognition**	*How can emotion affect cognition?*	• Buchanan and Lovallo (2001) • Luethi and Sandi (2009) • Sapolsky et al. (1990) • Luby et al. (2013)

• *All answers should be supported by evidence.*
• *Essay responses in Paper 1, Part B should include critical evaluation of the answer and the evidence.*
• *Students should also be prepared to discuss research methods and ethical considerations related to the relevant studies for the above topics.*

Multi-store model

How does the multi-store model explain memory formation?

The multi-store model of memory attempts to explain the formation of memories by identifying multiple stores and explaining how information travels between them.

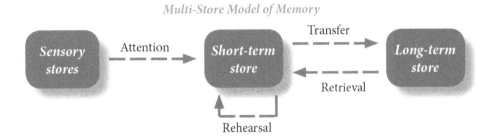

Multi-Store Model of Memory

Key Details

- There are numerous versions of the multi-store model (MSM), but Atkinson and Shiffrin's that was proposed in 1968 is the most well-known. Atkinson and Shiffrin's MSM was based on a lot of prior research on memory processes, such as Peterson and Peterson's work on short-term duration.
- **Separate stores:** The MSM posits that our memory is composed of three separate stores of information: the sensory stores, short-term store and the long-term store.
- **Control Processes:** Memory is transferred between the stores by the control processes: sensory to STS through *attention*, STS to long-term store through *rehearsal* and from LTS back to the STS through *retrieval*.
- **Duration and Capacity:** The stores differ in terms of their duration (see table on the next page).
- Another claim of the MSM is that the more rehearsal there is, the stronger the memory trace (the biological change in the brain that supports the memory).
- The MSM led to other developments in cognitive science, like the working memory model.

Key Study

Trigrams and STS duration (Peterson and Peterson, 1959): This study supports the claim that our short-term store is limited in duration and only lasts about 20 seconds. Participants tried to remember meaningless trigrams (consonant triplets, e.g. PTR, MPT, XTB). After they heard the trigrams, they were asked to count backwards in 3s from a random number to prevent rehearsal so that the information couldn't travel to the LTS. They did this for 0, 6, 12 or 18 seconds. The results showed that as the time delay was increased, memory for the trigrams decreased. After about 18 seconds, there was almost zero recollection of the trigrams. Because the rehearsal from STS to LTS was inhibited through a distraction task, the researchers could measure the average duration of the STS and conclude that it is about 20 seconds. This provides evidence for the claim that our STS is limited in duration and transfer to the LTS is needed for long-term memory.

Exam Tips

- Studies won't support every claim of the model but will support specific claims instead. Make sure you can clearly explain how studies support specific claims of the models or theories you are explaining.
- In any exam question about the MSM, make sure you can fully summarize the model and draw an accurate diagram.
- When asked to outline or describe a model of memory in an SAQ, a common error is to focus too much on a supporting study and not enough on the description of the model. Make sure you can provide a *detailed* description of the model first before you use a study.

- Serial position effect (primacy and recency effects): This is a cognitive phenomenon whereby people tend to remember the first (primacy) and last (recency) items in a series. This provides evidence for the MSM: people tend to remember the first items because they have longer to rehearse the information and they may have paid more attention to it, so it has a higher probability of being transferred to the LTS. They tend to remember the most recent information because it is still in their STS. Information in the middle may be lost because of the limited capacity of the STS. This can be shown in the Glanzer and Cunitz's study.
- Biological evidence: One way for a cognitive model or theory to be strengthened is to find the biological evidence for the processes and structures it describes. Case studies on patients with brain damage have provided such evidence (see below).

Further Studies

Primacy and Recency Effects (Glanzer and Cunitz, 1966): In one of their experiments, 46 participants heard 15 words and were asked to remember them. The researchers used a repeated measures design by testing subjects individually and randomizing the order they experienced these three conditions:

1. Immediate Free Recall Condition (IFR): wrote words down immediately after hearing them
2. Delayed Free Recall Condition (DFR) - 10 seconds: wrote words down after a delay of 10 seconds.
3. Delayed Free Recall Condition (DFR) - 30 seconds: wrote words down after a delay of 30 seconds.

Like Peterson and Peterson's study, participants had a distraction task during the delay and had to count backwards in 3s to prevent further rehearsal.

The results showed that when there was no delay in recall (IFR), the primacy and recency effect was demonstrated as per usual (participants remember about 70% of the first and last words). However, in the DFR-30 group, only the primacy effect was present and the recency effect was gone (only 30% words remembered – about average for all words). This is further support for the MSM because it shows that the rehearsal has not changed the transfer to the LTS (because the primacy effect still exists). On the other hand, the recency effect has gone because there was no time for rehearsal (because of the distraction task) and the 30-second delay was longer than the short-term store's capacity, so the memories were lost.

HM's case study (Milner and Scoville, 1957): The case study of HM, who had his hippocampus removed, provides some support for the idea that our memory is composed of different stores and that memory needs to be transferred from the STS to the LTS in order to be retrieved. HM had his hippocampus removed to cure his epilepsy. The result was that while HM could hold information in his STS if he kept rehearsing it, it would not transfer to his LTS. This provides biological evidence for the fact that there are different stores because if all of our memories were stored in the same place and no transfer was needed, HM would not be able to use one memory (STS) while not being able to transfer these to another (LTS). It also suggests that there is a biological component (e.g. the hippocampus) responsible for memory consolidation (the transfer of memory from the STS to the LTS).

Use this code to read more about this study.

Critical Thinking Considerations

- How has the MSM contributed to the field of cognitive science? *Hint: think about the working memory model.*
- Can the MSM be equally applied to explain the formation and storage of all types of memory? For example, does it apply equally to declarative and procedural memory?
- Does the MSM take into consideration the role of emotion and the accompanying role of biological factors in memory?
- Do we need to rehearse all information in order to remember it? Can you think of exceptions?
- Are there generalizability issues in any of the above studies? For example, do they suffer from a lack of mundane realism?

Models of Memory

Working Memory Model
How does the working memory model explain short-term memory?

The working memory model elaborates on the MSM by proposing a model for how short-term (working memory) processes occur.

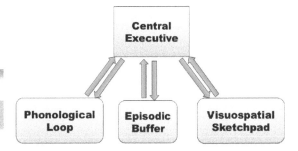

Key Details

• **Working memory** is the information that we are conscious of at any one time. More specifically, it is "…the small amount of information that can be held in mind and used in the execution of cognitive tasks" (Cowan, 2013). Baddeley and Hitch's (1974) **working memory model (WMM)** is an elaboration of the short-term store of the MSM. The "working" part of working memory refers to how we use information in our conscious minds.

• The central claim of the WMM is that our working memory is directed by the **central executive** because this controls the **slave systems**.

• The slave systems are names given to the processes that control the flow of specific **modalities** (types) of information. The **phonological loop** deals with auditory (verbal) information and the **visuospatial sketchpad** deals with visual and spatial information.

• The **episodic buffer** was a later addition to the WMM. Its role is to act as a temporary store of information that can keep chunks of information until it is needed. It also connects sensory and long-term memory with short-term memory.

Key Study

Dual-task study of working memory interference and chess (Robbins et al., 1996): This study provides evidence for the claim that there are different slave systems that control processes of different modalities of information. Twenty male chess players from Cambridge, UK, ranging in abilities, participated in this study. There were two conditions. In both conditions, the participants had to view an arrangement of chess pieces and then recreate this arrangement on a new board. In one condition (verbal interference), they had to repeat the word "the" while viewing the first chess set and also while recreating it on a new board. In the second condition (visual/spatial interference), they had

to tap a particular sequence into a keypad in their laps while viewing the first board and recreating the second. Verbal interference resulted in an average score of 16/25 (64%) correct, while visual/spatial interference was only 4/25 correct. The verbal condition has a higher score because "the" is using the phonological loop and recreating the chess board is the visuospatial sketchpad, so both systems are working independently and there is limited interference. However, the scores drop to 16% correct in the second condition because both tasks are using the one slave system and the capacity is limited. If working memory was all one system, this difference wouldn't be observed.

Exam Tips

• You may be asked about one specific model of memory (WMM or MSM) or either. SAQs will require you to write about one whereas essays could be one or two. It is a good idea to become an expert in one and have a second as a backup. I recommend becoming an expert in the WMM as it allows for the strongest answers.

• HL students should try to use studies on the effects of cognition on working memory in essays on the working memory model.

• In any exam question about a model of memory, make sure you can fully summarize the model and draw an accurate diagram.

- **Working memory training:** One of the major strengths of the working memory model is that it has provided the language and structures to discuss a range of cognitive problems, especially in young children. Working memory "…allows us to actively maintain and manipulate mental information for short periods of time" (Fougnie and Marois, 2009). Not surprisingly, having a good working memory capacity has been correlated with many important things, like intelligence, reading comprehension and the ability to avoid distractions and stay on task. For many children, low working memory capacity is a factor influencing their poor performance at school due to its role in the above behaviours. Because the model has identified the constructs underlying working memory, psychologists can try to develop interventions to help improve working memory capacity.

Further Studies

Effects of media-use on working memory capacity (Cain et al., 2016): The aim of this study was to see if there was a correlation between use of media (TV, cellphones, etc.) and working memory capacity (among other things). Seventy-four eighth graders from Boston participated in the study and data was gathered on their media use through questionnaires. The amount of time using media was correlated with the students' test scores of their working memory capacity (e.g. n-back and digit span tasks - activities that require remembering sequences of numbers). The results showed a statistically significant (yet moderate) negative correlation between working memory capacity and media usage, with a -0.27 for digit span tasks and -0.38 for n-back tasks. This is one example of how Baddeley and Hitch's development of the construct of working memory can help us better understand important cognitive processes and what might affect them.

Working memory games and improved attention (Klingberg et al., 2005): This study demonstrates the positive applications of understanding working memory processes because it shows we can design computer games to improve the working memory capacity of children and to reduce attention problems. Forty-two kids with ADHD were assigned to two conditions: either a computer game designed to improve working memory that gradually got harder or the same game but not designed to stretch their capacity. The results showed that those in the first condition had improved working memory capacity and reduced ADHD-related behaviours compared to the second condition. While the working memory model has helped to identify problems with working memory, it has also been used to develop tools to improve it.

Critical Thinking Considerations

- How can understanding working memory processes be applied to education (or other fields – see explanations of PTSD for more examples)?
- Is the WMM limited by the range of sensory information that it explains? It covers visual and auditory, but what about the others?
- It is important to note that research like Klingberg's is not free from criticism. For example, Hulme et al. (2016) conducted a meta-analysis on working memory training programmes and concluded that "…working memory training programs appear to produce short-term, specific training effects that do not generalize to measures of 'real-world' cognitive skills. These results seriously question the practical and theoretical importance of current computerized working memory programs as methods of training working memory skills."

Schema Theory

Cognitive Schema
How does our mind use cognitive schemas to make sense of the world?

Schema theory is a combination of ideas about how our mind organizes information and how this can affect our thinking and behaviour. Schema theory's central claim is that our knowledge of the world is organized and categorized in clusters called schemas and these can influence our cognition and behaviour.

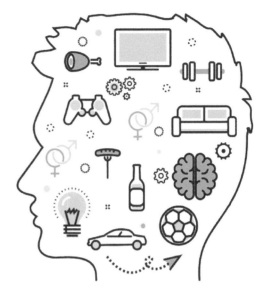

Key Details

- A **cognitive schema** is a cluster of knowledge or memory that is stored in the mind, or "organized packets of information about the world, events, or people stored in long-term memory." (Eysenck and Keane, 2010). They're also referred to as "cognitive frameworks" as they are a system for categorizing and organizing information and memory.
- Along with the very existence of schema, another central claim of schema theory is that their function is to help us make sense of the complex world of information that we live in. In doing this, schemas can affect our cognition and behaviour.
- One proposed function of schemas is that they save our cognitive energy and they make processing information easier. Another way schemas can influence cognition is that they can affect our ability to comprehend new information. When we're exposed to new information, we relate it to our existing knowledge (our schemas) and this can affect our **comprehension** of that information (as seen in Bransford and Johnson's study below). In this way, we learn by making connections between new information and existing schema.
- Unlike other theories in psychology, schema theory isn't attributable to a single psychologist but has had many contributions from various psychologists across almost 100 years of research. Some of the most notable contributors include Bartlett, Piaget and Vygotsky.

Key Study

Schema activation and comprehension (Bransford and Johnson, 1972): In this classic series of experiments, there were a few different procedures. One experiment involved the participants listening to a passage of information that was deliberately vague. There were three conditions: a) they were given the title of the passage ("Doing Laundry") before the reading, b) the title was given after the reading, or c) there was no title. After hearing the passage, the participants were asked to rank their comprehension of what they had just heard, as well as recall as many details as they could remember. Out of 18 total points, the title before group remembered 5.8 compared with 2.6 (title after) and 2.8 (no title). The title before group also ranked their comprehension of the passage higher, with a self-score of 4.5/7 compared with 2.1 and 2.3 for title after and no title, respectively. This study demonstrates how schemas can improve comprehension and memory of new information because when our schema is activated, it enables us to relate new information to our existing knowledge of a subject.

Exam Tips

- When asked about schema theory (or cognitive schemas), make sure you write a full description first before explaining studies. Your description of schema theory should include (a) a precise definition of schema, (b) functions of schema, and (c) at least one example of how they can affect our thinking and/or behaviour.
- When asked to evaluate or discuss a theory, remember the D.E.A.L acronym.
- Evaluating (or discussing) schema theory is very difficult. If you are planning to write an essay for the cognitive approach, make sure you can clearly explain at least 2-3 limitations of the theory or the evidence.

- Schema theory can be applied to understanding stereotypes and social interactions. For instance, schema theorists could explain the formation of stereotypes by saying there are too many individual people in the world for us to consider. Thus, in order to save our cognitive energy, we think about groups of people and make generalizations about them.
- In this way, stereotypes are examples of social schemas because they are a generalized cluster of ideas about a particular group of people. Having a set schema for a group of people could then affect how we think about people based on the group that they belong to.

- The process of relating new information to existing schema can also influence our processing of new information and can lead to **confirmation bias** – a cognitive bias whereby we are more likely to focus on (and remember) information that is consistent with our existing beliefs.
- For instance, we may fall victim to confirmation bias and focus on people's characteristics and behaviour that are consistent with our stereotypes (schemas) and ignore contradictory details. This could have the effect of strengthening our existing stereotypes. This can be seen in Cohen and Stone's studies (below).

Further Studies

Schema, stereotypes and confirmation bias (Cohen, 1981): In this experiment, 96 college students watched a video of a woman having dinner in a restaurant with her husband. Half of the participants were told she was a librarian and the other half were told she was a waitress. After watching the video, they were asked to recollect details of the video. The results showed that participants were more likely to remember schema-consistent information. For example, the librarian condition increased memory of the fact she had spent the day reading and she liked classical music, whereas those in the waitress condition remembered she was drinking a beer and eating a hamburger. This study provides evidence for the function of schemas to simplify our complex world and save our cognitive energy by focusing our attention on information that is consistent with what we already know (which is easier than trying to comprehend information that challenges our existing beliefs).

Perceptions and judgements of basketball players (Stone et al., 1997): The participants were told they were participating in a study comparing listening to a radio with watching TV, but they were really the subject of a study about stereotypes. They were given the name

of a basketball player and were told to listen carefully to a radio recording of his performance because they would be asked to evaluate it. Half of the participants were told the athlete was white, the other half were told he was black. After the recording, they completed a questionnaire based on evaluations of natural ability, performance, and contributions of the player. The results showed that black athletes were rated as making a contribution to the team through good positional play, whereas white athletes made a contribution through smart plays and hustle. The researchers concluded that the ratings were "…remarkably consistent with the stereotypes discussed in the sports media: perceivers reported that Black men have more athletic ability and are better at playing the game of basketball, but White men can contribute because they are more intelligent and make up for their lack of physical ability through effort."

Loftus and Palmer's study on leading questions could be used for schema theory, but you need to make sure you can explain clearly how it is linked to schema – the phrasing of the question is activating a particular schema, which is then altering the memory of the event.

Critical Thinking Considerations

- Two common applications of schema theory are in social psychology (especially the study of stereotypes) and in education (especially reading and literacy). How do you think ideas from schema theory could be applied to these fields?
- Some psychologists have argued that the concept of schema is too vague to be helpful. To what extent do you agree with this claim?
- What limitations can you find in the above studies? Are there ethical considerations? Are there reasons to suspect the results might not generalize to other contexts?

Thinking and Decision Making

The Dual Processing Model
What is one model or theory of thinking and decision making?

The dual processing model of thinking and decision making outlines two systems that humans rely on to make decisions – system one (fast, intuitive) and system two (slow, rational).

Key Details

- Numerous theorists have proposed dual processing models of judgement and decision making. They share similar characteristics and are based on the idea that there are two distinct systems that are used when we are making a decision: system one and system two.
- **System one processing:** Intuitive (automatic), fast, unconscious, based on experiences.
- **System two processing:** Rational (controlled), slow, conscious, based on consequences.
- The system used to process information will affect our judgement, which will affect our decision making, which could affect our behaviour.
- Neuroimaging studies have provided evidence of different neurological systems being involved in the different systems of processing.

- The dual processing model could be used to explain relationships between the brain and behaviour. For example, impulsive behaviour has been linked with prefrontal cortex dysfunction, and this could be due to an inability to use system two processing when making decisions.

Key Studies

Dual processing and heuristics (Kahneman and Tversky, 1974): These two psychologists devised many ways of testing and experimenting people's mental shortcuts that are used when making decisions. In one task, they had 95 participants and they gave them the following scenario: *A certain town is served by two hospitals. In the larger hospital, about 45 babies are born each day and in the smaller hospital, about 15 babies are born each day. As you know, about 50 percent of all babies are boys. However, the exact percentage varies from day to day. Sometimes it may be higher than 50 percent, sometimes lower. For a period of 1 year, each hospital recorded the days on which more than 60 percent of the babies born were boys. Which hospital do you think recorded more such days?*

1. *The larger hospital*
2. *The smaller hospital*

3. *About the same (that is, within 5 percent of each other)*

The correct answer is the smaller hospital because statistical probabilities suggest that the larger the sample size (e.g. the more babies born), the closer it will get to the average, so it is more likely that a small hospital will have more disproportionate days. However, 78% of participants got this wrong and most answered "about the same" (56%) "...presumably because these events are described by the same statistic and are therefore equally representative of the general population." In other words, because birth rate is 50/50 for boys/girls, they assumed the probability in this scenario would also be 50/50. They were using system one and were going with intuition, rather than using system two and using logic and reasoning to deduce the correct answer.

Exam Tips

- Make sure you can remember 3-4 adjectives to describe system one and two processing. You may be asked specifically about intuitive (automatic) and rational (controlled) thinking, so you should definitely remember these terms.
- If asked to write about one study related to thinking and decision making, Bechara et al.'s (see next page) or Kahneman and Tversky's studies would be suitable, but perhaps Kahneman and Tversky's is better since it's their model.
- Bechara et al.'s study could also be used to show localization of function and the use of brain imaging technology.

- **Heuristics**: The problem in the study by Kahneman and Tversky is an example of what they call **heuristics**. These are cognitive biases (or shortcuts) that people use when making decisions, or "rules of thumb that are cognitively undemanding and often produce approximately accurate answers" (Eysenck and Keane, 2010). There are different types of heuristics and the test above is an example of people using the "**representativeness heuristic**." This is used when people are making judgements based on probabilities. Instead of assessing the problem logically (system two), they think of an object or event as being representative of other similar objects or events, so they use the same probability across multiple scenarios. In other words, one probability is used to represent (and to calculate) other similar probabilities. For example, in the above problem, they are using the average birth rate of 50/50 boys/girls to represent the other probabilities about birth rates in specific hospitals, even though this is incorrect.

- **Biological evidence**: One way for a cognitive model or theory to be strengthened is to find the biological evidence for the processes and structures it describes. There may be specific parts of the brain that are responsible for using different systems in processing information. The ventromedial prefrontal cortex (vmPFC) has been associated with executive cognitive control and the ability to perform cognitive tasks that require system two processing (e.g. basing decisions on consequences). Studies have shown that if this part of the brain is damaged, it could affect our processing, judgment and decision making. This suggests that we have different parts of our brain may be linked to different systems.

Further Studies

The brain and processing – the role of the vmPFC (Bechara et al., 2000): Using the experimental procedure called the Iowa Gambling Task, the study showed that patients with lesions in their ventromedial prefrontal cortices (vmPFCs) continually made decisions based on impulse without thinking through the consequences of their actions (i.e. they only used system one). Healthy controls, on the other hand, were able to identify the pattern in the game and make decisions that were less beneficial in the short-term but more beneficial in the long-term (i.e. they were able to use system two). The results support other studies that indicate areas of our prefrontal cortex are responsible for inhibiting impulsive decisions (i.e. overriding system one processing) and making decisions based on consideration of more factors (i.e. using system two processing).

Wason Task Studies: In this common experimental procedure, participants are shown four cards face up and are given a rule to prove (if P, then Q). Less than 10% of participants give the correct answer (Roth, 1979), which requires careful consideration of the rules and the problem (system two processing). *More information can be found by searching Wason Task on our blog.*

This code will take you to a blog post with more information about the Iowa Gambling Task and this study.

Critical Thinking Considerations

- Do the above studies show that *all* people use heuristics (system one) when processing information? Why/why not?
- When participants provide answers to the above problem, there are not consequences for their decisions. Does this affect the generalizability of these results to other situations? Can you think of situations where people might be less likely to use system one (heuristics) to make decisions because of consequences?
- What factors might affect individual differences in processing information?
- Does the dual processing model and the associated studies suffer from cultural biases? Can you think of any reasons why we might not expect the same results in some cultures?
- Why is understanding how we process information a relevant field of study? Can you think of any potential applications of this research?
- Kahneman has said that there is no biological basis to system one or two thinking. Does this challenge the conclusions that can be drawn from Bechara et al.'s study?

Reconstructive Memory

Misinformation Effect

How does the misinformation effect demonstrate the reconstructive nature of memory?

Decades of research have shown that our memory does not work like a tape recorder. Instead, memory is a reconstructive process and, during this process, our memories can be distorted. This has had significant implications for the field of eyewitness testimony in court cases.

Key Details

- It was previously believed that our memory was like a tape recorder and, when we recalled details of events and facts, they would be reliable. However, there is a large body of research that shows our memory can be distorted. Elizabeth Loftus is the most prominent researcher in this field. She gives the analogy of memory as being more like a Wikipedia page that anyone can change and edit.
- One way our memory can be distorted is through having false information introduced after an event has happened. Many studies have shown that false information can be recalled by someone as if it was real. This creation of false memories because of inaccurate information is a phenomenon known as the **misinformation effect**.
- The misinformation effect may be due to the fact that memory is **reconstructive**: this means we don't encode and record information and store it accurately when it happens – we actually reconstruct (rebuild) memories when we're in the process of remembering them. This is how information we are introduced to after an event can implant itself and be recalled incorrectly.
- Memory reliability could also be influenced by schemas, as the influence of schema during the processing of information could affect its later recall (as shown in Loftus and Palmer below).

Key Studies

Leading questions and memory reliability (Loftus and Palmer, 1974) - Experiment one: In this first experiment, 45 participants were asked to watch several clips of car crashes, ranging from about 5 to 30 seconds long. After they watched the films, they were given a series of questions to answer, including one about how fast the car was going. The independent variable was the verb used in the question. The results showed that the stronger the verb, the higher the speed estimate (with the verb "contacted" having a mean of 32, "hit" having a mean of 34, "bumped" having a mean of 38, "collided" having a mean of 39, and "smashed" having a mean of 40). One explanation is that the verb was a leading question and directed students who weren't sure towards a particular guess. Another possible explanation is that the verb activated a different schema, which actually changed the way the participants were recollecting the event. To gather more evidence for the second explanation, the second experiment was conducted.

Leading questions and the misinformation effect (Loftus and Palmer, 1974) - Experiment two: This second experiment tested the hypotheses that the type of question asked after an event can actually change the memory of the event. The procedures were similar to the first experiment, except this time there were only two verbs (hit or smashed) and one control group (not asked anything). Another procedure was added: after one week, the participants were asked another question: did they see any broken glass? The results showed that 32% of the smashed condition said they saw broken glass (there was no broken glass in the clip), compared with only 14% in the hit condition and 12% in the control condition. This second study provides more solid evidence for the misinformation effect occurring: the smashed verb introduced after the video led participants to actually recall the crash with a greater impact and to produce a false memory of something that didn't happen (glass breaking).

Exam Tips

- The best explanations of Loftus and Palmer's study will mention both experiments, as the second is needed to support the explanation of the misinformation effect.
- If you are asked about "one study" then it's fine to write about both experiments in this study as they count as "one study."

- **Eyewitness testimony**: Before the decades of research on memory *un*-reliability, eyewitness testimony was previously enough to prove someone was guilty of committing a crime. With new DNA testing techniques, hundreds of innocent men have been released and acquitted of crimes they never committed, with some of these men being released after having been in prison for over 30 years. In most of these cases, eyewitness testimony played a significant role in their trials and "proving" their guilt. Because of the research of Loftus and others, there are major changes being made to many parts of the legal process, including how witnesses and the accused are interviewed.

Further Studies

False memories of committing a crime (Shaw and Porter, 2015): The aim of this study was to see if it was possible in a laboratory setting for researchers to implant a false memory of committing a crime. The researchers gathered 70 Canadian college students who were randomly assigned to either the "criminal condition" or the "non-criminal condition." They were interviewed three times over three weeks. In each interview, the participants in the criminal condition were asked to describe two events: a true event (details were provided by a family member) and a fictional account of committing a crime when they were about 10-14 years old (the participants were led to believe the details of this had also been given by their family member). The crimes were either theft, assault, or assault with a weapon. In the non-criminal condition they were led to believe they had experienced an emotional event (e.g. a dog attack) and this is the false memory researchers tried to plant. To facilitate the production of false memories, the researchers encouraged the participants to practice visualization techniques at night and they also used subtle social pressure by saying most people can remember these kinds of things if they try hard enough. By the third interview, 21/30 (70%) of the participants in the criminal condition had a false memory of committing the crime, some even giving specific details of their contact with the police at the time. The results also showed a similar rate of false memories for those in the non-criminal condition. This study provides evidence for the fact that how people are questioned can lead to false memories.

Lost in the mall (Loftus and Pickrell, 1995): In this study, Pickrell and Loftus used 24 participants who were led to believe they were taking memory tests. They asked family members to provide details of three stories from when the participants were 4 - 6 years old. They also asked about details that could be plausibly added to a fictional story - being lost in the mall. For instance, the family members might give details like the name of the mall, or when they might have been shopping there. The family members also validated that the participant was never actually lost in the mall as a child. The participants read the descriptions of the four events that had been prepared by the researchers with the help of descriptions from the family members. The participants were interviewed soon after they read the descriptions of the events and then again in one week. The results showed that 5/24 (i.e. 21%) of the participants recalled being lost in the mall, sometimes in great detail. They did, however, rate the memories as being less clear than the other memories.

Critical Thinking Considerations

- While the above results can be interpreted in a way that provides evidence for the unreliable nature of memory, how can they also be interpreted to show that our memory *is* actually quite reliable?
- These studies take place in a controlled environment. What factors might influence the memory of a real-life event of something shocking or emotional, like a car crash? *Hint: read about the effects of emotion and cognition in Buchanan and Lovallo's experiment.*
- Loftus and Palmer's experiments were conducted on students. How might this affect its validity and/or generalizability?
- Shaw and Porter's study could explain how police interrogation tactics lead to false memories. Why might this study (or others) lack generalizability to the context of a police interrogation?

Confirmation Bias

How can one or more biases in thinking and decision making be demonstrated in studies?

Our thinking and decision making may be vulnerable to a number of cognitive biases. One of these is confirmation bias, which is the tendency to focus on information that is consistent with our beliefs. This could affect our behaviour.

Key Details

- **Confirmation bias** is one bias in thinking and decision making. The term describes the cognitive phenomenon whereby we tend to focus on (and remember) information that is consistent with our existing beliefs.
- Cognitive psychologists suggest that one reason why this happens could be that humans are "cognitive misers," which means we want to save our cognitive energy. The idea behind this idea is that we tend to focus on information that is consistent with our existing beliefs and opinions because it takes less mental effort and is more comfortable. Trying to comprehend and make sense of information that contradicts our existing knowledge or beliefs is mentally more difficult.
- One example of confirmation bias can be seen when looking at stereotypes. Stereotypes are a kind of social schema as they are a generalized way of thinking about a group of people. Stereotypes could influence our perception of people and affect how we make judgements about them. This is because they can lead to **confirmation bias** - since a stereotype is a type of schema, it means that if we have a stereotype about a group of people and we're making judgements about someone from that group, we're likely to focus on information that reinforces that stereotype and ignore information that contradicts it. This could affect how we judge that person and it could also reinforce stereotypes, making them harder to get rid of.

Key Study

Perceptions and judgements of basketball players (Stone et al., 1997): The participants of this study were 51 undergraduates from Princeton University. They were told that they were participating in a study comparing listening to a radio with watching TV, but they were really the subject of a study about stereotypes. They each listened to a 20-minute recording of a college basketball game and were given a written transcript. They were given the name of a player and told to listen carefully to his performance because they would be asked to evaluate it. Half of the participants were shown a photo of a white athlete and the other half a photo of a black athlete. After the recording, they completed a questionnaire based on evaluations of natural ability, performance, and contributions of the player. The results showed that black athletes were rated as making a contribution to the team through good positional play, whereas white athletes made a contribution through smart plays and hustle. The researchers concluded that the ratings were "...remarkably consistent with the stereotypes discussed in the sports media: perceivers reported that black men have more athletic ability and are better at playing the game of basketball, but white men can contribute because they are more intelligent and make up for their lack of physical ability through effort." Confirmation bias could explain these results because depending on the race of the player the participants thought they were listening to, they gave stereotype-consistent ratings because they focused on (and remembered) the details of the game that were consistent with these stereotypes.

Exam Tips

- Confirmation bias is one example of how stereotypes can affect behaviour, so Stone et al.'s and Cohen et al.'s studies (see next page) can also be used for this topic in the sociocultural approach. As stereotypes are examples of a social schema, these studies can also be used for schema theory.
- Either Stone et al. or Cohen's experiments could be used to demonstrate confirmation bias.
- The IB guide states that "...one or more of the following biases should be used: confirmation bias, cognitive dissonance, optimism bias, selective attention, or illusory correlations." (p30). Heuristics (see next page) are not on this list, but are widely regarded as biases in thinking and decision making.

- **Schema theory**: Confirmation bias is when we focus on information consistent with our beliefs (i.e. schema-consistent information). In this way, schema theory could explain confirmation bias because it is another of example of how we use schema to make connections between prior knowledge and new information.
- **Heuristics**: Kahneman and Tversky came up with biases in thinking that they call **heuristics**. These are cognitive biases (or shortcuts) that people use when making decisions, or "rules of thumb that are cognitively undemanding and often produce approximately accurate answers" (Eysenck and Keane, 2010). There are different types of heuristics and the test below in Kahneman and Tversky's study is an example of people using the "representativeness heuristic." This is used when people make judgements based on probabilities. Instead of assessing the problem logically, they think of an object or event as being representative of other similar objects or events so they use the same probability across multiple scenarios. In other words, one probability is used to represent (and to calculate) other similar probabilities.

Further Studies

Schema, stereotypes and confirmation bias (Cohen, 1981): In this experiment, 96 college students watched a video of a woman having dinner in a restaurant with her husband. Half of the participants were told she was a librarian and the other half were told she was a waitress. After watching the video, they were asked to recollect details of the video. The results showed that participants were more likely to remember stereotype-consistent information. For example, the librarian condition increased memory of the fact she had spent the day reading and she liked classical music, whereas those in the waitress condition remembered she was drinking a beer and eating a hamburger. These results could also be explained by confirmation bias – in order to simplify our processing of information, we tend to focus on information that is consistent with our existing beliefs (in this case, the stereotypical qualities of a waitress or librarian) and this affects our memory. In other words, the participants of this study had a tendency to remember schema-consistent information.

Dual processing and heuristics (Kahneman and Tversky, 1974): In one study, participants were given the following scenario: *A certain town is served by two hospitals. In the larger hospital, about 45 babies are born each day and in the smaller hospital, about 15 babies are born each day. As you know, about 50 percent of all babies are boys. However, the exact percentage varies from day to day. Sometimes it may be higher than 50 percent, sometimes lower. For a period of 1 year, each hospital recorded the days on which more than 60 percent of the babies born were boys. Which hospital do you think recorded more such days?*

1. *The larger hospital*
2. *The smaller hospital*
3. *About the same (that is, within 5 percent of each other)*

78% of participants got this wrong and most answered about the same (56%) "…presumably because these events are described by the same statistic and are therefore equally representative of the general population." In other words, they were using a representativeness heuristic because the birth rate was used as representative of the similar probability problem in the scenario so the same calculation was used. Just because birth rate is 50/50, they assumed the probability in this scenario would also be 50/50, which is inaccurate.

Critical Thinking Considerations

- In Stone et al.'s study, the participants' ratings were consistent with common existing stereotypes, but how do we know they were consistent with the participants' stereotypes? They can also be used to show confirmation bias. But how do we know what information they were focusing on during the experiment?
- Could there be individual differences in our vulnerability to confirmation bias in certain situations? For example, do you think a novice or an expert may be more prone to confirmation bias? Why?
- What are the ethical considerations associated with these studies? Can you see any other limitations with these studies?
- Why is it valuable to be aware of confirmation bias?

The Influence of Emotion on Cognition

Cortisol and Memory Consolidation
How can emotion affect cognition?

The emotion of fear can have positive and negative effects on memory due to its activation of the stress response and the subsequent release of stress hormones like cortisol. Cortisol could increase short-term memory, but prolonged cortisol release could have negative effects on the hippocampus, thus damaging memory capabilities.

Key Details

• Emotion could increase **memory reliability**. For example, when we experience fear, our amygdala is activated, which triggers the HPA axis and stress hormones are released as part of the "fight or flight" response. The stress hormone cortisol has been shown to have an effect on memory consolidation (the transfer of memory from short-term to long-term).

• This effect of fear on improving memory of emotional events could be an evolutionary adaptation. For example, if we can remember dangerous events, we can learn how to avoid them. Similarly, if we have a good memory for joyful events (like where and how to get food), we can increase our survival. Thus, humans might have evolved to have physiological responses to emotional situations in order to increase **memory consolidation** of these situations.

Key Study

Cortisol secretion and emotional memory consolidation (Buchanan and Lovallo, 2001): 48 participants (24 males and 24 females) were randomly allocated to receive 20mg of cortisol or a placebo. They were then shown 60 pictures on a TV monitor and told to focus on the images (they weren't told it was a memory test). The pictures were either "arousing pleasant," "arousing unpleasant" or "non-arousing neutral." Exactly one week later, they came back to the lab and completed a memory test where they had to describe the images to two scorers (who were "blind" to their condition). The results showed that when recalling the images, the cortisol condition recalled more images than the placebo group. Across all participants, the arousing images were recalled significantly more than the non-arousing slides. From these results, we can see that an increase in cortisol (both through the drug and the arousing images) can influence the reliability of our memory of emotional information. This shows how emotions (like fear and stress) can affect cognition.

Exam Tips

• The material from this topic can also be used to show how a hormone (cortisol) can affect behaviour (memory). It can also be used to support an evolutionary explanation of behaviour and the material on the next page can be used for the neuroplasticity topic.

• The specific emotion you should identify is "fear" because even though stress has the same physiological response, it is not technically considered an emotion.

• A good SAQ response will explain the positive effects with Buchanan and Lovallo, but will also briefly explain how prolonged cortisol may have a negative effect (without necessarily using further studies).

- While acute (short-term) stress can have a positive effect on memory, research has shown that chronic (long-lasting) stress might have adverse effects on the development of the hippocampus. This could affect the development of **neural networks** in the hippocampus by damaging the neurons and the synaptic connections they make.
- Animal studies have shown that prolonged release of the stress hormone, cortisol, damages neurons in the hippocampus (see Sapolsky et al., 1990 below).
- Human studies have also correlated stressful life events with hippocampus size and volume. For example, studies have shown that there is a correlation between socioeconomic status and hippocampus size. More specifically, children growing up in a poorer socioeconomic environment tend to have smaller hippocampi. This can be explained due to the increased stress and adverse childhood experiences (ACEs) that children from these areas tend to experience.
- Research also suggests that the effects of emotion on memory may differ depending on the type of memory (see Luethi and Sandi below).

Further Studies

The effects of cortisol on the hippocampus (Sapolsky et al., 1990): The aim of this study was to see if cortisol would damage the hippocampus. One group of rhesus monkeys had a pellet of cortisol surgically inserted into their hippocampi and were compared with a control group who had a cholesterol pellet inserted. After one year, the monkeys were euthanized and their brains compared. The results showed the cortisol group had damage to their hippocampal neurons. This study shows how stress might affect neuroplasticity in the brain and may explain why people who experience long-term stress tend to have smaller hippocampi.

Stress and memory function (Luethi and Sandi, 2009): This study tested the effects of stress (and cortisol) on multiple types of memory. Thirty-five adult male participants were randomly assigned to either the stress condition or the control group. The stress condition underwent the Trier Social Stress Test to create stress. This test lasts 15 minutes and includes giving a 5-minute speech in front of a group and also having to do difficult math without making a mistake. Cortisol was measured to ensure the participants were stressed. The results showed that stress had a strong negative impact on working memory, but did not appear to have an effect on declarative verbal memory. Stress also enhanced classical conditioning for negative stimuli, but not positive stimuli. This suggests that the effects of emotion could vary across different types of memory.

Poverty and brain development (Luby et al., 2013): The aim of this study was to see if poverty was correlated with brain development and to see if there were mediating variables related to stress and parenting that could explain this relationship. MRIs were used to measure correlations of poverty, stressful events and parenting styles with hippocampal volume in 145 children over a 10-year period. The results showed a negative correlation between poverty and hippocampal volume. They also found that parenting and stressful life events were mediating variables in this relationship. This suggests that poverty, parenting styles and stress are all factors that can negatively affect the development of neural networks in the hippocampus. This study shows how emotion (stress) could affect memory because it can lead to reduced development in the hippocampus, an important part of the brain for learning and memory.

Critical Thinking Considerations

- What are the limitations in using Buchanan and Lovallo's study to explain how emotion can increase memory reliability?
- In order to address the "to what extent" part of an essay question, you need to offer a counter-argument. How could emotion and the release of cortisol over a long period of time actually *decrease* memory reliability? How could this be shown in studies like Sapolsky et al.'s (1990) experiment on monkeys, research on PTSD patients and HM's case study?
- Can these explanations apply to all types of memory?

True Experiments

How and why are true experiments used in the cognitive approach?

True experiments (a.k.a. laboratory experiments) are used when the researchers manipulate an independent variable and create different conditions. They then, as much as possible, control for all extraneous variables and measure the effects of the IV on the dependent variable. By carefully controlling the extraneous variables, the researchers can maximize the chances that any differences in the DV can be explained by the IV. This allows for conclusions about causality to be made.

Key Details

• **True experiments in the cognitive approach to understanding behaviour**: In this approach, the focus is on the study of relationships between cognition and other factors. Typically, these experiments are looking at factors that can affect cognition, so the IV is some factor hypothesized to affect cognition (e.g. false information, cortisol, stress, or computer game training). Cognition is measured using some behavioural task that requires participants to complete a task that can assess their cognition (e.g. recalling items from a list, remembering images, or performing working memory tasks)

• By conducting experiments in carefully controlled environments and isolating the IV as the only factor affecting the DV, researchers are able to draw causal relationships between cognition and other factors.

Key Studies

Reliability of cognitive processes: In studies investigating the reliability of cognitive processes, researchers can manipulate the factor that they think might affect cognition. In the studies of reconstructive memory and cognitive biases, for example, researchers can compare the effects of variables like activating schemas, leading questions, and misinformation. The controlled lab also allows them to carefully measure the cognition via the participants' responses to particular tasks (e.g. memory recall).

Loftus and Palmer (1974), Shaw and Porter (2015), Cohen (1981), Stone et al. (1997), Bransford and Johnson (1972)

Emotion and cognition: In controlled environments, researchers can test the effects of emotion on cognition by manipulating the emotion to create different conditions and measuring the results. For example, they can test the effects of stress on memory by manipulating cortisol levels (a hormone released during stress) and see how this might affect memory.

Buchanan and Lovallo (2001), Luethi and Sandi, (2009)

Critical Thinking Considerations

• Are true experiments inherently limited in generalizability because of their artificial environments?
• How can correlational studies inform true experiments?
• What are the ethical considerations associated with true experiments?
• When studying emotion and cognition, how can correlational studies like Luby et al.'s be valuable?

Exam Tips

• If asked about "cognitive processing" you can use research related to the reliability of cognitive processing. You can actually write essays about research methods and ethical considerations by looking at the effects of emotion on the reliability of memory.
• For additional methods, see the HL extension on how technology can affect cognition – there, you can read about examples of correlational studies used to study cognition.

Ethical Considerations

Informed Consent in True Experiments
How and why are ethical guidelines considered in the cognitive approach?

At the heart of **ethics** *in psychological research is considering the impact the research might have on others, especially the participants.* **Informed consent** *is one consideration that can reduce some of the stress and other negative effects of participating in a study. Informed consent means you get an agreement from participants that they want to be in the study (consent) and that they are basing this decision on information you have given them (informed).*

Key Details

- In true experiments in the cognitive approach, **informed consent** is an important consideration because researchers must carefully consider how much information to reveal to participants and when. In true experiments that investigate how certain factors can affect our cognition, our cognition is often manipulated in some way so the researchers can compare conditions.

- Informed consent is important because manipulating someone's cognition could be unpleasant and stressful. Similarly, in some studies, stress is the IV -- not everyone is comfortable experiencing stress, so informed consent allows them to make an informed judgment before they are subjected to the conditions of the experiment.

Key Studies

Reliability of cognitive processing: In studies on false memory, some participants may be led to believe things that never happened (e.g. like committing a crime in Shaw and Porter's study). Researchers cannot provide all the details in their consent forms, so they need to consider carefully what information they have in their consent forms to begin with.

Loftus and Palmer (1974), Shaw and Porter (2015), Cohen (1981), Stone et al. (1997), Bransford and Johnson (1972)

Emotion and cognition: In experiments on how emotion can affect the reliability of memory, participants may have their physiology altered or may be placed in stress-causing situations, so they should be made aware of this before the study. However, in some studies, they cannot know which group they're in, so researchers can't reveal all of the information. Because we know that too much cortisol could have negative effects, in order to make an informed decision about taking part in the study the participants should probably be told about this beforehand. Debriefing afterwards also becomes important.

Buchanan and Lovallo (2001), Luethi and Sandi, (2009)

Critical Thinking Considerations

- You may be asked about two ethical considerations for an essay question – how and why is anonymity (or any other consideration) relevant to experimental studies on cognition?
- How might informed consent affect the validity of a study? For instance, should researchers reveal *everything* in their informed consent forms? How can withholding information and/or deceiving participants improve the validity of the study?
- Are there other ethical considerations relevant to true experiments at the cognitive approach?

Exam Tips

- Any ethics or research methods question about cognitive research can be answered using Buchanan and Lovallo and Luethi and Sandi, while Shaw and Porter can be added for reliability of cognition essays.
- A good way to start any ethical consideration question is to state the relevant consideration(s) and to provide a definition.
- The best answers will clearly explain why informed consent is relevant and what exactly must be considered *before* describing the relevant studies.
- Prepare one consideration for SAQs and essays but have a second study as a backup, just in case. Debriefing works well in conjunction with informed consent.

4 Sociocultural Approach

Sociocultural Approach to Understanding Human Behaviour

Topic	Content
The individual and the group	<ul><li>Social identity theory<ul><li>*Social groups*</li></ul></li><li>Social cognitive theory</li><li>Stereotypes</li></ul>
Cultural origins of behaviour and cognition	<ul><li>Culture and its influence on behaviour and cognition<ul><li>*Cultural groups*</li></ul></li><li>Cultural dimensions</li></ul>
Cultural influences on individual attitudes, identity and behaviours	<ul><li>Enculturation<ul><li>*Norms*</li></ul></li><li>Acculturation<ul><li>*Assimilate*</li></ul></li></ul>
Ethical considerations and research methods	<ul><li>Students need to understand the use of research methods and relevant ethical considerations for each <u>topic</u>.</li></ul>

Terms it italics <u>may</u> be used in short-answer questions from May 2020 onwards.

Sociocultural approach to Understanding Human Behaviour

	Content	Key Questions	Key Studies
The individual and the group	**Social identity theory**	*How does social identity theory explain behaviour?*	• Park and Rothbart (1982) • Tajfel and Turner (1971) • Cialdini (1976)
	Social cognitive theory	*How does social cognitive theory explain behaviour?*	• Bandura et al. (1961 and 1963)
	Stereotypes	*What are the origins and effects of stereotypes?*	• Park and Rothbart (1982) • Stone et al. (1997) • Cohen (1981)
Cultural origins of behaviour and cognition	**Culture and its influence on behaviour and cognition**	*How can culture influence behaviour and cognition?*	• Cohen et al. (1996) (Multiple experiments)
	Cultural dimensions	*How can cultural dimensions influence behaviour?*	• Bond and Smith (1996) • Berry (1967) • Barry et al. (1959)
Cultural influences on individual attitudes, identity and behaviours	**Enculturation**	*How can enculturation influence behaviour?*	• Berry (1967) • Barry et al. (1959) • Lamm et al. (2018) • Bond and Smith (1996)
	Acculturation	*How can acculturation influence behaviour?*	• Torres et al. (2012) • Lyons-Padilla et al. (2015) • Nap et al. (2014)

- *All answers should be supported by evidence.*
- *Essay responses in Paper 1, Part B should include critical evaluation of the answer and the evidence.*
- *Students should also be prepared to discuss research methods and ethical considerations related to the relevant studies for the above <u>topics</u>.*

Social Identity Theory

In-Groups and Out-Groups
How does social identity theory explain behaviour?

Tajfel and Turner's Social Identity Theory attempts to explain the occurrence of conflict between groups (e.g. prejudice and discrimination). It focuses on the effects of identifying with an in-group and categorizing others as out-groups.

Key Details

- **Social identity theory (SIT)** was devised by Tajfel and Turner to explain intergroup behaviour. Specifically, it helps to explain intergroup conflict, including sources of intergroup conflict such as stereotypes, prejudice and discrimination.
- SIT was developed after realistic conflict theory (RCT). Whereas RCT states that conflict is caused by competition for resources, SIT explains how conflict can occur between groups even when there is no competition for resources.
- Essentially, SIT claims that belonging to a **social group** and identifying with that group can affect how we treat members of the out-groups. The theory also outlines a number of concepts involved in this process, including **social categorization, social comparison, positive distinctiveness and the self-esteem hypothesis**.

- Social categorization is the process of distinguishing who is a member of an in-group and who is in the out-group. After we categorize, it is natural for people to make comparisons between the groups and their members. According to SIT, comparisons serve to emphasize the distinctions between groups, with the in-group being seen more favourably (this is called positive distinctiveness).
- The **self-esteem hypothesis** of SIT posits that we tend to make biased comparisons which favour our in-group because we have a natural desire to have high self-esteem (and belonging to superior groups will do this). This bias can then lead to prejudice, as we judge others by their group identity and we may discriminate against them in favour of our own in-group members.

Key Study

Sororities and in-group bias (Park and Rothbart, 1982): The researchers worked with three sororities at the University of Oregon who were similar to one another. There were 90 participants (about 30 from each sorority). The data was gathered using questionnaires. The girls were asked to rank their own sorority and an out-group sorority on ten characteristics. In the questionnaire, the girls were asked to rank their own sorority and the other two in terms of how much each group personified these characteristics (there were 8 favourable characteristics and 2 unfavourable characteristics). Questions were asked for all ten characteristics and the results were compiled. For the eight favourable characteristics, all groups said that they were more typical of their own sorority than the other sororities. This shows in-group bias and can support social identity theory's explanation of how belonging to a group can

lead to in-group bias and favouritism, possibly as a result of wanting to boost one's self-esteem and positive social identity. Similarly, for the two unfavourable characteristics, in-group bias was shown in two of the sororities as they ranked the unfavourable characteristics as being more characteristic of the other sororities than their own. This is more evidence to explain how the cognitive process of social identity – social categorization and social comparison – can lead to in-group bias.

This code will take you to a blog post that has more information, including tables of specific results for this study and a video explaining it

Exam Tips

- Social Identity Theory can also be applied to the "group dynamics" topics in the Human relationships option, as well as the formation of stereotypes.
- When discussing (or evaluating) social theories of behaviour (e.g. SCT and SIT), try to think of biological explanations for the same behaviour(s) to use as counter-arguments.
- When answering SAQs about SIT, make sure you fully explain the theory first before writing about the supporting studies.

Extension: More Evidence for SIT

• **The out-group homogeneity effect** is the term used to describe the psychological phenomenon of perceiving out-group members as being more similar to one-another than in-group members. This could explain stereotypes of out-groups because a stereotype is a generalization about a group of people – if we think that an out-group of people are similar, this generalization becomes easier. Park and Rothbart's study demonstrates this phenomenon.

• **The minimal group paradigm**: In their early studies, Tajfel and Turner used British schoolboys to test their ideas about how identifying with an in-group can lead to in-group bias. They found that even when participants know they are being randomly assigned to groups, they still demonstrate in-group bias by offering more rewards to other anonymous in-group members compared to out-group members.

Further Studies

Sorority groups and the out-group homogeneity effect (Park and Rothbart, 1982): The results showed that girls in all three groups viewed their own sorority members as being less similar than the other girls thought they were. In other words, they thought out-group members were more similar to one-another than their own in-group members were to each other. Thus, they were demonstrating the out-group homogeneity effect. It could make it easier to be prejudiced and to discriminate against out-group members if you think they're all the same. This could also explain the formation of stereotypes.

Minimal group paradigm experiments (Tajfel et al., 1971): The minimal group paradigm is an experimental procedure that involves randomly putting people into groups based on meaningless criteria. They are then asked to assign points or rewards to other anonymous participants who are either in their in-group or out-group. They have to use matrices that influence what rewards they can give. The results of these studies show that participants will demonstrate in-group bias for anonymous in-group members even though the criteria

to create that in-group was meaningless. This could explain why some people favour members of their own group at the expense of others. *(For more information about SIT and supporting studies, visit our blog and search "social identity").*

Social identity in college students (Cialdini, 1976): In this study, the researchers wanted to see if victory in a college football game would have an effect on how students' identified with their college. The independent variable was whether or not the students' college football team won on the weekend and the dependent variable was how many wore clothing with their college's logo. The results showed that a victory increased the wearing of college-logo clothing. This is similar to other studies where fans will use the pronoun "they" when describing their team if they lose, but "we" if the team wins. Both these studies show social identity and provide support for the self-esteem hypothesis – we want to identify with victorious groups (e.g. teams) because they boost our self-esteem and we distant ourselves from losing teams.

Critical Thinking Considerations

• SIT aims to explain conflict between groups. Are there **alternative explanations** you can think of (hint: RCT and the Robber's Cave)?
• Are there individual differences that might make some people more likely to discriminate against others based on group identity (hint: SCT and biology)?
• Could in-group bias be explained from an evolutionary perspective?
• Can you apply SIT to explain any real-life examples of intergroup conflict? Is it limited in explaining extreme examples, such as genocide and mass murder? Can these extremely immoral behaviours be explained just by looking at social identity?
• SIT was developed in Western cultures. Can you think of any reasons why it might not fully explain intergroup conflict in other cultures?

Exam Tips - How many studies?

• SAQs: At least one study (most of the time one is enough, but you can use two if it helps your point).
• Essays: Aim for three studies, if possible. If you are asked to discuss or evaluate one study, first try to evaluate the methodological limitations (e.g. generalizability). Then try to find ways that other studies support or contradict the original. This means you need to choose the study you evaluate carefully. For example: If asked to discuss/evaluate one study related to SIT, I would use RCT and the Robber's Cave to show how competition for resources is another explanation of conflict between groups. Additionally, I would include a study to show that biology can be a factor, as well.

Social Cognitive Theory

Observational Learning and Triadic Reciprocal Determinism
How does social cognitive theory explain behaviour?

Bandura's social cognitive theory was originally called social learning theory and a key premise is that behaviour can be learned by observing others. Another key concept in this theory is that of triadic reciprocal determinism, which means our behaviour, internal characteristics and external factors all interact and affect one another.

Key Details

- Bandura's social learning theory (SLT) claims that behaviour can be learned through observation. This has helped to explain aggression, among other behaviours.
- Albert Bandura proposed his original theory (social learning theory) in the 1960s. SLT was renamed in the 1980s to 'social cognitive theory' to emphasize the role of cognition in observational learning.
- One key concept in SCT is **observational learning** – learning through the observation of others, including friends, family and in the media.
- Bandura claims that there are certain processes that will increase the likelihood that **modeling** (someone performing a behaviour) will lead to a learned behaviour by the observer of the model:
  - **Attention processes** (paying attention to the model)
  - **Retention processes** (remembering what the model did)
  - **Motor reproduction processes** (being able to physically replicate the behaviour)
  - **Reinforcement and motivational processes** (if a model is rewarded for their behaviour, the learner will be more motivated to imitate it)
- SCT has been used to explain how children may become aggressive adults by learning the aggressive behaviour through the observation of others, such as their siblings, parents or on TV.
- Bandura's theories were a response to the idea of **behaviourism**, which claimed that all behaviour was learned through conditioning – receiving rewards and punishments for behaviour.

Key Study

Bobo doll study #1 (Bandura, Ross and Ross, 1961): In this now famous experiment, children were exposed to different models. In one condition, the kids observed an adult model acting aggressively towards a large inflatable clown. In another condition, they observed the adult model playing peacefully with the doll. In the control condition, they didn't observe any model. The results showed that observing aggressive behaviour from the model increased the aggressive actions of the children. This study demonstrates that observation of a model can lead to imitated behaviour. It also supports the idea that identifying with a model could influence imitated behaviour, as boys who observed a male model and girls who observed a female model were more likely to imitate the behaviour.

Bobo doll study #2 (Bandura, Ross and Ross, 1963): The procedures of this study were similar to the original, although there were three aggressive conditions in this experiment: a real-life model, a televised model and a cartoon model. There was also a control condition. Similar to the original study, this experiment showed that the modelled behaviour was more likely to lead to imitated behaviour by the children. The results also showed that observing the cartoon model led to the highest number of imitated aggressive acts. It could be that cartoon versions attract and maintain children's attention more than the other conditions, as children seem to be drawn to cartoons.
For more information on these key studies, search "bobo doll" on our blog.

Exam Tips

- You need to be able to provide one explanation for how stereotypes are formed and explain how they could affect behaviour.
- The out-group homogeneity effect could be used to explain *how* stereotypes are formed, and schema theory could be used to explain *why*.
- SAQs will probably ask about either the effect or formation, so be prepared to answer both questions in an SAQ.

- **Triadic reciprocal determinism (a.k.a. triadic reciprocal causation)**: This is a key addition to Bandura's early theory of behaviour. Originally, social learning theory claimed that we learn by observation, so the direction of this relationship was singular: Environment → Behaviour. Triadic reciprocal determinism is the idea that external factors, internal factors and our behaviour all interact.

  o An example of this can be seen with the MAOA gene. The combination of childhood trauma or abuse (environment) and the MAOA gene (internal) can increase the likelihood of aggression (behaviour).

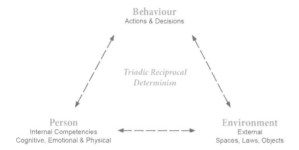

Behaviour
Actions & Decisions

Triadic Reciprocal
Determinism

Person
Internal Competencies
Cognitive, Emotional & Physical

Environment
External
Spaces, Laws, Objects

o Another example of this is the culture of honour: our cultural environment (environment) can influence our testosterone levels and desire to react to a challenge (internal) which can increase chances of aggression (behaviour).

- **Self-efficacy** is defined as "an individual's belief in his or her own ability to organize and implement action to produce the desired achievements and results" (Bandura, 1997). In other words, it is the confidence in one's ability to do something. For example, there is a bulk of evidence (i.e. many studies) that shows high self-efficacy in academics is associated with high academic achievement.

This code will take you to my YouTube video where I explain how to evaluate models and theories in psychology by using the DEAL structure. I also use SCT as an example throughout the video.

Further Studies

Longitudinal study of MAOA-L variants, childhood abuse and antisocial behaviour ("The Dunedin Study") (Caspi et al., 2002): This study followed over 1,000 children in Dunedin, NZ over 25 years and took measures every few years. They found that the MAOA-L gene moderated the effects of experiencing child abuse on adult aggression – that is to say, those participants with the MAOA-L gene variant and who were abused were more likely to be antisocial and aggressive adults. If participants experienced abuse as children, they were more likely to be antisocial, but the chances were almost 3 times as high for those with the MAOA-L variation (compared with the MAOA-H variation). This can be used to demonstrate triadic reciprocal determination, as the environment (abuse) is affecting the individual (genes) which affects behaviour (aggression).

Correlations between self-efficacy and GPA (Ismail et al., 2017): This study investigated the correlation between self-efficacy and GPA in 60 students of sports science at a university in Malaysia. The researchers gathered data on self-efficacy by using questionnaires and used university grades to record their GPA. The results showed that the correlation between self-efficacy and GPA was 0.67 for male students and 0.85 for female students. This is one example of how self-efficacy is correlated with academic achievement.

MAOA Gene, self-efficacy and academic boredom (Liu and Lu, 2017): In a study on Chinese students, it is not surprising that these researchers found a negative correlation between self-efficacy and academic boredom (lower self-efficacy linked with being more bored). What is interesting, however, is that differences in the MAOA gene moderated this relationship. In other words, the type of MAOA gene the students had affected how strongly their self-efficacy was linked with their academic boredom. This is another interesting example of triadic reciprocal determinism.

Critical Thinking Considerations

- SCT can be used to explain aggression in that aggressive behaviour is learned through observation (as demonstrated by the bobo doll studies). Can you offer an **alternative explanation** for aggression?
- Are their **methodological limitations** in any of the above studies? For example, Bandura's studies take place in an artificial environment. Can you think of reasons why this might not generalize to the real-life setting of a family home?
- In the late 1980s, when Bandura revised SCT, the concept of triadic reciprocal determinism would have been revolutionary. However, the interaction of nature and nurture is now almost common sense. Does this limit the value of this theory?

Stereotypes

Formation and Effects
What are the origins and effects of stereotypes?

The formation of stereotypes could be explained by looking at the out-group homogeneity effect. Stereotypes are also an example of a social schema and may lead to confirmation bias, so one effect of stereotypes is that they could reinforce the stereotype. Another effect could be the stereotype threat effect.

Key Details

- A **stereotype** is a widely held generalization about a group of people. The **out-group homogeneity effect** is the term used to describe the psychological phenomenon of perceiving out-group members as being more similar to one another than in-group members. This could explain stereotypes of out-groups because a stereotype is a generalization about a group of people – if we think that an out-group of people are similar to one another, it makes generalization (i.e. stereotyping) much easier.
- Another explanation could be that **social identity theory** claims we categorize people into out-groups and in-groups and we make comparisons between groups in a way that make our in-groups seem superior. This could explain why we have negative stereotypes of out-groups – we raise our self-esteem by making our own in-group look superior.
- **Schema theory** provides an explanation that we form stereotypes in order to save our cognitive energy. It requires less cognitive energy to think about a group of people as being similar than to think of them as unique individuals.

Key Study

Effect of stereotypes on behaviour: Park and Rothbart (1982): In this study on college sorority girls in Oregon, the researchers studied in-group bias and out-group homogeneity effect. The results showed that girls in all three groups viewed their own sorority members as being more dissimilar than the other girls thought they were. In other words, they thought out-group members were more similar to one another than their own in-group members were to each other. Thus, they were demonstrating the out-group homogeneity effect. In terms of explaining stereotypes, we can see how this view of out-group members as being similar to one another could make it easier to make generalizations about that group of people. Since stereotypes are generalizations of groups, the out-group homogeneity effect could explain how stereotypes are formed. For example, there could be a stereotype that one sorority is full of party animals and another is full of geeks.

This code will take you to a blog post that has more information, including tables of specific results for this study and a video explaining it.

Exam Tips

- You need to be able to provide one explanation for how stereotypes are formed and explain how they could affect behaviour.
- The out-group homogeneity effect could be used to explain *how* stereotypes are formed, and schema theory could be used to explain *why*.
- SAQs will probably ask about either the effect or formation, so be prepared to answer both questions in an SAQ.

• **Confirmation bias**: Stereotypes could influence our perception of people and affect how we make judgements about them. This is because stereotypes can lead to confirmation bias. Why does this happen? Cognitive psychologists suggest that humans are "cognitive misers," which means we want to save our cognitive energy. This is why we tend to focus on information that is consistent with our existing beliefs and opinions more than we focus on contradictory information. In other words, we have a tendency to focus on schema-consistent information, as opposed to schema-contradictory information. This bias is known as confirmation bias. Since a stereotype is a type of schema, it means that if we have a stereotype about a group of people and we're making judgements about someone from that group, we're likely to focus on information that reinforces that stereotype and ignore information that contradicts it. This could affect how we judge that person and could reinforce stereotypes, making any stereotypes harder to get rid of.

• **Stereotype threat** occurs when someone feels they may end up conforming to a stereotype held about their group. This has been shown to affect performance in a range of tasks, including SAT scores and general academic tests. This is one way stereotypes can affect our behaviour.

Further Studies

Confirmation bias and stereotypical perceptions and judgements of basketball players (Stone et al., 1997): The participants of this study were told that they were participating in a study comparing listening to a radio and watching TV, but they were really the subject of a study about stereotypes. They each listened to a recording of a basketball game and were given the name of a player and told to listen carefully to his performance. Half of the participants were shown a photo of a white athlete and the other half were shown a photo of a black athlete. After the recording, they completed a questionnaire based on evaluations of natural ability, performance and contributions of the player. The results showed that the ratings were "…remarkably consistent with the stereotypes discussed in the sports media: Perceivers reported that Black men have more athletic ability and are better at playing the game of basketball, but white men can contribute because they are more intelligent and make up for their lack of physical ability through effort." *(See also Cohen et al.'s study in the schema theory section).*

Stereotype threat effect in race and the SATs (Aronson and Steele, 1995): In this famous study, the researchers compared the SAT scores of black students and white students. The researchers manipulated the stereotype threat by either telling students they were being tested on their intellectual abilities or that it was just a test of problem solving. When participants had to indicate their race and were told that it was a test of intellectual performance, the black students did worse than when they were simply told it was a test of problem solving strategies. This provides support for the effect of stereotype threat on behaviour.

Stereotype threat effect in Asian-American women (Shih et al., 1999): The aim of this study was to see if stereotype threat effect could have a *positive* influence on behaviour. Forty-six female Asian-American students from Harvard were randomly allocated into one of three conditions (Asian-identity condition, gender-identity condition and control). In the Asian-identity condition, they were asked questions related to their heritage. For the gender-identity condition, they were asked questions related to gender. In the control condition, they were asked meaningless questions. After these questionnaires, they took a math test and the results showed there was a significant difference in the percentage of correct answers in each condition: Asian-identity: 54% Control: 49% Gender identity 43%. This suggests that stereotype threat can have a positive or a negative effect on behaviour. *Search "stereotype threat" on our blog for more details about this topic.*

Critical Thinking Considerations

• SIT can explain negative stereotypes of out-groups and positive stereotypes of in-groups, but can it do the opposite?
• The above studies are all conducted in the USA. Are there reasons why these results might not be generalizable to other cultures?

Cultural Influences on Behaviour and Cognition

Culture of Honour
How can culture influence behaviour and cognition?

The values associated with a culture of honour could influence violence. This influence may occur because of biological and cognitive effects of the culture of honour.

Key Details

• Culture is "…made up of a set of attitudes, behaviours, and symbols shared by a large group of people, and usually communicated from one generation to the next." (IB Guide, p. 34). **Cultural groups** can be identified by their distinct **cultural norms**, which are shared expectations of appropriate ways of thinking and behaving. A "**culture of honour**" is one type of cultural group that shares cultural norms and has been identified by anthropologists and psychologists.

• A culture of honour is characterized by the importance that is placed on maintaining one's honour, especially in the face of threat. In these groups, "… small disputes become contests for reputation and social status." (Cohen et al., 1996). In other words, if you are threatened or insulted, you are expected to respond in order to defend your honour.

• While there are many examples of cultures of honour around the world, one particular cultural group that has been studied is the South in the United States. In Cohen et al.'s key research, the focus was primarily on white,

Southern males. In their original 1996 study, Cohen et al. reported that white male homicide rates are higher in the South than the North and in the South there is a higher number of murders that are related to arguments and conflict.

• Early studies also showed that Southerners were more accepting of some types of violence over others. More specifically, they were more accepting of violence for self-protection or retaliating in response to an insult. These cultural norms that are persistent in a culture of honour could influence the likelihood that someone would response to a threat or insult with violence.

Key Study

The culture of honour and a comparison of reactions to insult (Cohen et al., 1996): In this study, there were 148 white male college students. Half were from the North and half were from the South of the US. The participants were told they were in a study on personality and they filled out a questionnaire. Then they were then asked to walk down a long hallway to place their questionnaire on a table. Halfway down the hallway, a confederate (an actor working for the researchers) bumped into the participant (on purpose but made to look like an accident) and then the confederate called the participant an a**hole (this was the threat). After this, the participant continued walking down the very

narrow hallway (wide enough for only one person) and another confederate walked towards them. This second confederate was big: 6'3" (1.91m) and 250lbs (114kg). The researchers had set up a game of "chicken" and wanted to see how close the participants would get before "chickening out" to the bigger man. The results showed that the Southerners who had been bumped got much closer to the bigger man before chickening out (0.94m) compared to the Northern participants (2.74m). The conclusion we can draw from this study is that Southerners are more likely to react with hostility after being insulted compared to Northerners.

Exam Tips

• If you are asked about culture and behaviour, you can also use the material on cultural dimensions (next topic) or from the personal relationships topic in the Human Relationships option.

• If you are writing about aggression for any biological topics (e.g. hormones, neurotransmitters, etc.), the culture of honour studies make for good counter-arguments (and to explain the *reactive* part of impulsive, reactive aggression).

• While it's highly unlikely, you may be asked an SAQ about cultural influences on cognition (not behaviour). The example of cognitive priming is the best example to use to answer this question.

• **Biological factors**: The relationship between culture and aggression could be moderated (influenced) by other factors, including internal biological and cognitive factors. For example, testosterone is a hormone that has been directly linked with levels of aggression. Studies such as Radke et al.'s (see hormones topic) show that testosterone increases activity in the amygdala, which could bias the amygdala towards dealing with a threat. Increases in testosterone could further increase the likelihood of responding aggressively to a challenge or threat. Cohen's studies below show that Southerners experience a higher spike in testosterone (and cortisol) levels after being insulted.

• **Cognitive factors**: Culture influences behaviour through its effect on our thinking – our cultural values and norms affect how we think and this affects our actions. Cohen also studied how different cultural backgrounds (North vs South) had an effect on cognition.

Further Studies

Other experiments:
Cohen and colleagues conducted a series of experiments in their original report. Along with measuring their willingness to display "dominance behaviour," (as shown in the previous study) they also measured other factors. They used similar experimental designs, which included comparing Northerner and Southerner responses to insults.

• **Testosterone**: In one experiment, saliva samples were taken before and after the participants received the insult. The testosterone levels of the Southerners increased by 12%, compared to only 4% for the Northerners.

• **Cognitive priming**: In another experiment, the researchers measured how the insult might have influenced cognitive priming. Cognitive priming refers to the effect something has on one's perception, thinking or behaviour. In this context, it refers to the effects of the insult on the perceptions and judgements of the participants. After the insults, the participants were given a series of tasks to complete. One of these was a story completion task. After the insult, participants read the start of a story about an engaged woman being hit on by another man at a party. They were then asked to finish the story. The results showed that insulted Southerners were more likely to complete the story with the threatened male (the guy who was engaged to the girl) responding violently in some way: 75% of Southerners ended the story with the threatened male injuring or threatening to injure his challenger compared to only 20% of the Northerners.

Critical Thinking Considerations

• Could these experiments have a **methodological limitation** because they never directly measured aggression? Why might a Southerner's reaction in a real-life situation be different?

• Can cultural values of a culture of honour explain *all* types of violence? What are some examples of violence that it might not explain?

• These studies focus mainly on the cultural factors influencing aggressive behaviour. What **alternative explanations** (e.g. biological or cognitive factors) are important to consider (hint: think about studies such as Radke, Bandura, Passamonti, and Caspi)?

• Are there ethical considerations associated with this series of experiments?

Cultural Dimensions

Individualism/Collectivism and Conformity
How can cultural dimensions influence behaviour?

Cultural dimensions are descriptions of cultural values that can be placed on a continuum. The most commonly studied is individualism/collectivism. This could affect conformity.

Key Details

- A **cultural dimension** is a group of related cultural values. One cultural dimension includes values at two ends of a spectrum, so the cultural dimension of individualism/collectivism has individualistic values at one end of this spectrum and collectivistic values at the other.
- Individualistic values include focusing on individuals, having loose connections with wider groups and looking after one's immediate family.
- Collectivistic values put the group before the individual and they form strong in-group bonds. They focus more on maintaining norms and group harmony over personal interests.

- People with individualistic values might be less likely to conform because they value their own opinion over the opinion of the group. People with collectivist values, on the other hand, may be more likely to conform to social norms since they wouldn't want to be seen as disrupting social harmony.
- *See table on the opposite page for a more complete summary of differences.*

Key Study

Meta-analysis of Asch Paradigm studies (Bond and Smith, 1996): The Asch paradigm is an experimental procedure that involves a group of people answering questions about the length of lines, except only one participant is a real participant and the rest are confederates instructed to occasionally give wrong answers. The original studies by Asch found that about 75% of participants conformed with the group at least once. After his famous studies, many replications were conducted around the world over the following 50+ years. Bond and Smith gathered these together to see if there were any correlations between culture and rates of conformity. They collected the data from 17 countries and a total of 133 studies that used the Asch paradigm. They correlated levels of conformity with individualism/collectivism scores. The results showed that countries high on the individualistic scale like the UK, the USA and France had lower rates of conformity, whereas countries high on the collectivistic scale like Hong Kong, Fiji and Japan had higher rates of conformity. There are multiple possible explanations for these results, including the differences placed on group harmony.

Exam Tips

- The material from the interpersonal relationships topic in the Human Relationships option can also be applied here. Similarly, Barry's and Berry's studies from the next topic (enculturation) can also be used to explain possible economic reasons how and why some cultures might develop collectivist or individualistic values.
- For any question about cultural dimensions, aim to write about 5-6 characteristics for individualism and collectivism.
- Remember that individualism and collectivism is *one* cultural dimension. The IB guide states you can learn about "one or more." Therefore, learning about individualism/collectivism in-depth is an effective strategy.
- You could be asked about only one behaviour or you could have the chance to write about various behaviours.

Individualism	Collectivism
• Focus on the "I" • Have an identity that comes from their individuality • Loose ties between individuals (look after yourself and your immediate family) • Competition exists between individuals and is encouraged • When carrying out a task, the task comes first and the relationship may come afterwards • Confrontations are okay and can sometimes be viewed as healthy	• Focus on the "we" • Identity is defined by relationships with others and belonging to various groups • Form strong in-groups. This could be the immediate family, extended family, tribe, village or whole community • Competition is between whole groups • When carrying out a task, relationships come first and the task comes second • Value harmony in the in-group, even if some members disagree - the group harmony is important

- **Origins of cultural values:** There have been numerous theories proposed as to why different cultural dimensions (i.e. values) have emerged in some parts of the world. The list below can provide further insight as to why some cultures may develop values associated with individualism and collectivism that may lead to higher rates of conformity.

  - **Enculturation and economics**: Cultures relying on agriculture may encourage conformity with norms and obedience because these are important qualities that will ensure that crops and animals are properly raised. On the other hand, low food accumulating cultures can afford to take more risks and experiment with new ideas, since a failed innovation will only have short-term consequences but a success can have long-term benefits. Thus, people in these cultures are likely to value independence and innovation *(read more about this in the next topic).*

- **"Rice Theory"**: Talhelm et al. (2014) proposed a theory that the differences in staple crops (rice vs. wheat) could explain differences in the value placed on conformity and co-operation compared to independence. Rice is a labor-intensive grain - with traditional methods, it required co-operation from the whole village for sowing and harvesting, as well as sharing waterways. Wheat, on the other hand, could be grown by a single farmer, so self-reliance and independence are more beneficial.

- *For a fascinating theory of how genetics might have influenced the development of individualism and collectivism, visit our blog and search "culture-gene coevolution."*

Further Studies

Cross-cultural correlational study on economic factors and child training practices (Barry et al., 1959): This study compared 46 cultures from around the world ranging from low to high food accumulation. They gathered data to measure the child training practices in each culture and focused on things like obedience, responsibility, self-reliance, achievement, independence, etc. They studied the practices used on children from around 5 years old to adolescence. The results showed that high food accumulating cultures placed more emphasis on responsibility and obedience training, whereas low food accumulating cultures placed more emphasis on training children in ways that would encourage independence, achievement and self-reliance. In conclusion, parents raise their kids with the cultural values that are going to help them be successful in the economies in which they live. These values may explain why some cultures are more likely to conform to group norms than others are.

Critical Thinking Considerations

- Can you think of any **alternative explanations** for conformity? For example, how might an evolutionary psychologist explain conformity?
- Can the enculturation and economics explanation of cultural values explain why Central and South American and Asian cultures are more collectivist, while European cultures are more individualistic?
- Barry's studies date back to the 1950s. What are the limitations in applying these studies to modern societies?

Enculturation

Parenting, Cultural Values and Conformity
How can enculturation influence behaviour?

Enculturation is the process of acquiring the values of one's home culture. Parenting is one way in which enculturation happens and different types of parenting could affect levels of conformity in a society. This is because parents raise their children with the cultural values and norms that will help them succeed in that culture and so these values and norms will vary depending on the economic system of that culture.

Key Details

• **Enculturation** is a broad term that refers to the process of acquiring the cultural norms and values of one's home culture. Berry defines it as a type of cultural transmission, a process "...by which cultural features of a population are transferred to its individual members." (Berry, 2010).

• There are many ways that people can become enculturated, including through education, parents, peers and other social influences like the media. Parents naturally want their children to adopt the cultural values and cultural norms of the home culture so they can be successful individuals in that culture. Thus, they will teach them these values and norms.

• How parents raise their children and the values they encourage will vary depending on the culture. For example, Barry et al. proposed that cultures traditionally relying on agriculture and farming may encourage

obedience and conformity with norms because these are important qualities that will ensure both crops and animals are properly raised (they have short harvest seasons, so if rules aren't followed, survival could be jeopardized because crops may fail and food could be ruined). On the other hand, the researchers argue, cultures that are more hunter-gatherer can afford to take more risks and experiment with new ideas. This is because a failed innovation will only have short-term consequences, but a success can have long-term benefits. Thus, people in these cultures are likely to value independence and innovation.

• In terms of effects on behaviour, if cultures value obedience and compliance with cultural norms, they are probably more likely to have high levels of **conformity**, whereas those that value independence would be less likely to conform to group norms.

Key Study

Cross-cultural correlational study on economic factors and child training practices (Barry et al., 1959): This study compared 46 cultures from around the world ranging from low to high food accumulation. They gathered data to measure the child training practices in each culture and focused on things like obedience, responsibility, self-reliance, achievement, independence, etc. They studied the practices used on children from around 5 years old to adolescence. The results showed that high food accumulating cultures placed more emphasis on responsibility and obedience

training, whereas low food accumulating cultures placed more emphasis on training children in ways that would encourage independence, achievement and self-reliance. In conclusion, parents raise their kids with the cultural values that are going to help them be successful in the economies in which they live. These values may explain why some cultures are more likely to conform to group norms than others are (use Barry's study for evidence of cross-cultural differences of conformity as based on economic factors).

Exam Tips

• Berry's study can show the example of cultural differences in conformity and Barry's study can show why they happen.
• If conformity is too difficult to explain, use delayed gratification and the Marshmallow test study by Lamm et al. for an SAQ.
• Barry's theory and study can also be applied to explain origins of cultural dimensions.
• Bond and Smith's research shows: culture → conformity. Adding the above information to the explanation looks like this: economics → culture → parenting → conformity. (See cultural dimensions section for more info on this study).

- **Enculturation and delayed gratification**: Parenting (i.e. one way enculturation occurs) could also explain why some kids are able to delay gratification and wait for rewards, while other kids are more impulsive. We can make conclusions about enculturation may affect behaviour by seeing how parenting styles and attitudes across cultures may be linked with their kids' abilities to delay gratification. This was done in one study comparing German and Cameroonian kids in a famous test called the Stanford Marshmallow Test (see study below).

Further Studies

Marshmallow experiments – a cross-cultural comparison (Lamm et al., 2018): When kids take the marshmallow test, they sit in a room by themselves and they are given a marshmallow. The researcher tells them that if they wait ten minutes, they can get a second marshmallow. This is a test of their ability to delay gratification. Studies have found that kids who can wait for the bigger reward when they are younger grow up to do better in school, have higher SAT scores, get better jobs and be less likely to commit crimes. Most of these studies have taken place in the USA and other Western countries. This particular study compared the ability of German and Cameroonian four-year-old preschool children to delay gratification and wait for a treat (the Cameroonian children did not have marshmallows, but instead were given a similar treat that is popular for Cameroonian kids). In the first study, the results showed that almost 70% of the Cameroonian kids were able to wait for a treat, compared to around 30% of German kids. The researchers also gathered data on the values of the parents and their parenting styles. They found that Cameroonian mothers placed more emphasis on "hierarchical relational socialization" (e.g. obeying and respecting elders) and they placed strict emphasis on conforming to social norms. The German mothers, on the other hand, had more emphasis on "psychological autonomous socialization," which means they allowed more individuality and personal freedom. This study provides us with another example of how different enculturation processes (e.g. different parenting styles and values) can have an effect on the behaviour of children.

Cross-cultural comparison of the Asch paradigm (Berry, 1967): This study compared people from a tribe in Africa (the Temne people of Sierra Leone) with Inuit (Eskimo) people from Baffin Island in North America. The researchers used the Asch paradigm (judging line lengths in the presence of confederates giving wrong answers) to measure conformity. The results showed that the Temne people had higher rates of conformity than the Inuit. This is because, Berry argued, the Temne people were an agricultural society, so they needed higher rates of cooperation in order to survive. The Inuit, on the other hand, encourage more individualism as their method of gathering food does not require as much cooperation as agricultural societies. Barry (1959) would explain the difference by focusing on the different food production systems.

Critical Thinking Considerations

- What are some **alternative explanations** for these behaviours? For example, what other factors besides culture and parenting might affect the ability to delay gratification?
- Barry's theory and study come from the 1950s. Are there reasons why these might not apply to modern societies? (e.g. globalization)
- Parenting is one way enculturation can happen. Can you think of other factors that might affect this process?

Acculturation

Acculturation Strategies and Psychological Distress
How can acculturation influence behaviour?

Acculturation may refer to assimilation, but it can also refer to Berry's model of acculturation which outlines four way in which someone may adapt to a new culture. The type of acculturation a person experiences can affect their behaviour. More specifically, it may moderate the effects of prejudice and discrimination.

Key Details

- **Acculturation** is the process of adapting and changing as a result of living in a new culture (Berry, 2002). To explain the effects of acculturation on behaviour, we can look at how different acculturation strategies can have different effects on behaviour.
- Berry's model of acculturation identifies four **acculturation strategies**: assimilation, integration, separation and marginalization *(see the next page for definitions and an illustration)*.
- Numerous studies have shown that those who have integrated have better mental health outcomes than those adopting other strategies. Similarly, integrating could act as a buffer against the harmful effects of prejudice and discrimination. For example, marginalized individuals who have no sense of their home culture *and* have not integrated into their new culture may be more likely to sympathize and may even join extremist groups. It has been argued that they may join extremist groups (e.g. ISIS) not because they hold the same beliefs, but because they are missing a sense of group identity, purpose and belonging. This can have significant implications for understanding origins of Islamic extremism and terrorism. Evidence for this can be seen in Lyons-Padilla et al's study below.

Key Study

Acculturation, discrimination and extremism in Muslim immigrants (Lyons-Padilla et al., 2015):
In this study, the researchers surveyed 200 first- and second-generation Muslim immigrants across the USA using a range of questionnaires. One result was that there was a strong correlation between feeling marginalized and feeling a sense of "significance loss" (a term the researchers used to describe a feeling of a lack of meaning, purpose and belonging). This is one example of how acculturation can have an effect on our behaviour. In addition, there was also a strong correlation between feeling significance loss and adopting a more radical interpretation of Islam. Another finding from the study was that discrimination moderated the effects of marginalization on significance loss. That is to say, participants who felt they had experienced discrimination and were marginalized had more of a sense of significance loss than those who weren't discriminated against. This is important to note, because they also found a positive correlation between feelings of significance loss and support for a fundamentalist Islamic group. In other words, discrimination and marginalization can increase support for fundamentalist Islamic groups. Here, we see numerous ways that the acculturation strategy of marginalization can affect behaviour.

Exam Tips

- The explanation of acculturation and extremism can be used for the HL extension as it shows how globalization (e.g. immigration) may affect behaviour. Lyons-Padilla et al.'s research can also be used to show the effects of prejudice and discrimination and perhaps even origins of conflict (this will help for the human relationships option).
- Remember to prepare one key explanation of a topic and one key study when writing SAQs. The term "assimilation" may be used in an SAQ. You could define it synonymously with acculturation (as the IB has done) or define it as *one* acculturation strategy (as Berry et al. have done).
- The examples for this topic show cultural influences on identity (belonging to an in-group), attitudes (interpretations of Islam and support for fundamentalist groups) and behaviour (significance loss).

- **Acculturation strategies**:
  - **Assimilation**: when an individual loses a sense of belonging to his or her heritage culture and completely adopts and adapts to the norms and values of their new culture.
  - **Integration**: the individual adapts to the new culture by adopting the cultural values and norms but they still have strong connections with their heritage culture.
  - **Separation**: the individual maintains their norms and values of their home culture, and rejects those of their new culture.
  - **Marginalization**: when an individual loses their sense of belonging to their heritage culture *and* does not adapt to their new culture.
- Numerous studies have shown that individuals who acculturate by integrating have the best psychological outcomes and reduced **acculturative stress** (negative mental health outcomes that come about because of interacting with a new culture). For example, they suffer from fewer mental health problems like depression, anxiety and stress. Integration can also protect against the negative effects of experiencing

Cultural Adaptation (relationship sought among groups)

		Low	High
Maintenance of heritage culture	**High**	Separation	Integration
	Low	Marginalization	Assimilation

Berry's model of acculturation that shows the difference between the four acculturation strategies. This diagram can be recreated in exam answers.

discrimination: people who adopt an acculturation strategy of integration experience less acculturative stress, depression and anxiety, whereas those who are separated or marginalized are more at risk for these types of mental health problems.

Further Studies

Correlational study of Latino-Americans, integration and discrimination (Torres et al., 2012): This study surveyed 669 Latinos from a range of countries (50% born outside of the US) who were living in the Midwest of America. They completed questionnaires to measure their acculturative stress, mental health and experiences of perceived discrimination (e.g. in school). The results showed a positive correlation between discrimination and acculturative stress, but they also found that participants who had a "higher Anglo behavioural orientation" (i.e. were more integrated) had lower levels of acculturative stress. This is one example of how the acculturation strategy used by people adapting to a new culture can affect behaviour.

The influence of acculturation on mental health (Nap et al., 2014): This study surveyed 5000 Moroccan, Surinamese and Turkish immigrants who had moved to the Netherlands. They were all seeking treatment in mental health facilities. One finding was that not all cultures integrated equally – Surinamese had the highest integration while Turkish participants had the least. This suggest that one's heritage culture could affect the acculturation strategy used. The researchers also gathered data on their levels of social integration (among other factors) and correlated this with their mental health symptoms. The results showed a modest (but statistically significant) negative correlation between social integration and mental health symptoms (-0.24, $p<0.0025$). They also found that those who were integrated needed less future care.

Critical Thinking Considerations

- Berry's model makes the **assumption** that everyone has a heritage culture. Can you think of people who might be exceptions to this, meaning this model may not apply?
- Is Lyons-Padilla et al's study **reliable**? At the time of writing, this was the first study of its kind and it has not yet been replicated.
- These studies are correlational. Can you explain any possible examples of bidirectional ambiguity in these studies? Can you think of other external variables that might affect (or explain) the correlations found?
- What are the possible applications of these findings on acculturation?

True Experiments

How and why are true experiments used to study the individual and the group?

True experiments (a.k.a. laboratory experiments) are used when the researchers manipulate an independent variable and create different conditions. They then, as much as possible, try to control for all extraneous variables and measure the effects of the IV on the dependent variable. By carefully controlling the extraneous variables, the researchers can maximize the chances that any differences in the DV can be explained by the IV. This allows for conclusions about causality to be made.

Key Details

• **True experiments in the sociocultural approach to understanding behaviour**: The key benefit of a true experiment is that the researchers can manipulate the independent variable that they hypothesize will have an effect on behaviour in some way. They can also do this in a controlled environment so the IV is the only variable affecting the DV. This is valuable in studies that investigate the effects of social factors on behaviour, such as social influence (Asch), social learning and observational learning (Bandura) and belonging to an in-group (Tajfel and Turner). In these experiments, the researchers can manipulate the social variable and create different conditions for comparison in tightly-controlled experiments. This is valuable because it is often difficult to observe social influence in natural settings and to control the social factor.

• On the other hand, they are limited for studies on the effects of culture on behaviour because culture is an independent variable that cannot be contrived or created in an artificial environment. For this reason, correlational studies are most commonly used in the study of the effects of culture on behaviour.

Key Studies

The individual and the group – examples of true experiments:

> **Bandura's bobo doll experiments**: We can have correlational studies that compare exposure to violent TV and violence, but the researchers can't control all the possible extraneous variables (like the child's natural levels of aggression). Using a matched-pairs experimental design, Bandura was able to control for this factor and to isolate the exposure to violence as the only variable influencing the behaviour of the kids.

Stone et al. and Cohen et al.'s experiments on stereotypes: These studies activated a particular stereotype (social-cognitive factor) and measured its effects on behaviour (memory and judgement). This is another example of how experiments can study the influence of social factors on behaviour. Note: this is referring to the Cohen's waitress/librarian study, not the culture of honour study (different Cohen).

Critical Thinking Considerations

• Are true experiments inherently limited in generalizability because of their artificial environments?
• How can correlational studies strengthen the results of true experiments?
• What are the ethical considerations associated with true experiments?

Exam Tips

• Correlational studies are commonly used to study cultures effects on behaviour. For more information about this, see the Sociocultural HL extension and the research method section in the Human Relationships option. We also have a blog post explaining this.

Informed Consent in True Experiments

How and why are ethical guidelines considered in studies on the individual and the group?

In order for a study to be considered ethical, participants should leave the study in the same (or improved) psychological and physical health as when they began the study. Informed consent means you get an agreement from participants that they want to be in the study (consent) and they are basing this decision on information you have given them (informed). **Informed consent** *is one consideration that can reduce some of the stress and other negative effects of participating in a study.*

Key Details

• **Informed consent**: Experiments involving the investigation of social factors on behaviour can be very troubling and problematic for participants because humans are social animals that are heavily influenced by the thoughts and actions of others. For this reason, researchers should ideally obtain informed consent before the experiment begins. As always, however, they need to strike a balance between giving too much information away in the informed consent and affecting the validity of the study (because of the fear of participant expectancy effects or other confounding variables).

Key Studies

Bandura's bobo doll experiments: These studies were conducted on young children so parental consent is essential. In order for the parents to make an informed decision, they would need to know that their child wouldn't experience any long-term harm or suffering and the researchers may even explain the procedures.

Stone et al. and Cohen et al.'s experiments on stereotypes: Stereotypes are a socially sensitive area of study.

In order to make participants completely comfortable with taking part in the study, the researchers may inform them that this is what they are studying. However, if they did so, this might affect the participants' answers because of the social desirability effect (the desire to be viewed positively by others). For this reason, some information in the informed consent may be withheld, which highlights the need for debriefing after the study has finished.

Critical Thinking Considerations

• You may be asked about two ethical considerations for an essay question – how and why is anonymity (or any other consideration) relevant to experimental studies on the individual and the group?
• How might informed consent affect the validity of a study?
• How much detail should researchers reveal in their consent forms?
• Are there other ethical considerations relevant to true experiments at the sociocultural approach?

Exam Tips

• By focusing on one common method (true experiments) and one ethical consideration (informed consent) you can reduce the content you need to revise and improve the quality of your explanations.
• A good way to start any ethical consideration question is to state the relevant consideration(s) and provide a definition. The best answers will clearly explain why informed consent is relevant and what exactly must be considered *before* describing the studies.
• Prepare one consideration for SAQs and essays but have a second as a backup, just in case. Debriefing works well in conjunction with informed consent.

5 HL Extensions

As a Higher Level IB Psychology student, you get the opportunity to explore some really interesting extra topics. The topics, concepts and research used in this chapter are designed to build on your existing learning from the other units.

The material from the extensions will be assessed in Paper 1, Part B (essays). One, two or all three of the essay questions will be based on the HL extension material.

A good strategy is to prepare one extension for the exams. You should also choose one approach that is the same as the extension you feel most confident with. This means that you do not have to review lots of studies for all three approaches.

For example, you may decide to prepare the biological approach + animal studies extension for essays. You would skip the other extensions. This means that no matter what essay question comes up under the biological approach, you would be able to write about it. This will also allow you to exploit the overlaps in content between the core topics and the extensions because many of the same studies can be used for both.

Biological Approach: Animal Studies
The theme of this topic is the value of using animal models to provide insight into the role of genetics, hormones, and brain function in human behaviour.

Cognitive approach: Technology and Cognition
The major theme of this topic is the positive and negative effects of technology on cognitive processes and their reliability.

Sociocultural Approach: Globalization
The major theme of this topic is how individuals may be influenced by changes occurring in the physical and cultural environment as a result of globalization.

Biological Approach - HL Extensions

Biological approach: The role of animal research in understanding human behaviour
- The value of animal models in psychological research
- Whether animal research can provide insight into human behaviour
- Ethical considerations in animal research

Core Topics	Core Concepts	Supporting Studies

The brain and behaviour	*The value of animal models is that they can provide insight into localization of function and how damage to the brain may affect behaviour.*	• Weiskrantz (1956)
		  • *SM's case study (Feinstein et al. 2011)*
		• Rosenzweig and Bennett (1960s)
		  • *Perry and Pollard (1997)*
		  • *Luby et al. (2013)*
		• Sapolsky (1990)

Hormones and behaviour	*The value of animal models is that they can provide insight into how hormones may affect behaviour.*	• Sapolsky (1990)
		  • *Luby et al. (2013)*
		• Albert et al. (1986)
		  • *Radke et al. (2015)*

Genetics and behaviour	*The value of animal models is that they can provide insight into how genetics may affect behaviour.*	• Van Oortmerssen and Bakker (1981) • Mosienko et al. (2012) • *Caspi et al. (2002)*

(Animal models)

Core Topics	Core Concepts	Supporting Studies
The brain and behaviour	*Psychologists need to consider the justifications for harming animals in order to study genetics and behaviour. Where harm is justified, they should keep suffering to a minimum.*	• Weiskrantz (1956) • Sapolsky (1990)
Hormones and behaviour		• Sapolsky (1990) • Albert al (1986)
Genetics and behaviour		• Van Oortmerssen and Bakker (1981) • Mosienko (2012)

(Ethical considerations in animal research)

- *Tip: The biological approach extensions have the most predictable questions and if you can comprehend the explanations provided in these topics, you could write excellent answers. However, the material tends to be more complex than the cognitive approach.*
- *Human studies are written in italics*

Animal Research on the Brain and Behaviour

Localization and neuroplasticity

To what extent can animal studies provide insight into relationships between the brain and behaviour?

Non-human animals have neurological similarities that make them valuable in studies on relationships between the brain and behaviour. These studies may provide insight into localization of function and neuroplasticity.

Key Details: Localization

- An **animal model** is the use of non-human animals to demonstrate a biological or psychological phenomenon. For example, **localization of function** is one phenomenon that has been demonstrated using animal models.
- Animals were especially important for research on localization before the invention of modern brain imaging technologies like fMRI. This is because psychologists could research localization of brain function by damaging the brains of animals in experimental research and measuring the effects.
- In these experiments, there are typically two conditions: one condition has a group of animals that have areas of their brain scarred (lesioned) or removed entirely (ablated). There is a control condition that has no damage to the brain. The researchers measure the behaviour of the different conditions, compare them and draw conclusions.
- If the damage to a particular area of the animal's brain results in a change in behaviour, the researchers can conclude that the part of the brain that was damaged must have some sort of function related to that behaviour.
- The reason why animals are valuable in these experiments is because it would unethical to conduct these studies on humans (and impractical, too, since humans wouldn't volunteer to have their brain damaged).

Key Studies

Key Study: Lesioning of the amygdala in rhesus monkeys (Weiskrantz, 1956): In this study, the researchers wanted to study the relationship between the amygdala and emotion. Earlier research (in the late 1800s) had found connections between the temporal lobe and emotion. This experiment went one step further by isolating the amygdala as the particular part of the temporal lobe that might be connected with emotion. There were two conditions in the experiment: one group of monkeys had their amygdalae lesioned and the other condition had a different part of the temporal lobe lesioned. The results showed that it was damage to the amygdalae specifically that led to a lack of fear in the monkeys. The use of monkeys in this experiment helped to develop the understanding of the amygdala's role in emotion and fear.

Human Study: SM's case study (Feinstein et al. 2011): The above study provides insight into the role of the amygdala in experiencing emotions, like fear. More modern human studies have supported this connection, like the case study on SM. SM has bilateral amygdala damage and cannot feel fear. Researchers have tested this by observing her behaviour in places like haunted houses, exotic pet stores and when watching scary films *(see localization of brain function in the biological approach for more details)*.

Exam Tips

- The value of animal models is that they can provide insight into human behaviour. You have to assess "whether" they can by explaining limitations.
- You can use the effects of hormones on the brain (next topic) for this topic, as well (e.g. Sapolsky, 1990).

- Animal experiments have also been valuable in studying **neuroplasticity** – the brain's ability to change as a result of experience.
- Similar to studies on localization, the benefit of animal experiments for neuroplasticity is that researchers can control the extraneous variables and isolate the environmental factor that they think might have an effect on the developing brain.
- Early animal experiments were able to disprove the common belief that the human brain was fixed from birth. By using rats and putting them in different environments (enriched and deprived), researchers like Rosenzweig and Bennett were able to show how our brain can change depending on the environments we grow up in. This has since been further demonstrated in human studies that compare naturally-occurring environmental variables on the developing brain, including poverty and stress (**see Luby et al. for more information**).

Further Studies

Effects of enriched and deprived environments on the brain (Rosenzweig and Bennett, 1960s): The aim of this study was to investigate the effects of the environment on brain growth and development. Rats were placed in different cages and lived for 30 to 60 days before they were euthanized. A post-mortem study was conducted to measure the thickness and heaviness of the brain cortex as well as the amount of acetylcholine receptors and synapses. Male rats were chosen from different litters (to control for gender and genetics) and were randomly allocated to two different conditions: enriched condition (EC) or the deprived condition (DC). In the EC, there were about 10-12 rats and there were a range of toys that the rats could play with. This group also received "maze training". On the other hand, in DC they were alone in a cage with no toys and just food and water. The results showed that rats living in the EC developed a heavier and thicker brain cortex. More specifically, the frontal lobes of the rats in the EC were heavier and they had developed more acetylcholine receptors (a neurotransmitter associated with learning and memory). Further studies found that the brain weight of the rats can increase by 7 – 10% and the synapses can increase by about 20% as a result of the EC. The results were quite groundbreaking at the time; the researchers were so surprised by the results that they replicated the research numerous times and obtained the same results with each replication. This study may provide insight into neurological and cognitive developmental differences that are commonly found in human kids that come from different backgrounds. Similar results have also been found in kids who have come from extremely deprived environments, like Romanian kids who grew up in orphanages.

Neglect and brain development (Perry and Pollard, 1997): Using MRI scans, this study used naturally-occurring neglect in human children as a variable that was correlated with brain development. They found that kids who suffered from multiple types of neglect (including emotional, physical and social) had reduced volume in their cerebral cortices. This suggests that Rosenzweig and Bennett's findings also apply to humans.

Correlations between poverty and hippocampal development (Luby et al., 2013): This study used brain scanning techniques to measure correlations between socioeconomic status and brain volume. The results showed that there was a positive correlation between socioeconomic status and development of the amygdala and hippocampus, which suggests findings like Rosenzweig and Bennett's can also apply to humans (*more details are located in the PTSD chapter*).

This code will take you to our blog post with more information on Rosenzweig and Bennett's study.

Critical Thinking Considerations

- What are the ethical considerations related to using animals to study the brain and behaviour? For example, what are the arguments for and against the justifiable use of animals to further our understanding of human behaviour?
- What factors need to be considered in terms of the generalizability of findings from animal studies to humans? In order to fully explain issues of generalizability, you need to think about differences between animals and humans that might affect the extent to which findings from animals could be applied to humans.
- To what extent has the invention of brain imaging technology made the use of animals in research unnecessary?

Animal Research on Hormones and Behaviour

Testosterone and cortisol

To what extent can animal studies provide insight into the effects of hormones on behaviour?

The value of animal models is their insight into how hormones may affect behaviour, which includes how they may affect the brain.

Key Details: Testosterone

- Testosterone is the male sex hormone and it is produced in the testes (and in female ovaries, but at a lower level). It has been associated with aggression in numerous studies.
- Animal experiments are useful when studying the effects of testosterone on aggression because they can be conducted in environments where all extraneous variables can be controlled for, which allows researchers to deduce cause-and-effect relationships. The IV (levels of testosterone) can be directly manipulated and the effects this has on the DV can be measured.

- Testosterone has also been linked to social status and it could be that status and aggression are linked - aggression is needed to maintain high social status.

Key Studies

Castration and aggression in rats by (Albert et al., 1986): Alpha males were identified from groups of rats. Testosterone levels were manipulated through castration and testosterone replacement. There were four different conditions that allowed the researchers to directly manipulate the levels of testosterone in a way that could not be done with human studies (e.g. through castration and re-injecting testosterone). The results showed that when alpha male rats were castrated, they displayed decreased levels of aggression towards other rats placed in the same cage. When they had their testosterone replaced (through injections), their aggression returned to normal levels. They also found that the submissive (not alpha) males rose in status and the castrated alpha males lost their alpha position. This study shows a cause-and-effect relationship between testosterone levels and aggressive behaviour in rats. This is similar to some human studies that have also found correlations between social rank and testosterone levels.

Correlations between testosterone and aggression in violent criminals (Ehrenkranz et al., 1974): In this study, the researchers compared the average levels of testosterone for three groups of selected prisoners. One group had high levels of violence and aggressive behaviour, the second group were "socially dominant"

and the third group were nonaggressive and not dominant prisoners. The results showed that the average testosterone levels were higher in the first two groups than in the third. This suggests that testosterone levels are linked with aggressive behaviour and social dominance in human males. Albert et al.'s study can provide causal evidence to support the correlational link shown in this study.

For more information about Albert et al., use this QR code

Testosterone's effects on the brain by (Radke et al., 2015): This is a more modern study that uses fMRI technology to show how testosterone may be linked with aggression through its effects on the brain. Animal studies like Albert et al.'s helped to pave the way for studies like this because they showed there was a connection in the first place. This study is similar to Sapolsky's as it shows how a hormone may affect the brain. *(See more details of this study in the biological approach).*

Exam Tips

- Animal studies can be used in essays about human behaviour provided that they are linked with a human study. This also goes for explaining research methods and ethical considerations **if the research method you are identifying is a *true experiment*** (an "animal study" is not a research method).

- **Cortisol** is a stress hormone that is released from the adrenal gland. It is released in times of stress when the amygdala activates the HPA axis.
- A common finding in people who have experienced chronic (long-term) stress (e.g. those who have PTSD or suffered severe childhood trauma) is that they have reduced volume in their hippocampus (i.e. their hippocampus is smaller). Animal studies have been used to see if the reduction in size of the hippocampus could be a direct result of the release of cortisol.
- We again can see that the primary value in animal

studies is that they allow researchers to control extraneous variables and isolate the IV as the only variable affecting the DV. In this case, the IV is cortisol and the DV is the brain. There is no way that humans would participate in this study because no one would want to volunteer to be in a study that could potentially damage your brain (and not telling people of the dangers of such an experiment would be unethical). This is why animal studies are valuable, but they will also raise ethical considerations.

Further Studies

The effects of cortisol on the hippocampus (Sapolsky et al., 1990): The aim of this study was to see if cortisol would damage the hippocampus. One group of four rhesus monkeys had a pellet of cortisol surgically inserted into their hippocampi and were compared with a control group who had a cholesterol pellet inserted into the same area. After one year, the monkeys were euthanized and their brains were compared. The results showed that the cortisol group had damage to their hippocampal neurons whereas the cholesterol group did not have any damage. This study shows how stress might affect neuroplasticity in the brain and may explain why people who experience long-term stress tend to have smaller hippocampi.

Meta-analysis of MRI studies on patients with PTSD (Karl et al., 2006): This meta-analysis gathered data from 50 different studies that investigated correlations between PTSD and brain regions. The results showed that the strongest correlation was between reduced hippocampal volume and PTSD (with an effect size of -0.28). This study highlights the benefits of studies like Sapolsky's because the monkey study could explain why this correlation exists. Sapolsky's study provides a potential explanation that perhaps the prolonged stress

experienced by people with PTSD leads to an increase of cortisol over a long period of time, which would atrophy their hippocampi.

Poverty and brain development (Luby et al., 2013): The aim of this study was to see if poverty was correlated with brain development and to see if there were mediating variables related to stress and parenting that could explain this relationship. MRIs were used to see if poverty, stressful events and parenting styles were correlated with hippocampal volume in 145 children over a 10-year period. The results showed a negative correlation between poverty and hippocampal volume. They also found that parenting and stressful life events were mediating variables in this relationship. This suggests that poverty, parenting styles and stress are all factors that can negatively affect the development of neural networks in the hippocampus. Again, Sapolsky's study could be used to explain the findings here – the increased stress caused by poverty results in long-term release of cortisol, which causes a shrinking of the hippocampus. Without the animal experiment that showed the causal link between cortisol and the hippocampus, we would not have the evidence to make this link.

Critical Thinking Considerations

- While the above explanation about the link between PTSD, cortisol and the hippocampus seems to make sense, it has been a rather shocking finding in research that people with PTSD actually have lower than normal levels of cortisol. Does this highlight a limitation of the animal model or a limitation of the human studies? Or maybe both? Similarly, Gilbertson's twin study (in the PTSD unit) can also be used to counter the claim that PTSD causes a small hippocampus and shows how it might be the other way around.
- Animal models are useful because of the similar physiologies of animals and humans. However, what are the differences that make generalization an issue? *Hint: think about society, culture and cognition.*

Animal Research on Genes and Behaviour

Heritability and genetic knockouts
How and why are animals used to study links between genes and behaviour?

Links related to genetics in general can be studied by using selective breeding techniques. Specific genes can be studied in relation to behaviour using genetic "knockouts" (which are animals with specific genes turned off).

Key Details: Selective Breeding

- Animal modeling is used in the study of genetic influences on human behaviour through selective breeding. This is when animals that demonstrate particular traits are selected to mate with one another and have babies that will share their genes. Rats and mice are used because they begin reproducing after they are about two months old, so several generations of mice can be bred in a year. This means that the effects of genetic inheritance over multiple generations can be studied in a relatively short period of time.
- **Selective breeding** is done by selecting rats based on their **attack latency**, which is how long it takes a mouse who is used to living in a particular cage (a resident mouse) to attack another mouse that is put in this same cage (the intruder mouse). Mice are determined to have a long attack latency if they wait before attacking, or do not attack the intruder

at all. On the other hand, a short attack latency means that the resident mouse is quick to attack; these mice are considered more aggressive. This commonly-used experimental paradigm for measuring aggression in mice is known as the **resident-intruder paradigm**.
- Researchers investigating the link between genetics and aggression selectively breed mice based on their attack latency. They can separate mice based on their latencies and then develop different strains (groups) of mice. This allows comparisons to be made between a short-attack latency strain (more aggressive mice) and a long attack latency strain (less aggressive mice). By creating more aggressive and less aggressive strains of mice through selective breeding, the researchers can show that aggression has a genetic base.

Key Studies

Selective breeding and aggression in mice using the resident-intruder paradigm (Van Oortmerssen and Bakker, 1981): These researchers selectively bred mice from a group of wild mice that were found in a barn. They tested this first group of wild mice using the resident-intruder paradigm and selected the mice with the shortest latency attack scores (the most aggressive mice) to produce offspring and create one strain of aggressive mice. They also selected the mice with the longest latency attack scores (the least aggressive mice) and had these mice produce offspring. The latency scores were analyzed over 11 generations of the mice from this selective breeding program. Their results showed that the latency scores gradually decreased with each generation in the short latency group (the aggressive strain of mice). This group of mice were quicker to respond with aggression towards an intruder that was put in their cage. What this suggests is that with each generation, the

mice were becoming increasingly aggressive. Because all other variables were controlled in the laboratory, this increase in aggression over generations can be attributed to genetic inheritance. The results also corroborated earlier findings by demonstrating a heritability of 0.30 for aggressive behaviour (remember that heritability refers to how much the variations in behaviour can be explained by genetics. The closer the number to 1.0 the more genetics is a factor).

Human studies: The above study provides insight into the possible link between genetics and aggression, but links aggression to both environment and genetics (since heritability was not 100%). This is similar to human twin studies such as Baker et al., Grove et al. and Mason (*see "Twin and kinship studies" in the biological approach for more details*).

Exam Tips

- It is important in any essay about research methodology, including animal experimentation, that you can explain how and why the methods are used. This is the key thing you need to show you understand in any HL extension that focuses on research methodology. Therefore, try to focus equally on the explanation and not just on the studies and the critical evaluation.
- The example of genetic 'knockouts' could be used also for the brain and behaviour, as it shows the links with serotonin and the PFC in aggression.

- Selective breeding has been used in recent studies where specific genes are identified and mice are selectively bred based on the identification of a particular gene. In fact, researchers can actually ablate (remove) an individual gene from an animal and then observe the effects this has on behaviour. This experimental process of **gene ablating** is similar in concept to brain ablation shown in other experiments – if the removal of a gene changes behaviour and all other factors are kept controlled, then we can conclude that this particular gene must be linked with the behaviour in some way.

- This process is called "knocking out" and the animals are called "**knockouts**." Animal experiments are valuable here because humans would be unwilling to volunteer to have their genes "knocked out".

- Studies using knockouts have been used to research the link between genes, serotonin, the brain and aggression. The explanation for this could lie in the relationship between serotonin and the function of the prefrontal cortex (PFC): low serotonin levels reduce activity in the PFC, which could interfere with an ability to inhibit aggressive reactions. Animal studies using ablating and lesioning techniques have shown that even in rats, damage to the prefrontal cortex can increase aggression and that disrupting serotonin specifically in the PFC can also increase aggressive behaviour (Takahashi and Miczek, 2014).

- Serotonin (also called 5-hydroxytryptamine, or 5-HT) is made from an amino acid called tryptophan. The **TPH2 gene** (tryptophan hydroxylase 2) plays a role in this conversion of tryptophan into serotonin; the TPH2 gene sends information from the nucleus in a cell to begin the process of converting tryptophan into serotonin. If this gene is knocked out, it will affect the ability to convert tryptophan to serotonin, thus resulting in reduced levels of serotonin in the brain. This could then lead to increased aggression.

- What could cause "knocking out" in humans? Animal studies have shown that high levels of stress early in a rat's life will reduce the expression of the TPH2 gene, resulting in less serotonin. This could explain connections between serotonin dysfunction, childhood trauma and aggression.

Further Studies

TPH2 knockouts and aggression (Mosienko et al., 2012): In this study, the researchers ablated TPH2 genes in order to create a group of TPH2 knockout mice and compared their genetically modified mice with a control group. A number of tests were conducted to study the effects of knocking out the TPH2 gene. One of these tests was the resident-intruder test. The results of this test were that the TPH2 knockout mice attacked six times faster than the control group. The total number of attacks and the total time spent attacking was also seven times more than the control group of mice. The resident-intruder test lasts for a total of ten minutes, but 100% of the TPH2 knockout mice attacked within five minutes of the test beginning compared to 22% of the control group. These results show that knocking out the TPH2 gene caused a significant increase in aggressive behaviour. The experiment provides a possible explanation for how serotonergic dysfunction could be the result of the TPH2 gene being turned off, which could help psychologists understand how genes, behaviour, the brain, and neurotransmission are connected. As with other types of variables in animal studies, the manipulation of genetics by researchers in a controlled environment could not be replicated in humans. However, studies like Mosienko et al.'s can still help psychologists to understand the role of genetics in human behaviour because we also have TPH2 genes.

Human studies like Caspi et al. (2002) show how childhood abuse is linked with aggressive behaviour and the MAOA gene. It might also be that the childhood abuse is reducing the expression of the TPH2 gene, which is leading to aggression. Moore et al.'s study also shows a link between serotonin and antisocial behaviour (e.g. aggression), which might also be linked with genetics. In addition, human studies have found links between aggression and the TPH2 gene.

Critical Thinking Considerations

- What are the possible ethical considerations for these studies? Are there possible ethical issues with the potential application of findings from studies that link specific genes with behaviours?
- Why is generalizability an issue when measuring aggression with the resident-intruder paradigm? Is this similar to human examples of aggression or is it too different to be a valuable comparison? What types of aggression might this paradigm not reflect in humans?

Ethical Consideration #1: Animal Welfare

How and why is animal welfare an important consideration in animal studies?

Animal welfare is a general consideration that refers to the need for researchers to take good care of the animals they are experimenting on, including avoiding any unnecessary harm or suffering.

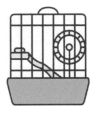

Key Details

- Even though the experimental procedures might result in the animals experiencing distress, this should not happen unnecessarily. For example, researchers may damage the brains and change the physiology of the animals, but this is done for a reason. In addition, when animals are being operated on, the researchers need to make sure that they are not suffering unnecessarily by using ethical methods (e.g. using an anesthetic during surgery so that the animals do not feel any pain).
- All steps should be taken to ensure that **animal welfare** is a top priority and that the animals have proper food, water, and living conditions while they are being studied.
- However, an element of suffering may be an unavoidable result of irreversible experimental procedures. If animals are experiencing severe trauma or pain, researchers need to consider euthanizing them to minimize suffering. Similarly, in post-mortem studies, the animals should be killed in a humane way.
- Researchers need to consider the possibility of terminating a study early if their experimental procedures result in behaviour that is damaging to the animal. For example, one side effect found in Weizkrantz's study was that those mice with amygdala damage started behaving in peculiar ways and doing things like eating their own feces. It might be considered unethical to allow animals to continue to live if they are behaving in ways that are causing suffering.
- In studies using the resident-intruder paradigm, researchers need to be ready to end the experiment if one rat is in danger of being seriously harmed.

Key Studies

Brain and behaviour: These studies often include doing irreparable damage to the brain. Researchers need to make sure their surgeries result in as little pain as possible. At the end of the study, the animals should be euthanized in a humane way. Examples that demonstrate these points are Rosenzweig and Bennett's (euthanizing) rat study and Sapolsky's study (surgery and euthanizing).

Hormones and behaviour: Sapolsky et al. and Albert et al.'s studies involved keeping animals in cages and conducting surgery, so many of the above points apply including avoiding unnecessary suffering and humanely euthanizing animals if necessary.

Genes and behaviour: Van Oortmensen and Bakker and Mosienko et al.'s studies kept mice in cages and used the resident-intruder paradigm, so many of the above points apply, including avoiding unnecessary suffering and humanely euthanizing animals if necessary.

Exam Tips

- Avoid making definitive statements like "it is unethical to study animals" or "it is ethical to study animals." This shows a lack of understanding of the nuance and subtleties of the debate. You need to discuss both sides of the argument – the value added to our knowledge by these studies but the suffering needed for this knowledge.
- When you write about the studies in relation to ethics, make sure your conclusion is highlighting how the study demonstrates a particular ethical consideration.

Critical Thinking Considerations

- Do the ends justify the means? This is the central argument when discussing ethical considerations with animal research. You can use the material in the next section to help you discuss this point. For example, how might causing suffering for some animals reduce suffering for humans?
- Do these considerations apply equally to all non-human animals?

Ethical Consideration #2: Justification

How and why is "justification" an important ethical consideration in animal experimentation?

It is inevitable that animals may experience suffering in experimentation and a study is only considered ethical by common standards if that suffering is justified.

Key Details

- Whether studying the brain, hormones or genetics, the ethical considerations involved in animal research are pretty much the same. One of the central debates at the heart of animal research in psychology is whether or not it's acceptable to harm animals for the sake of science.
- The core ethical consideration is whether or not causing harm and suffering to animals is justified. In order to fully explain this consideration, we need to think of (a) the extent of suffering caused and (b) the potential applications of the studies.
- Be wary of making judgements like 'it is unethical to kill animals for research." For example, what if we could kill an ant to cure cancer? It would arguably be highly unethical to allow millions of people to suffer because we did not want to kill one ant. However, with all things related to ethics, it is subjective and based on context.
- Animals in experiments do suffer, whether it is having brain surgery, being put in a resident-intruder situation, or having their testicles removed. We need to consider whether or not this is worthwhile. In order to do that, we need to think of how the findings from the animal study may potentially benefit humans.

Key Studies

Brain and behaviour: Studies like Rosenzweig and Bennett's (and Sapolsky's) have provided tremendous insight into how the environment can shape the brain. Findings like these could be used to improve the lives of many people because neuroplasticity research is used to address common causes of neurological and cognitive deficits, especially in lower socioeconomic groups. Weiskrantz et al.'s study can also be used for this topic.

Hormones and behaviour: Albert et al.'s study has helped us to understand aggression. If we want to reduce violence in society, we first need to know what causes it so there's a justifiable reason for conducting these studies. Also, these animals were not euthanized and the treatment (i.e. castration) they received was no different to what many farm animals experience.

Genes and behaviour: Van Oortmensen and Bakker and Mosienko et al.'s studies can help us understand links between genes and behaviour and, as previously mentioned, we have to know what the causes are if we want to reduce antisocial behaviour.

Critical Thinking Considerations

- Perhaps part of the debate includes the animal in question. Should we apply the same ethical considerations to sea slugs and chimpanzees? One has far more complex social networks and is able to perform more cognitive processes. This means they are able to experience more "emotion" than other animals, so does the way we consider animal research depend on the animal model we are using?
- If animal research has been carried out under unethical circumstances but the findings could have significant applications, should we be able to use that research? Who should make that decision? This could have implications for our use of historical research that was conducted before ethical guidelines were published.

Exam Tips

- The key to writing a good explanation of a study for this topic is to explain (a) what the suffering was and then (b) how that suffering is justified because of the potential application(s) for humans.
- When you are writing about ethical considerations, you are not expected (or recommended) to give judgements about whether studies are ethical or not. Instead, you are supposed to write about what the researchers must consider during the research process.

Cognitive approach: Cognitive processing in the digital world
- The influence of digital technology on cognitive processes.
- The positive and negative effects of modern technology on cognitive processes.
- Methods used to study the interaction between digital technology and cognitive processes.

	Positive effects	Negative effects	Methods
Reliability of cognitive processing	Computer-based training could improve working memory reliability • Klingberg (2005) • Simons et al. (2016) • Kuhn et al. (2014) • West et al. (2017)	Technology (e.g. television, Google, smartphones) could reduce memory reliability and working memory capacity • Sparrow et al. (2001) • Mueller and Oppenheimer (2014) • Cain et al. (2016) • Christakis et al. (2004) • Lillard and Peterson (2011)	True experiments and correlational studies
Emotion and cognition	VRET could be used to reduce anxiety, which may improve working memory function. • Parsons and Rizzo (2008) • Roy et al. (2014)	Using social media could increase anxiety, which reduces working memory capacity. • Vytal et al. (2013) • Weinstein et al. (2015)	True experiments and correlational studies

Exam Tip: *If you are asked about the effects of technology on the reliability of cognitive processes and you are writing about working memory, make sure that you are focusing on the reliability of working memory. Reliability can be defined as being trustworthy or performing consistently well and so any study related to working memory capacity can be used to show the performance (i.e. reliability) of working memory*

Technology and Cognition #1

Positive effects of technology on working memory
How can technology have a positive effect on working memory?

Computer games have been designed to help improve the reliability of working memory problems and attention disorders (e.g. ADHD) that many children are diagnosed with. However, there is some debate about their actual effects.

Key Details

- **Working memory** is information that we are conscious of at any one time. More specifically, it is "…the small amount of information that can be held in mind and used in the execution of cognitive tasks" (Cowan, 2013). **Working memory capacity** refers to **how much** information we can hold in our minds at any one time. This capacity has been linked to many things, including intelligence and academic achievement. Therefore, kids with poor working memory capacity (i.e. unreliable working memory capabilities) struggle in school and often get in trouble. This is a problem for the kids, their parents and teachers, so researchers have been looking at ways to help improve working memory capacity.

- One method that has been developed to improve working memory is the use of computer games. This has become a multimillion-dollar industry. These games are designed to be fun and engaging, like ordinary video games, but they require kids to use their working memory.

Key Studies

Working memory games and improved attention (Klingberg et al., 2005): This study demonstrates the positive applications of understanding working memory processes because it shows we can design computer games to improve the working memory capacity of children in order to reduce attention problems. In the study, 42 kids with ADHD were assigned to two conditions: a computer game designed to improve working memory that gradually got harder (treatment group) or the same game but not designed to stretch their capacity (control group). The kids were expected to play the games for around 40 minutes a day for five days a week. The kids were tested after five weeks of treatment and again after three months. The results showed that the kids in the treatment group had significant improvement in their working memory capacity. Their parents also reported reduced symptoms of inattention and hyperactivity. This is one example of the positive effects of technology on the reliability of cognitive processes, in this case working memory capacity and attention.

Review of the effects of video games on working memory (Simons et al., 2016): This was not so much a study as a review of a range of existing studies. The review was conducted after two teams of psychologists engaged in serious disagreements about the effectiveness of video games for working memory training. To draw their conclusions they reviewed a wide range of studies that tested the effectiveness of computer-game training on working memory. What they concluded from their review was that these games can help performance on closely-related tasks (e.g. n-back or span board tasks). However, they found that the tasks had limited transfer to other related or general cognitive tasks. What this means, for example, is that the games might improve the kids' scores on the span-board task (one task that was used in Klingberg et al.'s study), but improving on that task does not mean it will transfer to other cognitive skills like reading comprehension, the ability to inhibit impulsive thoughts and actions or improving long-term memory. They also found numerous flaws in many of the studies that claimed to demonstrate the positive effects of these programs.

Exam Tips

- Any study that examines working memory can be used to demonstrate the applications of the working memory model.
- If you revise the effects of technology on the reliability of cognition, you only need to study two topics for the cognitive approach because if the question asks about "cognitive processes", you can write about the reliability of cognitive processes.
- Using an example of a negative effect of technology on working memory would make for a good discussion.

Extension: Technology and Neuroplasticity

• We know from many MRI studies that our brain changes as a result of experience – this is called **neuroplasticity**. Therefore, hours spent playing video games could have significant effects on important parts of the brain, like the **hippocampus** (which is associated with memory) and the **prefrontal cortex**. In particular, the dorsolateral prefrontal cortex is important because it has been linked with working memory and cognitive control. It might be that playing video games can improve brain function, which can improve cognition.

• Understanding the effects of video games on the brain and cognition is important because video game addiction is a growing concern, especially for young people. However, it is also important for older people, too. As we age, our brains start to deteriorate and it is thought that keeping the brain active could help delay or prevent diseases like Alzheimer's and dementia. Video games can be used in this way and have been the subject of many studies related to this topic.

Further Studies

Video game playing and the brain – a correlational study (Kuhn et al., 2014): This study gathered data on 152 teenagers (14 years old). They measured how much time they spend playing video games and used an MRI to measure the cortical thickness in various parts of the brain including the dorsolateral prefrontal cortex (dlPFC). The results showed a "robust positive association between cortical thickness and video gaming duration," meaning that those kids that played more video games tended to have thicker dlPFCs (correlation = 0.30). The researchers concluded that these differences could explain findings in studies like Klingberg et al.'s that show computer gaming can have a positive effect on working memory. An interesting (but maybe not surprising) finding from the study was that boys played video games more than girls and there were no boys who said that they did not play video games. However, even after the researchers controlled for gender, age and parent education levels, the correlation still remained.

The effects of playing Mario Brothers on the hippocampus (West et al., 2017): This study randomly allocated participants to one of three conditions: (1) playing Super Mario 64, (2) taking online piano lessons and (3) a control group that did not do any technology training. The researchers used MRI scans to measure their hippocampal volumes before and after six months. The results showed that only the Super Mario group had a significant increase in grey matter in their hippocampi. They also showed an improvement in short-term memory tests and improvement in memory was correlated with an increase in hippocampal grey matter. Interestingly, the music group had increases in their dlPFC but not their hippocampus and, unfortunately, the control group experienced a shrink in their hippocampal volumes. These results show more potential positive effects of computer gaming on the brain. The music condition can also show the value of technology to learn new things, which can also increase brain function in areas like the dlPFC.

Critical Thinking Considerations

• Klingberg has worked with computer program developers and this could be a very profitable industry that he could financially benefit from. For example, one estimate found that in 2014, people spent over $750 million dollars on computer-based brain training games (Yong, 2016). To what extent do you think this conflict of interest affects the validity or credibility of his research?

• Kuhn et al.'s study is correlational. One way of explaining a limitation in such a study is to give an example of bidirectional ambiguity – while it is logical to conclude that video gaming increased dlPFC volume, could this be explained in the other direction?

• What are the potential negative effects of computer gaming on cognition?

• Are there any ethical issues with these studies?

Technology and Cognition #2

Negative effects of technology on memory
How can technology have a negative effect on memory?

Overuse of some technology can have a negative effect on our memory, including relying too much on the internet to remember things and watching too much TV.

Key Details

- The old saying "use it or lose it" applies to the brain – it might be that modern technology is not encouraging us to use our brains in positive ways, causing our thinking skills to deteriorate. For example, we used to have to try to remember information if we wanted to access it later. Now, we can rely on our phones to store information and we have everything we need to know if we just "Google it." This could be negatively affecting our memory.
- How we try to learn things in the first place might also be having an effect on our memory. Students are using laptops in classes more than ever and it might be detrimental. Because we can type quickly without thinking, the processing of information is quite shallow and it doesn't transfer to our long-term memory. Taking notes by hand forces us to think about our notes and the information, which may be better for our memory in the long run.
- Digital media on the internet is also catering to short attention spans and we are constantly distracted by all kinds of media. This might be having a detrimental effect on our working memory, which is our ability to hold information and to pay attention.

Key Studies

Google and Memory (Sparrow et al., 2001): This experiment wanted to investigate if knowing about having access to saved information later (like we do with the internet) would affect semantic memory (memory of facts and information). The researchers asked participants to type out a series of trivia (random facts). One group were told that the information would be saved and that they could access it later. The other group were told that it would not be saved. Afterwards, they did a test and the results showed that if participants thought they had access to the information, they scored worse on a test of the facts that they wrote down.

Handwriting vs Typing (Mueller and Oppenheimer, 2014): In this experiment, 67 students from Princeton University participated and were asked to take notes on a lecture. The students were told to take notes how they normally would (typing on a laptop or by hand).

Afterwards, they were given a test on the content of the lecture. The results showed that there was not much difference in remembering facts from the lectures. However, there was a significant difference in test scores based on conceptual understanding (comprehending the meaning and significance of the facts) – those that wrote notes by hand had better scores on these questions. This suggests that using technology to take notes might affect our ability to remember and understand important ideas about what we are learning.

Effects of media use on working memory capacity (Cain et al., 2016): This study found a correlation between the number of hours teenagers spend using various media (including TV, internet, video games, etc.) and working memory capacity. *(You can read more about this in the Working Memory Model section of the cognitive approach chapter).*

Exam Tips

- You may be asked specifically about either positive effects or negative effects in an essay question. If the question is general and just asks to discuss the effects, you can write about both positive and negative effects.
- Sparrow et al.'s study could also be used in support of the multi-store model – participants are not rehearsing the information if they think it is being saved, so the memory is not transferring from STM to LTM.

• Numerous studies have investigated the effects of watching television on working memory and executive functions because kids in developed countries tend to watch a lot of television. Watching TV for long periods of time might be harmful for cognition because it doesn't require us to use our working memory, unlike other activities like reading or playing an instrument.

• As with anything, spending hours watching TV could have an effect on the brain. Research in Japan has shown a negative correlation between TV watching and grey matter in the prefrontal cortex (Takeuchi et al., 2013). Perhaps this could also explain why studies have found correlations between watching too much TV and having attention and working memory problems.

• Could this depend on the type of television we watch? Perhaps watching educational documentaries or foreign films that require careful concentration could be beneficial. However, watching TV that has lots of quick cuts and things happening so quickly that we do not really have to think very carefully about what we're watching could have negative effects. Studies have shown that it is not necessarily watching TV that is bad, but it is the type of TV.

Further Studies

Longitudinal study of TV watching and attention problems (Christakis et al., 2004): This longitudinal study was conducted on over 1,000 American children with the aim of seeing if watching TV as a young child (ages 1 and 3) would increase the chances of having attentional problems when they got older (at age 7). After conducting their correlational analyses, the results showed that the main predictor for attentional problems at age 7 was hours spent watching TV at ages 1 and 3. One finding from the study was that for every hour on average they watched TV at age three, they were 10% more likely to have attentional problems at age seven.

Different types of TV and working memory (Lillard and Peterson, 2011): In this study, the researchers randomly allocated 60 four-year-old children to one of three conditions. In the fast-paced TV condition, the kids watched SpongeBob SquarePants (which has an average scene length of 11 seconds). The slow-paced TV condition watched another cartoon, Caillou (which has an average scene length of 34 seconds). A third group watched no TV and did drawing activities instead. The children watched TV (or drew) for nine minutes before completing a range of tests on their working memory, including a digital span task. The results showed that the kids who watched nine minutes of SpongeBob (fast-paced condition) scored significantly less on the digit-span and other tests of executive function compare to the group in the drawing and slow-paced TV conditions. This suggests that it is not just about how much TV a child watches but also the type of TV being watched.

Critical Thinking Considerations

• Christakis et al.'s study is correlational. One conclusion could be that the watching TV increases attention problems, but could bidirectional ambiguity be an issue with this study? How could the results be explained in the other direction?

• In Lillard and Peterson's study, the children did the working memory tasks immediately after watching TV. What is one limitation in using these results to explain why watching TV at home might affect attention at school?

• Can you think of other limitations of these studies? For example, could the study on Princeton University students be critiqued based on its population validity?

Technology, Emotion & Cognition

Effects of technology on emotion and cognition
How can technology have positive effects on emotion and cognition?

Technology could causing increases in anxiety, which then has negative effects on cognition, especially in young people. However, technology like VRET could be used to treat anxiety and thus improve cognition.

Key Details

• In order to explain how technology can influence the relationship between emotion and cognition, we first need to establish the link between emotion and cognition.

• A common finding in people who suffer from anxiety issues is that they have reduced working memory capacity and other cognitive problems. For example, it is commonly reported that people with PTSD suffer from memory loss, poor executive function and working memory capacity. People with generalized anxiety disorder (GAD) also tend to have working memory problems. Even in healthy people, stress and anxiety can reduce working memory capacity.

Interestingly, some research shows that if we are doing something cognitively easy anxiety will affect our performance, but if the task becomes more demanding, our anxiety decreases and we perform better.

• One possible explanation for the link between anxiety and working memory is that they are both using similar cognitive processes – if we are anxious, it is usually because we are thinking of something that's causing the anxiety, so this reduces our ability to concentrate on whatever else we are supposed to be doing.

Key Study

Anxiety and working memory performance under threat of shock (Vytal et al., 2013): In this study, the researchers compared the working memory capacity of participants when they were in an anxious state and when they were calm. To make them feel anxious, participants were told that the might get a small shock on their wrist. The shock is uncomfortable but not painful. In the "safe" condition, they were told they would not be shocked. To test their working memory, they were given an n-back task (a task that requires you to keep information in your working memory). The results showed that when participants were under a threat of shock, their working memory was worse than when they felt safe (on average, they made about 5% more errors in the shock condition). Interestingly, as the task got harder (by having participants remember 3

pieces of information instead of one), participants actually did better in the threat condition. This is one of many experimental studies that shows how increased anxiety can negatively affect cognition. In the next section, we will look at how technology can influence this relationship.

This code will take you to a site where you can try the n-back tasks so you know what it is

Exam Tips

• It is unlikely that you will be asked about the effects of technology on emotion and cognition because it is not clear how this question could be answered.

• While the effects of technology on anxiety is a common field of study, it is not a cognitive process. This is why if you are asked this question, you need to make the links between anxiety and cognition.

• The material in this topic could be used for the "Emotion and Cognition" topic.

• If you are asked about the effects of technology on the reliability of cognitive processes and you are writing about working memory, make sure that you are focusing on the reliability of working memory. Reliability can be defined as being trustworthy or performing consistently well and so any study related to working memory capacity can be used to show the performance (i.e. reliability) of working memory

- **Negative Effects**: Rates of anxiety disorders in developed countries are rising, especially in teenagers and young adults. Many researchers have hypothesized that this could be because of our increased access to technology and the rise in popularity of smartphones. This correlation is not just found in Western countries, but has been found in other parts of the world such as Korea and Taiwan. In particular, internet addiction has been commonly linked with anxiety and depression. As we can see in studies that create anxiety, this could have a negative effect on our cognition, including working memory.

- **Positive Effects**: The effects of technology on emotion are not all bad. Virtual reality exposure therapy (VRET) is one example of how technology can be used in a positive way to reduce anxiety for people, including those who suffer from PTSD and phobias. This treatment works by exposing people to the things that cause them anxiety. By using computer technology, the images seem as realistic as real life but the patient is safe in knowing that they are not real. In this way, they can feel comfortable being exposed to their emotional triggers and eventually their brain will realize they are safe and that there's nothing to fear. This will reduce anxiety. A reduction in anxiety could help improve working memory and executive functions.

Negative effects: A correlational study of internet addiction and social anxiety (Weinstein et al., 2015): This study gathered data from 120 adult participants (60 male and 60 females). Their levels of internet addiction were measured using the Internet Addiction Test (IAT) and their social anxiety was measured using the Liebowitz Social Anxiety Scale. The results showed that there was not a difference between the genders in levels of internet addiction but there was a significant correlation between internet addiction and social anxiety. The correlation was similar for males and females, although it was slightly stronger in males (0.40 and 0.34, respectively). This is consistent with numerous other studies that have found associations between internet addiction and anxiety. Our increasing use of the internet (especially now that most people carry the internet with them in their pockets) could put us at risk for anxiety issues, which may in turn limit our cognitive abilities.

Positive effects: A meta-analysis of VRET used to treat disorders (Parsons and Rizzo, 2008): The researchers analyzed data from 21 studies (over 300 total participants) that used VRET to treat anxiety disorders. They found a significant effect in using VRET to treat a range of anxiety-related disorders, including PTSD and phobias. Their results showed an effect size of 0.87 for PTSD when comparing VRET with other treatments. Thus, it could be that technology can be used to reduce anxiety, and by reducing anxiety it might help to improve working memory.

Exposure therapy and brain function for PTSD (Roy et al., 2014): The aim of this study was to assess the effectiveness of exposure therapy for treating PTSD. The participants were 19 US combat veterans who were randomized to receive virtual reality exposure theory (VRET) or PE (prolonged exposure – a type of imagination therapy). fMRIs were used before and after treatment to assess changes in brain activity and a PTSD questionnaire (CAPS scores) was used to measure PTSD symptoms. The results showed that the VRET group had significant reduction in CAPS scores (20%), while there was no reduction in CAPS in PE group. However, both groups had increased vmPFC and ACC activity as well as reduced amygdala activity. This suggests that VRET may be more effective than imagination therapy for treating PTSD. Also, both types of exposure therapy can reduce PTSD symptoms by improving activity in important areas of the brain associated with PTSD.

- Weinstein et al.'s study is correlational. Why must we be careful when drawing conclusions from this study? What are the other factors that could affect the relationship between social media and anxiety?
- One limitation of the above argument is that the studies do not show a direct link between VRET and improving working memory. At the time of writing, I was unable to find any study that investigated this relationship. Why do you think this has (apparently) not been studied or the studies have not been published?

Research Method #1: True Experiments

How and why are true experiments used to study the effects of technology on cognition?

True experiments (a.k.a. laboratory experiments) *are used when the researchers manipulate an independent variable and create different conditions. They control for all extraneous variables to the best of their ability in order to measure the effects of the independent variable (IV) on the dependent variable (DV). By carefully controlling the extraneous variables, the researchers can maximize the chances that any differences in the DV can be explained by the manipulation of the IV. This allows for conclusions about causality to be made.*

Key Details

• **True experiments on technology and cognition:** The main benefit of using a true experiment is you can directly compare the effects of technology with control groups. In these experiments, participants are randomly assigned to a condition, which would involve one condition that is designed to test the effects of cognition.

This group is compared to one or more control groups. The dependent variable is measured using some kind of test, which is often a working memory test. We can then make conclusions about the effects of that technology on the specific cognitive process.

Key Studies

Different types of TV and working memory (Lillard and Peterson, 2011): This experiment showed how different types of TV affect working memory capacity in young kids.

Google and memory (Sparrow et al., 2001): This experiment showed how our memory could be affected by our ability to access information from an external storage system.

The effects of playing Mario Brothers on the hippocampus (West et al., 2017): This experiment showed that playing video games can affect the brain and cognition.

Working memory games and improved attention (Klingberg et al., 2005): This experiment showed how computer game training can improve working memory and attention.

Critical Thinking Considerations

• Most students say something basic like "true experiments lack ecological validity because they take place in artificial environments." In order to fully explain this point, you need to explain why we might not expect the same results in a specific real-life situation. Can you give a detailed critique of any of these experiments based on ecological validity?
• How can correlational studies and true experiments be used together to create strong arguments? How can correlational studies be used to highlight limitations of true experiments?
• Do true experiments always have to take place in a laboratory?
• In order to deduce a causal conclusion from an experiment, you need to control all variables. What are some of the variables that may not have been controlled in the above studies?

This code will take you to a blog post where I explain how to assess ecological validity using examples

Exam Tips

• It is very unlikely you will be asked about research methods used to study the effects of technology on emotion and cognition. If asked about research methods, it will probably be more general like "Discuss the use of one or more research methods used to study the effects of technology on cognitive processes."

Research Method #2: Correlational Studies

How and why are correlational studies used to study the effects of technology on cognition?

Correlational studies *measure how strongly two (or more) variables are related. Unlike experimental methods that include a direction of causality (IV→DV), correlational studies have co-variables, like use of technology and cognition.*

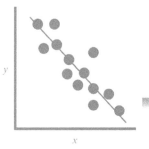

Strong Positive Correlation

Strong Negative Correlation

Key Details

- **Correlational studies on technology and cognition**: Correlational studies are commonly used in studies where one or more of the variables would be difficult to manipulate in a laboratory but those variables may be commonly occurring. This is why studies on the effects of technology are so common, especially in looking at the long-term effects. It might be unethical to expose children to hours of watching TV for months and months (it would also be impractical), but we can gather data on kids' natural habits and then see if this is related to cognition.

Key Studies

Longitudinal study of TV watching and attention problems (Christakis et al., 2004): This study found correlations between the amount of TV watched by children and attentional problems when they were a few years older.

Effects of media use on working memory capacity (Cain et al., 2016): This study found a correlation between the number of hours teenagers spend using various media (including TV, internet, video games, etc.) and working memory capacity.

A correlational study of internet addiction and social anxiety (Weinstein et al., 2015): This study found a link between internet use and anxiety (which is not a cognitive process but is linked with cognitive impairments).

Video game playing and the brain – a correlational study (Kuhn et al., 2014): This study found a correlation between hours spent playing video games and grey matter in the brain.

Critical Thinking Considerations

- The major limitation with correlational studies is that they do not show causation. One way of demonstrating this point is to explain an example of **bidirectional ambiguity** – this is where we are not sure in which direction the relationship is working. Can you explain one or more examples of bidirectional ambiguity from any of the above studies?
- One area of uncertainty with research methods is that it is often difficult to tell which method is being used. For example, **correlational studies are very similar to quasi and natural experiments**. Why? What is the difference? Could a study use both methods?
- What are the ethical considerations associated with correlational studies?

Exam Tips

- These same studies can be used for any question about research methods and cognitive processes (i.e. not just about technology and cognition).

Sociocultural Approach - HL Extensions

The influence of globalization on individual behaviour
- How globalization may influence behaviour
- The effect of the interaction of local and global influences on behaviour
- Methods used to study the influence of globalization on behaviour

Summary

In theory, the above three points could be asked in relation to the three topics from the sociocultural approach:
- The individual and the group
- Cultural origins of behaviour and cognition
- Cultural influences on individual attitudes, identity and behaviours

However, it is difficult to see how these topics could be combined with the extension points and how they could be answered. Technically speaking, a question could be: "Discuss the effect of the interaction of local and global influences on cultural influences on individual attitudes, identity and behaviours." This would be very difficult to answer, but it would also be unlikely to be an exam question.

Therefore, the approach I am recommending in this book is to review how globalization has changed cultures and how this change might have affected behaviour. We will look at the cultural dimension of individualism/collectivism in Japan and acculturation of Muslim immigrants. Both these examples and their studies can be used in the core, so it does not necessarily add to more revision.

An advisable revision strategy for the HL extensions is to prepare for either the biological or cognitive extensions, as their questions are more predictable. However, studying the material in this chapter will get you prepared for the most likely questions that will be asked about globalization:
- Discuss how globalization may influence behaviour
- Evaluate one or more research methods used to study the influence of globalization on behaviour

Models Summarizing the Findings of Lyons-Padilla et al. (2015)
The following models have been reproduced with permission from the author.

These diagrams are very complex and so they will not be understood easily. However, if you take the time to read and study them carefully, you'll get a much deeper understanding of the findings and conclusions of Lyons-Padilla et al.'s study and how it can be used to demonstrate the effects of globalization, as well as the effects of discrimination and acculturation.

Figure 1. Model showing the effect of marginalization on support for a radical interpretation of Islam is not direct but occurs via significance loss. The effect of marginalization on significance loss is exacerbated by experiences of discrimination.

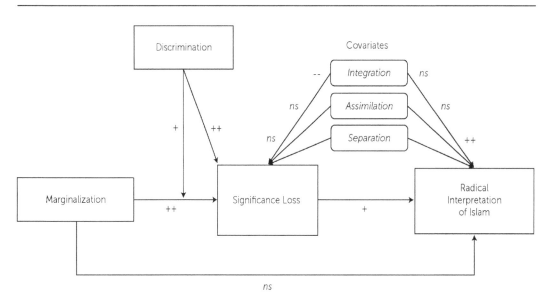

ns = the relationship between the variables was not significant; + = a significant positive relationship at the *p* < .05 level; ++ = a highly significant positive relationship at the *p* < .001 level. -- = a highly significant negative relationship.

Figure 2. Model showing the effect of marginalization on support for the fundamentalist group is not direct but occurs via significance loss. The effect of marginalization on significance loss is exacerbated by experiences of discrimination.

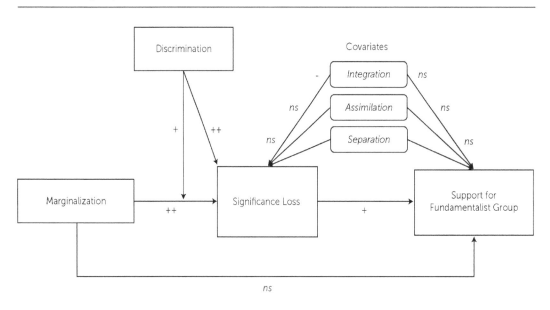

ns = the relationship between the variables was not significant; + = a significant positive relationship at the *p* < .05 level; - = a significant negative relationship; ++ = a highly significant positive relationship at the *p* < .001 level.

Globalization and Behaviour

Effects of globalization on culture and behaviour
How can globalization influence behaviour?

Globalization can affect individual behaviour in numerous ways. One way is through its change on cultural values. Another is through immigration.

Key Details

- Globalization is "a process by which cultures influence one another and become more alike through trade, immigration, and the exchange of information and ideas" (Arnett, 2002). One effect of globalization is that cultural values might change as a result of this bidirectional influence. However, it is often referred to as Westernization due to the media spreading Western beliefs and values through the internet, TV shows, films, books, and music. In this way, the effect is not bidirectional but is instead unidirectional.
- This Westernization may be affecting cultural values, especially those related to the cultural dimension of individualism/collectivism as Western culture is mostly individualistic. As countries like Japan have become increasingly Westernized, there has also been an increase in individualism.
- The increase in individualism in Japan has been measured through a number of statistics (Hanamura, 2012). These statistics include increasing economic wealth (GDP), increased divorce rates, smaller families and a decrease in three-generation households.
- This rise in individualism could have negative effects for Japanese people because individualistic cultures place emphasis on the "I" and encourage competition, but the competition could have negative effects by hurting interpersonal relationships. In order to counter the negative impact of competition, people in individualistic cultures learn the interpersonal skills needed to actively seek friendships and relationships. This would help to reduce the negative effects of being an individual and competing with one another (Ogihara and Uchida, 2014). However, when individualistic values are adopted by people in cultures that have not adopted the strategies to combat the effects of competition, it might have negative consequences. In countries like Japan that are increasing in individualism, the competitiveness and the desire to place emphasis on the individual could become part of a person's values, but this might not come with the additional strategies to protect against the isolation that this might cause. Because humans have an innate desire to belong and to feel connected with one another, this change could have negative effects on happiness and general life satisfaction.

Key Study

Individualism and mental health in Japanese students (Ogihara and Uchida, 2014): This study investigated how a change in values might be influencing the subjective well-being of young Japanese students. In their study, researchers gathered data from 114 students from two universities – one in Kyoto, Japan and the other in Wisconsin, USA. Participants completed questionnaires measuring their level of individualism or collectivism, how many close friends they had, their happiness, life satisfaction and their physical and psychological emotional states. The results from the statistical analyses showed a negative correlation between individualism in Japanese students and their overall subjective well-being. That is to say, the more individualistic the Japanese students were, the less happy they were and less life satisfaction they had. In addition, the number of close friends a Japanese student had was a mediating variable - the inability to make friends is *why* the individualistic values led to being less happy and less content with life. This correlation was not found in the American students. This study highlights a possible negative effect of globalization - as Western ideas spread to foreign countries, it can bring a change in values and beliefs, especially amongst young people. As people adopt these new ideas and beliefs they may find themselves at odds with their home culture and this can affect behaviour as it has negative consequences for our psychological health.

Extension: Immigration

- Globalization does not only refer to the spread of ideas, like individualism, but also the physical spread of individuals (e.g. through immigration). When someone immigrates to a new culture, they need to acculturate. Berry outlines four different acculturation strategies that a person might adopt: assimilation, integration, separation and marginalization *(see the Acculturation topic for more detail)*. Immigrants who integrate tend to have the best mental health, while those who marginalize themselves are at risk for negative psychological outcomes and are more negatively affected by discrimination. In extreme examples, they may also be radicalized and join extremist organizations. With the rise in Islamic extremism and terrorist groups in recent times, this has become a growing concern and something for psychologists to study.

- Lyons-Padilla et al. have hypothesized that the marginalization of Muslim immigrants in the USA could increase the likelihood of those individuals joining extremist organizations (e.g. ISIS). It is important to note that marginalization is a two-way street: residents of a country can exclude and marginalize immigrants but immigrants may also exclude themselves through their acculturation strategies.

- In summary, globalization is increasing the rate of immigration and how immigrants acculturate can affect their behaviour. Another way globalization is affecting behaviour is that the increase in immigration, especially by Muslims to Western countries, may be increasing the rates of discrimination and prejudice. This can also affect the psychological well-being and behaviour of immigrants.

Further Studies

Acculturation, discrimination and extremism in Muslim immigrants (Lyons-Padilla, et al 2015):
In this study, the researchers surveyed 200 first- and second-generation Muslim immigrants across the USA using a range of questionnaires. One result was that there was a strong correlation between feeling marginalized and feeling a sense of "significance loss" (a term the researchers used to describe a feeling of a lack of meaning, purpose and belonging). This is one example of how acculturation (and globalization through immigration) can have an effect on our behaviour. In addition, there was also a strong correlation between feeling significance loss and adopting a more radical interpretation of Islam. This could make those immigrants more likely to join extremist groups.

Another finding from the study was that discrimination moderated the effects of marginalization on significance loss. That is to say, participants who felt they were marginalized *and* had experienced discrimination had more of a sense of significance loss than those who were not discriminated against. This is important to note, because they also found a positive correlation between feelings of significance loss and support for a fundamentalist Islamic group. In other words, discrimination and marginalization can increase support for fundamentalist Islamic groups. In conclusion, globalization is increasing rates of immigration; how immigrants are treated as well as how they integrate into new countries can affect their attitudes and behaviour.

Critical Thinking Considerations

- What are the possible applications of Lyons-Padilla et al.'s findings?
- Some European countries are now making laws which state immigrants must pass language exams in order to claim benefits. Based on studies like Lyons-Padilla et al., do you think this will be effective?
- Ogihara and Uchida's study uses college-aged participants. Do you think this is representative of the broader population? Do you think these findings can apply to other collectivist cultures? Why/why not?
- Lyons-Padilla et al's study looks at Muslim immigrants in the US. Could we apply these findings to Europe and other places? Why/why not?

Exam Tips

- If you are writing about globalization and behaviour, explain the Japanese example (Ogihara and Uchida) first as this is the most directly related to globalization. The Muslim immigration example is more loosely linked to globalization (but it is still relevant).
- Ogihara and Uchida's studies are relevant for cultural dimensions and the culture topics in the core, while Lyons-Padilla et al's study is relevant for acculturation. When you are writing about these studies for various topics, it is essential you can clearly explain how they are relevant to each topic in your conclusions.

Research Method: Correlational Studies

How and why are correlational studies used to study the effects of globalization on behaviour?

Correlational studies measure how strongly two (or more) variables are related. Unlike experimental methods that include a direction of causality (IV→DV), correlational studies have co-variables, like the acculturation strategy of an immigrant and psychological outcomes.

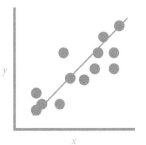

Strong Positive Correlation

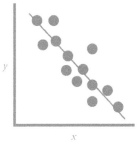

Strong Negative Correlation

Key Details

- **Correlational studies on globalization and behaviour**: Correlational studies are commonly used in studies with the goal of investigating how strongly variables are linked with one another and one or more of the variables would be difficult to manipulate in a laboratory. We would not consider culture to be an experimental variable as it is innate in the individual, so is not considered a "treatment" and thus most studies on culture are correlational. Correlational studies related to globalization measure a variable that is associated with globalization in some way, such as individualistic values or acculturation strategies used by immigrants. The other co-variables are cognition or behaviour.

Key Studies

Individualism and mental health in Japanese students (Ogihara and Uchida, 2014): This study found correlations between individualism in Japanese students and mental health. It also shows another use of correlational studies whereby mediating and moderating variables can be studied. A mediating variable is one that explains why one factor is correlated with another, while a moderating variable influences the strength of the relationship between the two variables. Mediating and moderating variables are commonly investigated in correlational studies.

Acculturation, discrimination and extremism in Muslim immigrants (Lyons-Padilla et al. 2015): This study measured correlations between acculturation strategies, discrimination, radical interpretations of Islam and support for extremist groups.

Critical Thinking Considerations

- The major limitation with correlational studies is that they do not show causation. One way of demonstrating this point is to explain an example of **bidirectional ambiguity** – this is where we are not sure in which direction the relationship is working. Can you explain one or more examples of bidirectional ambiguity from any of the above studies?
- One area of uncertainty with research methods is that it is often difficult to tell which method is being used. For example, **correlational studies are very similar to quasi and natural experiments**. Why? What is the difference? Could a study use both methods?
- What are the ethical considerations associated with correlational studies?

Exam Tips

- When writing about correlational studies, it is imperative that you highlight their value in calculating the strength of relationships between co-variables. If you miss this out and only explain that they are valuable in studying naturally-occurring variables, the examiner might think you are getting confused with quasi and natural experiments.

6 Human Relationships

The Psychology of Human Relationships

Topic	Content
Personal Relationships	• Formation of personal relationships • Role of communication • Explanations for why relationships change or end
Group Dynamics	• Co-operation and competition • Prejudice and discrimination • Origins of conflict and conflict resolution
Social Responsibility	• Bystanderism • Prosocial behaviour • Promoting prosocial behaviour
Ethical considerations and research methods	• Students should also be prepared to discuss one or more of the three approaches (biological, cognitive and sociocultural) in relation to each topic • Students should be able to discuss one or more research methods and ethical considerations related to the relevant studies for one or more of the three topics in this option

Psychology of Human Relationships

	Content	Key Questions	Key Studies
Personal relationships	**Formation of personal relationships**	*How can one or more factors affect the formation of personal relationships?*	• Johnston et al. (2001) • Buss (1989) • Levine et al. (1995) • *See also pheromones research*
	Role of communication	*How can communication affect personal relationships?*	• Gottman and Levenson (1985& 1992) • Rehman and Holtz-Munro (2007)
	Explanations for why relationships change or end	*Why do personal relationships change or end?*	• Gottman and Levenson (1985& 1992) • Rehman and Holtz-Munro (2007) • Fincham et al. (2000) • Levine et al. (1995)
Group dynamics	**Co-operation and competition**	*What are the causes and/or effects of co-operation and competition?*	• Sherif et al. (1961) • Bridgeman (1981) • *See also studies on aggression*
	Prejudice and discrimination	*What are the causes and/or effects of prejudice and discrimination?*	• Lyons-Padilla (2015) • Tajfel and Turner (1971) • Phelps (2000) • Park and Rothbart (1982)
	Origins of conflict and conflict resolution	*What are some origins of conflict and how might conflict be resolved?*	• Sherif et al. (1961) • Park and Rothbart (1982) • Tajfel and Turner (1971) • Pettrigrew and Tropp (2006) • Bridgeman (1981)
Social responsibility	**Bystanderism**	*Why does bystanderism occur?*	• Darley and Latane (1968) • Levine (1994 & 2001) • Steblay (1987)
	Prosocial behaviour	*How can one or more factors affect prosocial behaviour?*	• Darley and Latane (1968) • Levine (1994 & 2001)) • Steblay (1987) • Batson (1981)
	Promoting prosocial behaviour	*How can one or more strategies be used to promote prosocial behaviour?*	• Cialdini (2008) • Bickman (1974) • Bushman (1988)

- *One question will be based on each topic.*
- *All answers should be supported by evidence.*
- *Students should also be prepared to discuss one or more of the three approaches (biological, cognitive and sociocultural) in relation to each topic*
- *Students should be able to discuss one or more research methods and ethical considerations related to the relevant studies for one or more of the three topics in this option.*

Formation of Personal Relationships

Attraction and Marriage

How can one or more factors affect the formation of personal relationships?

A major factor affecting the formation of personal relationships is who we find attractive. Humans have evolved to find particular traits attractive because these traits are those that will ensure healthy offspring that have a high chance of survival. However, cultural factors are also important to consider and both may affect whom we form a relationship with.

Key Details

Evolutionary explanations

• **Testosterone**: Humans have evolved to be attracted to members of the opposite sex who have healthy genes and characteristics that will help their offspring to survive. For example, testosterone is the male sex hormone that has been linked to a strong immune system and healthy genes. Thus, it makes sense from an evolutionary perspective for females to want to procreate with a male who is high in testosterone as this will result in healthier children, meaning there is a higher chance the parents' genes will be passed on.

• **Gender roles**: Men and women may have evolved to find different traits attractive, due to the different roles they have in child bearing and rearing. Since females bear the children and have to devote more time and effort towards rearing them, they tend to be attracted to male partners who have access to more resources (e.g. they have higher social status and more ambition). Males, on the other hand, are more likely to focus on physical characteristics (e.g. youth and physical attractiveness) since these are signs of fertility and healthy genes. Therefore, gender differences in mate preferences could be explained by the different roles each gender has in ensuring the survival of their offspring.

Key Studies

Female preference for high testosterone (Johnston et al., 2001): The aim of this study was to see what types of faces females found more attractive. They had 42 female participants from New Mexico State University manipulate faces on a computer screen until they reached an optimal "target" (e.g. they changed the face until it was what they thought was most attractive). The results showed that when females were ovulating (highest chance of pregnancy) they had a stronger preference for facial features that signal high levels of testosterone. High testosterone could be attractive for a female because this hormone is correlated with a healthy immune system, so procreating with a man with these features could provide for healthy offspring.

A cross-cultural study on mate preferences (Buss, 1989): The results of this study showed cross-cultural similarities in mate preference for men and women. Traits that can be explained evolutionarily include age (males preferred younger partners and females preferred older partners), qualities such as domestic skills (males desired this more) and social status (females desired this more) (see next page for more details).

Exam Tips

• You can use the same material for this topic as you can for evolution and behaviour and cultural dimensions. For example, if asked about how culture or cultural dimensions influences behaviour, the behaviour you can write about is "personal relationships." You can use the arguments and evidence for pheromones for this topic, too.

• When writing about attraction, be sure to clearly explain how it's linked to the formation of personal relationships.

- There may also be differences in what males and females find attractive based on **cultural values** related to **individualism and collectivism**. For example, in collectivist cultures, there tends to be more focus on the well-being of the extended family. This could be why females in these cultures may place more value on ambition and social status than in individualistic cultures (because marrying a man with these traits can bring pride and wealth to the wider family). These may be more important than other factors like physical attraction (which benefits only the individual)

Further Studies

A cross-cultural study on mate preferences (Buss, 1989): This study provides evidence for the gender and cultural differences in what traits individuals find attractive in the opposite sex. The study was conducted on over 10,000 participants from 37 different cultures. Participants were asked to complete questionnaires on a range of different questions about what they wanted in a romantic partner. The results showed that there were universal differences in preference between men and women in what they found attractive. Traits that can be explained evolutionarily include age (males preferred younger partners and females preferred older partners), qualities such as domestic skills (males desired this more) and social status (females desired this more). They also found differences across cultural dimensions, including collectivist females having a preference for ambition and social status and individualistic males having a tendency to place lower value on domestic skills.

A cross-cultural comparison of the importance of love in marriage and divorce (Levine et al., 1995): This study compared college students from 11 different cultures (a mix of individualistic and collectivist). They gathered their data using questionnaires and one question asked, "If a person had all the qualities you desired, would you marry them if you weren't in love with them?" The results showed that students from individualistic cultures like the USA, UK and Australia placed more emphasis on love in a marriage compared to those from more traditional and collectivist cultures, like India, Pakistan and Thailand. Here we can see that in some cultures love is a crucial reason why someone might decide to get married (i.e. form a relationship), whereas in other cultures there are other factors to consider (like the feelings and opinions of extended family members).

To read more about Buss's study check out this blog post.

Critical Thinking Considerations

- What are the strengths and limitations of the supporting research? *See the summary of Buss's study for more critical thinking considerations.*
- Buss's study and Johnston et al.'s study could be explained from a biological perspective. However, could it also be explained from a social perspective? For example, how might gender differences in mate preferences be a result of socialization and/or social learning?
- Johnston et al.'s study only looks at female preferences. Why does this give us a limited understanding of how hormones may affect attraction?
- Are there alternative explanations for why females may find a man with high testosterone attractive?
- What are the ethical considerations related to studying factors that affect the formation of relationships?

Role of Communication

Communication Patterns and Marital Satisfaction
How can communication affect personal relationships?

One role of communication in a marriage is that it can help maintain and increase marital satisfaction. However, negative communication patterns might increase the chances of divorce.

Key Details

- Decades of research into marital satisfaction and the factors that predict divorce shows that the way in which a couple communicates is a key factor in marital satisfaction. Dr. John Gottman is a leading researcher in this field and he has concluded that it is not the frequency or intensity of arguments that couples engage in, but rather it is *how* they communicate. Couples who are able to engage in healthy communication patterns are more likely to have higher marital satisfaction and avoid divorce. Thus, one key role of communication in romantic relationships (e.g. marriage) is that it helps couples maintain a healthy and happy relationship.
- Through decades of research, some communication patterns have emerged and have been described. One of these is the **demand/withdraw pattern** (also known as the **wife demand/husband withdraw**, as this is the common trend). Gottman calls this "**stonewalling**." This common communication pattern been associated with decreases in marital satisfaction.
- The reason this could be associated with increased dissatisfaction in a marriage is that if one partner starts a

conversion or has an issue to discuss with their partner and the other partner withdraws (stonewalls), then that issue is never resolved. This could lead to problems accumulating over time, which explains the increase in dissatisfaction with the marriage, which may ultimately lead to divorce. Stonewalling is also part of what Gottman calls his "Four Horsemen of the Apocalypse," which are four common patterns of negative communication that are signs of problems in a marriage. The other three are defensiveness, criticism and contempt.

Key Study

Communication and marital satisfaction (Gottman and Levenson, 1992): 73 couples were studied over a four-year period (between 1983-1987). Throughout the duration of the study, the couples would be periodically invited into the "Love Lab" (an ordinary apartment equipped with recording devices) where they would have discussions with one another in the presence of a researcher. The couples did not see each other all day before the interview and they were asked to discuss three topics: one neutral, one pleasant and one that is a source of conflict. The discussions were recorded and the "Rapid Couples Interaction Scoring System (RCISS)" was used to quantify and code the communication patterns. The researchers used the data to identify two groups: regulated and non-regulated couples. A regulated couple was defined as a couple whose ratio of

positive to negative interactions increased throughout the discussion, meaning by the end of the interview their communication was more positive than negative. The regulated couples had higher marital satisfaction, more positive ratings of their interactions and more positive emotional expressions. The non-regulated couples, on the other hand, were almost three times as likely to divorce during the course of the study (19% compared to 7%) and they were also angrier, less affectionate, less joyful and less interested in their partners. The researchers also concluded that a healthy ratio of positive to negative interactions was 5:1. These results show how positive communication can maintain a healthy relationship, whereas negative communication might damage it.

Exam Tips

- The material in this topic can also be used to explain why relationships may change or end.

- **Cultural differences**: While Gottman et al.'s research suggests that communication patterns are strong predictors of marital satisfaction and divorce, this research has been carried out in America, an individualistic culture. It could be that the way couples interact and communicate might not be as important in marital satisfaction in other cultures. For example, in collectivist cultures, conflict might be avoided and the harmony of the group (which, in this context, could be the family or the marriage) might be valued more than individual expressions of emotion. For this reason, it is plausible that the same wife demand/husband withdraw patterns might not be observed. They might also consider numerous other factors in marital satisfaction and not just personal pleasure (see notes and summaries in the next topic <u>Why relationships change or end</u> for more).

- **Biological factors**: Gottman has identified that about 85% of males are stonewallers and that during arguments male stress levels (physiological arousal) is higher and takes longer to reduce than female stress levels. A difference in testosterone levels might be an explanation for this. During threat (e.g. a wife starting an argument with her husband), increased testosterone increases activity in the amygdala (see Radke et al.), which increases stress. High stress levels predicts stonewalling, so it might be a stress reduction strategy that males employ.

Further Studies

A comparison of Pakistani and American couples (Rehman and Holtz-Munro, 2007): This study compared three groups of married couples with about 50 couples in each group: American couples, Pakistani couples, and Pakistani immigrants living in the US. The researchers gathered data on communication styles and marital satisfaction. The results were similar to Gottman and Levenson's: couples with more positive communication had higher levels of marital satisfaction. However, the correlation was strongest in the American couples. This suggests that while communication might be an important factor in marital satisfaction across cultures, it could be a more significant factor in the West.

Correlations between physiological arousal and communication patterns (Gottman and Levenson, 1985): In this study, 21 couples were followed over a three-year period. Communication patterns were correlated with levels of physiological arousal (measured by taking heart rate and blood pressure). The results showed a strong correlation between high levels of physiological arousal (i.e. stress) and marital dissatisfaction. This included an incredibly strong negative correlation (-.91) between the husband's heart rate and marital satisfaction. This correlational study shows the relationship between biology and communication and how it might be a bidirectional path – an argument might increase the husband's stress levels so he stonewalls to try to reduce his stress, which only further frustrates his wife, so she makes more demands that lead to arguments (and the cycle continues).

Critical Thinking Considerations

- Is there bidirectional ambiguity in these studies? It is plausible that communication is increasing marital satisfaction- but how might this relationship work in the opposite direction?
- While communication may affect marital satisfaction, what are some other factors? See the next topic for more info.
- While comparing Pakistani and American couples does give some cross-cultural perspective, it is very limited. Why is this?
- Can you think of ways cultural values (e.g. collectivism or individualism) may moderate the effects of communication on a marriage?

Explanations for why relationships change or end

The Role of Communication, Cognition and Culture in Divorce
Why do personal relationships change or end?

Communication is a reason why marriages may end in divorce. However, cognitive patterns and cultural factors should also be taken into consideration.

Key Details

Communication
- *For more details on communication and marital satisfaction, see the previous topic and key studies.*

Cognitive explanation - attributions
- The study of **attributions** looks at how people explain behaviour. In the field of marriage and marital satisfaction, attributions are the most commonly studied cognitive factor. Decades of research have found that how couples make attributions can affect their marital satisfaction.
- If someone makes a positive attribution, it means they believe the cause of their partner's good behaviour is due to internal factors (e.g. their personality) and bad behaviours are due to external factors (e.g. the actions of others). A negative attribution is the opposite – good behaviour is a result of external factors and bad

behaviour is blamed on the person (internal factors). Not surprisingly, couples who make positive attributions tend to have higher marital satisfaction while those that make negative attributions tend to be less satisfied.

Key Studies

Cognition: Effects of attributions on marital satisfaction (Fincham et al., 2000): One aim of this study was to measure correlations between attributions and marital satisfaction. Participants were 130 white couples who had been married for 15-20 months from small towns in the Midwest of America. Marital satisfaction was measured using the Quality Marriage Index (QMI) and data was collected over three times using questionnaires during an 18-month time period. One result showed that marital satisfaction was negatively correlated with causal attributions at the beginning of the study (-.44) and after 18 months (-.41). In other words, when partners made a negative attribution of their partner's behaviour (e.g. by explaining a negative

behaviour was due to dispositional and internal factors) their marital satisfaction decreased. This finding supports many other studies that show the same thing – how we attribute our partner's behaviour can affect our marital satisfaction, which is one reason why relationships might deteriorate and eventually end in divorce.

Use this QR code to get an additional study that investigates attributions and cognitive explanations of why marriages may change or end.

Exam Tips

- The same arguments and studies can be applied to more than one topic. Here, you can use the same material for the role of communication and the reasons why relationships change or end topics - because communication is a reason why relationships change or end.
- If you are preparing only this topic, you need to be prepared to write about cognitive studies because you might be asked about the cognitive approach in relation to personal relationships. "Attributions" in relation to marital satisfaction is an excellent example to write about.

Extension

- While communication is one key reason for why marriages may end, we cannot ignore the cultural differences in divorce rates. For example, traditional, collectivist cultures such as India, Pakistan, and China have very low divorce rates, whereas more individualistic and modernized cultures, including the US and European countries, tend to have much higher divorce rates.
- This difference in divorce rates could be explained by differences in cultural values, including the value placed on love in a marriage. If a couple marries for love, it means they are placing their own personal decisions and feelings above the thoughts and feelings of others (e.g. their parents and families). This means if a relationship deteriorates, they may also be less likely to consult others or consider how others would be affected by the divorce and would make the choice that best suits them. However, if a couple is married based on an arranged marriage (which is still common in many cultures), and/or if they do not believe that marrying for love is the most important factor in getting married, they may not decide to end the marriage if a relationship deteriorates. This is because there are many more factors to consider, including the effect on parents and the extended families. The differences in attitudes towards love in a marriage can be seen in Levine et al.'s study.

Further Studies

A cross-cultural comparison of the importance of love in marriage and divorce (Levine et al., 1995): This study compared college students from 11 different cultures (a mix of individualistic and collectivist). They gathered their data using questionnaires and one question asked, "If a person had all the qualities you desired, would you marry them if you weren't in love with them?" The participants answered yes, no or neutral. Participants were also asked whether the disappearance of love from a marriage would be enough reason to end the marriage. The results showed that students from the USA, UK and Australia placed more emphasis on love in a marriage than those from India, Pakistan and Thailand. The results also showed that those cultures that placed more emphasis on the role of love in a marriage also had higher divorce rates. Thus, while communication might affect a relationship and could cause divorce, it might be less likely to do so in some cultures and more likely to do so in other cultures based on the importance placed on love.

A comparison of Pakistani and American couples (Rehman and Holtz-Munro, 2007): This study can be used to show how the correlation between communication and marital satisfaction may be similar across cultures, albeit stronger in America (see the previous topic for more details).

Critical Thinking Considerations

- While low divorce rates in traditional cultures like India and Pakistan could be explained through cultural values and norms, there could also be other factors that influence divorce rates. What economic or social factors could affect a woman's (or man's) decision (or ability) to get divorced?
- Could the above studies be questioned on their generalizability? For instance, do you think they cover enough cultures in order to draw strong conclusions? Are there reasons you can think of as to why these results might not apply to a specific culture?
- Some of the above studies use self-report data. Is there a reason why this might not be valid?
- Are there biological factors that may be involved in marital dissatisfaction (and divorce)?
- The trend for divorce rates across the world seems to be increasing in both individualistic cultures and collectivist cultures. Why do you think this might be?

Co-operation and Competition

Realistic Group Conflict Theory
What are the causes and/or effects of co-operation and competition?

When groups are in competition with one another, this can lead to conflict. However, having these same groups co-operate can reduce conflict. While these are social explanations, the role of biology (e.g. evolution and testosterone) should not be ignored.

Key Details

- In the 1950s and 1960s, many social psychologists in America were trying to understand the social and racial conflicts that were happening at this time. For example, they wanted to understand the prejudice and discrimination that many black people were facing at this time.
- Muzafer and Sherif were leading social psychologists in this field. They put forward a theory that conflict between groups is a result of direct competition for resources. Their theory is called realistic group conflict theory (RCT).
- There are three main claims to RCT. Firstly, conflict is a result of direct competition for resources between groups. Related to this idea is something called negative goal interdependence, which is the idea that one group

can succeed only if the other group fails. Thus, when competing for scarce resources, there is not enough to share and one group will go without the resource.
- The second claim is that conflict will not be resolved simply by having groups come in contact with one another and the final claim is that conflict can only be reduced or resolved by having groups co-operate and work towards a common goal. This is positive goal interdependence, which is when both groups are relying on one another to achieve a common goal.
- The claims of RCT have been applied to classrooms to reduce conflict between racial groups of children (see "Origins of Conflict and Conflict Resolution").

Key Studies

The Robber's Cave (Sherif et al., 1961): This field experiment can be used to show the effects of competition and co-operation. In this famous experiment, 22 white, middle-class, protestant, boys were sent on a summer camp (called "Robber's Cave"). The experiment had three stages: bonding, competition and co-operation. In the bonding phase the groups got to know one another and gave themselves names (Eagles and Rattlers). After a week, they met each other and the researchers put them in direct competition with one another for resources (prizes). They competed for points and the winning team was given pocket knives and a trophy. This second stage resulted in conflict between the two

groups, including cabin raiding, name calling and even fist fights. When asked to describe their groups, the boys also rated their own groups more favourably than the other. In the third phase, the groups had to co-operate to achieve a common goal, like fixing the water tank or a broken down truck. This served to reduce the hostility and conflict between the two groups. The manipulation of the competition and co-operation, and the subsequent effects, provide support for RCT.

Effects of the Jigsaw Classroom (Bridgeman): *See the section on "Origins of Conflict and Conflict Resolution."*

Exam Tips

- The material in this topic can also be used to explain "origins of conflict and conflict resolution." While RCT can be used to explain prejudice and discrimination, it may be difficult to use the Robber's Cave to support that explanation.
- You can use genetics as a counter-argument that provides alternative explanations of aggression and conflict.

Extension

- While RCT and the Robber's Cave experiment show how social factors can influence behaviour, they do ignore the role of biological factors. For example, testosterone is one hormone that has been associated with competition. For example, studies have shown that increased testosterone levels may bias the amygdala towards reacting to someone who has challenged or threatened us (e.g. Radke et al). This could provide an evolutionary advantage, as the activation of the amygdala would release stress hormones like adrenaline which would give us the necessary energy to compete with a potential rival for resources.
- Another theory for how testosterone may affect competition is outlined in Wingfield et al.'s (1990) "**challenge hypothesis**." According to this hypothesis, increased testosterone may help males compete with other males for a mating partner. The increase in testosterone may help them be more successful in competing with their challengers as it can increase their aggression.

Further Studies

Albert et al.'s (1990): study on testosterone and aggression in alpha male rats can be used to show how testosterone in alpha males can help them compete with and dominate other males, which enables them to maintain their position as alpha male on top of the social hierarchy. *See page 19 for more details.*

Radke et al.'s (2015): study on healthy females shows how increased testosterone levels can increase the activation of the amygdala when we are motivated to respond to a social threat (i.e. a challenge). This shows how testosterone may facilitate aggression in such situations because the increased amygdala activity could increase negative emotions like anger (as this is generated in the amygdala) and could also provide the physiological arousal needed to compete and be successful (e.g. by releasing adrenaline). *See page 19 for more details.*

Critical Thinking Considerations

- The above studies show how social and biological factors may affect our behaviour in competitive situations. How might culture also be a factor? For example, consider why people from a culture of honor might react differently than others to a challenge or treat.
- What are the strengths and limitations in using the Robber's Cave experiment to show the effects of competition on behaviour? For example, all the boys have similar characteristics. How could this be a strength and/or a limitation?

Prejudice and Discrimination

Causes and Effects of Prejudice and Discrimination
What are the causes and/or effects of prejudice and discrimination?

Prejudice and discrimination may be risk factors for radicalization of Muslim immigrants into the US. Social identity theory can explain the origins of prejudice and discrimination, which may even have a biological base as shown in studies on implicit racial bias and the amygdala.

Key Details

• Prejudice can be defined as "an unjustified negative attitude toward an individual based solely on that individual's membership in a group" (Worchel et al., 1988). Prejudice is commonly studied in relation to race, religion, gender and sexual orientation. Discrimination refers to the unequal and unfair treatment of individuals based on their group membership. Whereas prejudice refers to attitudes, discrimination refers to actions.

• Immigrants are common victims of discrimination and this can have serious effects on those individuals. However, the acculturation strategy that an individual adopts when adjusting to a new culture could moderate (e.g. reduce or increase) the effects of discrimination.

• For example, if immigrants are marginalized (they have no strong ties with their home culture and are excluded from the new culture) they may be more at risk of sympathizing with extremist groups and adopting radical ideologies. This could be due to something Lyons-Padilla et al. (2015) call "significance loss" – a lack of purpose and self-worth. According to their research, it might not be the case that Muslims join radical terrorists groups (e.g. ISIS) because they share the same beliefs. On the contrary, it could be that they adopt those beliefs because they want to feel like they belong to a group – something that's missing if they are marginalized and discriminated against.

Key Studies

Correlations between acculturation, discrimination and extremism (Lyons-Padilla, 2015): This study surveyed 200 first- and second-generation Muslim immigrants across the USA. The results showed that the more the Muslim Americans were marginalized, the more felt significance loss. Feelings of significance loss were also correlated with support for an Islamic fundamentalist group, meaning that those who felt strong significance loss were more likely to support the group. Discrimination also moderated this effect, which means that discrimination strengthened the connections between marginalization, significance loss, religious extremism and support for radical religious groups. *See HL extensions for more information.*

See also chapter 4, page 66, Torres et al. (2012) for more effects of discrimination on mental health.

Exam Tips

• Some of the material in this topic can also be applied to topics in the sociocultural approach (acculturation, social identity theory) and the HL extension (the effects of globalization on behaviour).

• It is most likely that you will be asked to discuss or evaluate research related to prejudice and discrimination. Therefore, it is advisable to make sure you can evaluate one study in this topic in-depth, and use other studies to help with your evaluation.

- **Social identity theory**: Tajfel and Turner proposed their social identity theory to explain prejudice and discrimination. They agreed that the Sherif's realistic group conflict theory provided a strong and empirically supported explanation for prejudice and discrimination when groups were competing for scarce resources, but they argued that this competition is not always needed in order for group conflicts to occur. Merely identifying with an in-group and categorizing other people as members of the in-group or out-group can lead to prejudice and discrimination. This could be explained by their self-esteem hypothesis, which posits that humans have a natural desire to increase their self-esteem and one way of doing this is to identify with groups who are successful. The only way to have a successful group is for other groups to be less successful, so we naturally bias our own groups and act favourably to in-group members and discriminate against out-group members. The out-group homogeneity effect could also explain the formation of stereotypes which could lead to prejudiced attitudes (see "Stereotypes" in the sociocultural approach to behaviour for more information). SIT's self-esteem hypothesis also states that low self-esteem is a motivator for discrimination.

- **Biological - implicit racial bias**: It is possible that there is a biological basis to racism. For one, it could be argued that in-group bias and out-group discrimination is an evolutionary adaptation because if our in-groups are successful, then we as individuals will have access to more resources (e.g. food and water) and have a higher chance of surviving and passing on our genes. This may explain why studies have found a neurological basis for racial biases in the amygdala. For example, the amygdalae of white participants is more active when perceiving a black face than a white face, even if the face is shown so fast that they are not consciously aware of seeing a face at all.

Further Studies

Minimal group studies (e.g. Tajfel and Turner, 1971): These studies can provide some evidence to support SIT's explanation of discrimination – boys who were placed in groups arbitrarily demonstrated in-group favouritism by selecting to give more rewards to members of their in-group rather than the out-group. Similarly, they also found that they were willing to sacrifice the rewards of their in-group so they could still get more than the out-group could. This is an example of discrimination – they were treating the other participants in the study differently based purely on their group membership.

Park and Rothbart (1982): This study demonstrates in-group bias and the out-group homogeneity effect, both of which could be origins of prejudice and discrimination. *Read the SIT topic in Ch4 for more details.*

Phelps (2000): In this study, white American participants took an Implicit Association Test (IAT) and the results showed they had some implicit racial bias tendencies (they showed unconscious biased attitudes in favor of white faces compared to black faces). The results also showed that their amygdala was more active when viewing black faces. Because this is the part of the brain that activates the stress response and evaluates social stimuli (e.g. whether someone is harmful or harmless), this finding suggests there could be a biological basis to prejudice. Another finding from the study was that there was a positive correlation between scores on the IAT and amygdala activity – the more implicit bias a person had, the higher their amygdala activity was when viewing black faces.

Critical Thinking Considerations

- Do you think the Implicit Association Test (IAT) is a useful predictor for behaviour? Forscher et al. (2016) conducted a meta-analysis and found that changing people's implicit bias might not actually affect their discriminatory behaviours. Does this question the validity of this construct?
- Prejudice and discrimination are mostly (and understandably) viewed negatively. Are there alternative explanations for these behaviours that could suggest why (and when) they could be beneficial?
- Much of the research cited above is correlational. What are the strengths and limitations of using correlational studies for this topic?
- Could we apply the concepts and studies in this topic to help devise strategies to reduce prejudice and discrimination?

Origins of Conflict and Conflict Resolution

Realistic Group Conflict Theory
What are some origins of conflict and how might conflict be resolved?

Competition is an origin of conflict, as outlined in realistic group conflict theory. This same theory, however, can also be used to explain how co-operation can be used to resolve conflict. That being said, there are also alternative explanations.

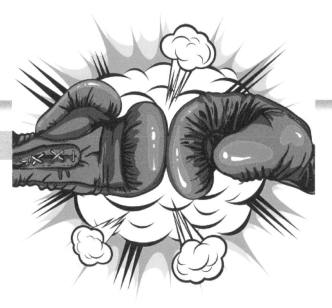

Key Details

- **Realistic group conflict theory**: Realistic group conflict theory (RCT) was proposed by Muzafer and Carolyn Sherif, who were leading social psychologists in the studies of prejudice and discrimination (i.e. conflict) in America in the 1950s and 1960s. The three main claims of this theory are that conflict is a result of direct competition for resources, conflict will not be resolved simply by having groups come in contact with one another and conflict can only be reduced or resolved by having groups co-operate and work towards a common goal. The claims of RCT have been applied to classrooms to reduce conflict between racial groups of children.
- **Social identity theory**: Tajfel and Turner's social identity theory came after Sherif's RCT. RCT posits that conflict is a result of competition for resources; SIT doesn't refute this claim, but it does explain how conflict may occur even when there is no direct competition for resources. The key idea behind social identity theory is that conflict may occur because of the psychological mechanisms involved in group identity. That is to say, belonging to a group and identifying with a group can affect how we think about in-group members, our out-group members and ourselves. The self-esteem hypothesis of SIT states that we discriminate against others because it boosts our self-esteem because it makes our own groups appear better.

Key Studies

Robber's Cave Experiment (Sherif et al., 1961): The two stages of this experiment can demonstrate the origins of conflict (competition) and how co-operation can be uses to resolve conflict. In the first stage, the boys were competing for scarce resources (e.g. prizes were given if they won competitions against each other) and this led to conflict. The conflict was reduced in the second stage of the experiment when the boys were forced to co-operate with each other

Sorority girls and in-group bias (Park and Rothbart, 1982): The results of this study can be used to support SIT as it demonstrates in-group bias, which could lead to discrimination.

Minimal group paradigm studies (Tajfel and Turner, 1971): These experiments can also support social identity theory's explanation of group conflict as the results show that just the identification with an in-group can lead to in-group bias and discrimination against members of an out-group. *Read the SIT topic in Ch4 for more details.*

Exam Tips

- The same material from this topic can be used to answer questions about competition and conflict resolution. If asked to evaluate or discuss one study, the Robber's Cave Experiment is a good choice as it focuses on competition, co-operation, origins of conflict and conflict resolution.
- Another origin of conflict could be cultural values associated with a "culture of honor." Conflict may be more common in these cultures as people are primed to react to threats and challenges with violence. Cohen et al.'s studies can be used to this effect.

- **Sherif's realistic group conflict theory (1961)**: A key part of RCT is that conflict is not resolved when groups are simply in contact with one another but that it can be resolved if they actively work together to achieve common goals (see notes in "Co-operation and Competition" for more detailed explanations).
- **Allport's contact hypothesis (1954)**: Allport was another psychologist who studied origins of prejudice and discrimination in the hope that if the root causes of inter-group conflict were understood, these causes could be targeted and the conflict resolved. The contact hypothesis outlines some conditions required in order for groups to resolve their conflicts. According to the hypothesis, contact between groups can reduce conflict when a) groups are of equal status, b) they share a common goal, c) their contact is supported by social norms and authority figures (e.g. the government and the police), and d) there is no competition between groups.
- **Jigsaw classroom**: This is a classroom teaching strategy devised by social psychologist, Elliot Aronson in Texas in 1971. During this time, schools had just been desegregated so kids from different races were interacting for the first time. This led to racial tension and conflict. Aronson used the findings from the Robber's Cave to design an activity that required all students to work together to achieve a goal (e.g. pass a quiz). The individual competition was removed and co-operation became imperative. Numerous studies have shown this classroom teaching strategy can have positive effects.

Further Studies

Robber's Cave Experiment: *See notes on the previous page.*

Meta-analysis of the effectiveness of the contact hypothesis (Pettigrew and Tropp, 2006): 515 existing studies on the contact hypothesis were part of a meta-analysis that aimed to determine its effectiveness in predicting conflict resolution. The findings suggest that inter-group contact can reduce conflict but there's a greater reduction when the conditions of Allport's theory are met.

Effects of the jigsaw classroom (Bridgeman, 1981): This study compared 120 fifth graders in an American school. Half of the students had been involved in a classroom that was using the jigsaw model while the other half were in traditional lessons. After two months, the researchers conducted a series of tests in perspective taking (the ability to consider someone else's point of view in a situation). They found the jigsaw students were more adept at perspective taking. This is a crucial skill in empathy that could help resolve conflict, as children could learn to understand the effects of their actions on others and be less likely to behave in ways that cause group conflict (e.g. they may be less likely to discriminate against someone based on race).

Critical Thinking Considerations

- The examples here have skipped biological factors involved in the origins of conflict. What are some biological factors that might make some people more willing to engage in conflict than others? Are there cultural factors that could explain origins of conflict? (Hint: honor)
- One claim of RCT is that contact alone will not reduce conflict – the groups have to work together towards a common goal. While this appears to be supported by the Robber's Cave study, there was no control condition in the experiment to test this claim. How might this affect the validity of the results?
- Why might studies such as the minimal group studies and Robber's Cave experiment be critiqued based on external validity (e.g. temporal and population validity)?

Bystanderism

Diffusion of Responsibility and Bystanderism
Why does bystanderism occur?

Diffusion of responsibility is one core explanation for bystanderism. Cultural values may also explain differences in rates of bystanderism across cultures.

Key Details

- **Bystanderism** is a term that can be used to explain when people do not help someone else is need. The more commonly used term in social psychology is "the bystander effect." This term refers to the phenomenon that occurs when someone sees someone else in need, but because there are other people around, they do not help. There are numerous explanations for bystanderism.

- **Diffusion of responsibility**: Darley and Latane are two social psychologists who have studied bystander behaviour in-depth. One explanation they provide for bystanderism is "diffusion of responsibility." If there are lots of people able to offer help, a person feels less personal responsibility to help because their responsibility is diffused (spread) across many people. This could explain why a common belief (which is supported empirically) is that people living in rural areas and small towns are more helpful than those living in big cities.

- **Informational social influence**: Another possible explanation is "informational social influence." This is a type of social influence that occurs when we are in ambiguous situations and we are not sure how to act, so we look to those around us for information as to what the right thing to do would be. This is different to normative social influence, where we follow the actions of others because we are afraid of standing out from the group.

Key Studies

The smoky room study (Darley and Latane, 1968): In this famous study, participants were asked to fill out a questionnaire in a room. While they sat, the room slowly filled with smoke. The researchers measured how long it took the participant to notify someone that the room was filling with smoke. The independent variable was how many people were in the room. In one condition, the participant was alone. In another, the participant was with two other participants. In a third condition, the participant was with two paid confederates who acted as if the smoke was not a problem. When there were three participants, only 38% of the participants helped.

This is evidence for diffusion of responsibility as this is much lower than when they were alone (75%). The rate of helping drops to 10% when they are with two passive confederates, which is evidence of the effects of information social influence. Because the smoke filling the room is ambiguous (it is not clear if there is an immediate emergency), the participants may be looking to others for guidance on how to act. Because the confederates did not respond, this influenced the participants to think that there wasn't an emergency and there consequently wasn't a need to respond.

Exam Tips

- Diffusion of responsibility could be considered a social explanation as it is affected by social factors (i.e. other people), but it could also be considered a cognitive explanation as it is considered a type of attribution.
- If you're ever asked about "one" explanation of something, you can group your explanation by a relevant approach. For example, one explanation of bystanderism is to use "the sociocultural approach." This allows you to use a lot of content to answer a specific question.

Extension

- **Sensory overload**: Milgram provided an alternative explanation for the bystander effect. He used the concept of "sensory overload" to explain why people in crowded cities might be less likely to help. Because we have a limited amount of cognitive energy to devote to sensory input (e.g. sights, smells, and sounds), we tend to block out information that is not personally relevant. If something does not immediately help an individual satisfy their wants or needs, it is ignored.
- **Cultural and economic explanations**: *Studies have shown that there are cross-cultural differences in rates of helping others. See the next topic for more details.*
- **Empathy**: *See the notes for the next topic on Prosocial Behaviour (if feeling empathy is a reason why people might help others, then not feeling empathy could be why people don't help).*

Further Studies

Comparison of helping behavior in major US cities (Levine, 1994): In this study, Levine gathered data from 36 major cities across the United States. In this study, confederates would pretend to be in need of some kind of help (e.g. needing help crossing the street). He found that population density and population size were negatively correlated with rates of helping other people. In other words, the more people in the city, the less helpful they tended to be. He also found that helping rates began to decline when the population size was around 300,000 or above.

Meta-analysis comparing helping rates in urban and rural areas (Steblay, 1987): This meta-analysis gathered and analyzed data from 65 studies that compared how helpful people were in rural (countryside) and urban (city) environments. The results supported the idea that people in cities were generally less helpful compared to people in the countryside.

Critical Thinking Considerations

- Are there alternative explanations to some of the results in Darley and Latane's experiment? For example, could the difference between the control group and the condition with three naïve participants be explained by the effects of normative social influence?
- Are there issues of generalizability with Darley and Latane's research? For example, why might it be difficult to use these findings to explain bystanderism in real-life situations (such as when intervening in an assault or trying to save someone's life)?
- Are there ethical considerations relevant to these studies?
- Can you think of evolutionary explanations for why we might not want to help other people in need?
- Levine's research is correlational. Why is this a limitation? Can you think of other reasons why people in large cities might not want to help?

Prosocial Behaviour

Empathy and Economics
How can one or more factors affect prosocial behaviour?

Prosocial behaviour is any behaviour that is done with the aim of benefitting other people. Empathy, cultural values and population density are factors that affect prosocial behaviour.

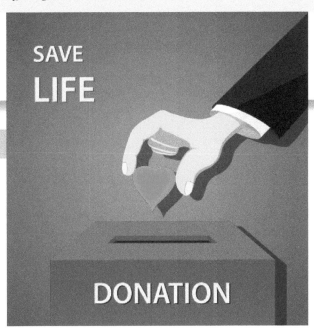

Key Details

- One form of prosocial behaviour is altruism, which is when someone helps another person with no expectation of reward for themselves. The reason this is an interesting and popular field of study is that altruism doesn't seem to make much sense from an evolutionary perspective: why would we help others if it's not going to benefit us?
- There have been many theories that have tried to explain altruism. One of those is Batson's empathy-altruism hypothesis. The key claim of this theory is that altruism is more likely to occur if the helper feels empathy for the person in need of help. According to this theory, we will help others for whom we feel empathy.

Key Study

Elaine and the empathy-altruism hypothesis (Batson, 1981): 44 females participated in this study and were asked to watch a video of a young woman named Elaine receiving electric shocks. However, Elaine wasn't really receiving electric shocks - she was a confederate who "turned up late" to take part in the exper-iment. The participants were deceived into believing that the experiment was testing how people worked under unpleasant circumstances. Part way through observing Elaine receive shocks, the participants were given a chance to take her place -- the experimenter pretends to have an idea to ask if the participant would want to change places for the remainder of the experiment. The researchers measured altruism by seeing how many people would volunteer to take Elaine's place in the experiment to be the "worker" receiving the shocks. In order to test the influence of empathy, before the experiment began, all participants filled out a person-ality questionnaire. Half of the participants were led to believe that Elaine was very similar to them (high empathy) while the other half were led to believe that she was quite different (low empathy). Research suggests that individuals may feel more empathy for people whom they identify with. The results showed that even when participants were able to leave the experiment without continuing to watch Elaine receive shocks, 91% in the high-empathy condition still agreed to take her position, compared to just 18% in the low-em-pathy condition. These results provide support for the empathy-altruism's explanation of prosocial behaviour. The results can also be used to explain bystanderism: perhaps people do not help others if they do not feel empathy towards them.

Exam Tips

- If the question asks about prosocial behaviour in general, you can discuss strategies used to promote prosocial behaviour.
- Questions about bystanderism and prosocial behaviour can be answered using the same studies because they can be used to explain why people might help others (prosocial behaviour) but also why they might not (bystanderism).

- Studies have shown that there are different rates of altruism and prosocial behaviour across different cultures. Two interrelated factors that might explain this finding are cultural values and economic factors. Studies like Levine et al.'s (see below) and others suggest that people from wealthier countries are less helpful than people from poorer countries. There are numerous possible explanations for this. Firstly, it might be because children from poorer areas have more responsibilities to help others in their family, including taking care of younger children. Poorer countries tend to have larger families so older children are given more responsibilities. Another possible explanation is that in order for a country to acquire wealth, its individuals must adopt values that focus on individual goals and economic productivity, which aren't always compatible with placing value on helping others in need. Thus, it might be that the same values that created the wealth can also explain a reduced willingness to help others.

Further Studies

Correlations between cultural factors and helping others (Levine et al., 2001): The aim of this study was to measure correlations between rates of helping behaviour and sociocultural factors. The study took place across 23 cities around the world. To control for population size being a factor, the study took place in the largest city in each country. Sociocultural factors were measured, including scores on the individualism/collectivism dimension, economic productivity and life pace. Helping behaviour was measured by having a confederate act as if they needed help (e.g. pretending to be a blind person needing help, dropping magazines or a pen). The results showed the strongest correlation was found between economic productivity and helping others – the negative correlation showed that the higher the gross domestic product (a measure of wealth) the lower the rate of helping. For example, countries like the USA, Netherlands and Singapore had low helping rates, compared to other countries like Malawi, El Salvador and Brazil. One possible explanation for this correlation is that in order to develop economically, people need to focus on individual goals more than the collective well-being of others.

Critical Thinking Considerations

- These examples and studies are mainly from a social approach to understanding behaviour – can you think of any possible biological reasons why we might (or might not) want to help other people?
- Levine's research is correlational. Why is this a limitation? Why is it difficult to conduct controlled experiments and studies on cross-cultural rates of prosocial behaviour?
- Batson's theory and study explains that altruism can affect prosocial behaviour, but what can affect levels of altruism? Is this an important area of uncertainty to consider? Can you hypothesize factors that might influence empathy?
- Is using the largest city in a control a suitable control?

Promoting Prosocial Behaviour

Authority and Compliance
How can one or more strategies be used to promote prosocial behaviour?

Social norms and people in positions of authority can be used to promote prosocial behaviour.

Key Details: Compliance

• Social psychologist Robert Cialdini has outlined six principles of persuasion that can be applied to gain compliance. **Consensus**, the idea of having others agree, is one of these. In social psychology, it refers to the process of making people aware of descriptive social norms so that the individual sees that others are in agreement on the correct way to act (there's "social proof").

• The compliance technique of using consensus can be used by asking a request and showing the potential complier that others are also following that request.

• This can work because decades of social psychology work have shown humans have a natural desire to belong to groups and to act in a way that is consistent with social norms. Therefore, they will want to comply with the request through fear of being left out or of seeming different (which is normative social influence).

Key Study

Hotel towel study (Cialdini, 2008): The aim of this study was to see if social influence could be manipulated to have an effect on reusing towels in a hotel. The study took place in a mid-priced hotel (they were not aware they were participants in a study) in the Southwest of America. Data was gathered over an 80-day period in 190 rooms. The independent variable was the phrasing of a card in the room that asked the guest to reuse towels. The card in the first condition read: "HELP SAVE THE ENVIRONMENT. You can show your respect for nature and help save the environment by reusing your towels during your stay." The card in the second condition read: "JOIN YOUR FELLOW GUESTS IN HELPING TO SAVE THE ENVIRONMENT. Almost 75% of guests who are asked to participate in our new resource savings program do help by using their towels more than once. You can join your fellow guests in this program to help save the environment by reusing your towels during your stay." The researchers gathered data on the percentage of participants who reused their towels. There was a significant difference in the percentage of reusing of towels depending on the card. For the first condition with the environmental focus, 35% of participants reused their towels. For the second condition, which implemented the use of consensus, 44% of participants reused their towels. These results suggest that using the strategy of consensus by making people aware of descriptive social norms can be used to encourage prosocial behaviour.

Exam Tips

• Content related to "promoting prosocial behaviour" can also be applied to general exam questions about "prosocial behaviour."
• The examples in this topic do not include studies directly relevant to the cognitive approach.

Extension

- People have a natural tendency to follow orders from people in positions of authority, so this can be used to get compliance.
- The effects of **authority** on compliance were studied in Milgram's famous experiments using electric shocks. These experiments were designed to provide plausible explanations for the behaviour of the Nazis during the holocaust.
- Subsequent social psychologists asked whether the concept of using authority to gain compliance could be used for social good.
- One reason people may have a natural tendency to comply with requests from people in positions of authority is because we rely on these positions to maintain order within society. We have been socialized to respect and obey people in positions of authority (e.g. parents, teachers, police officers) because this enables society to function in a civilized way.

Further Studies

Field experiments using authority to induce compliance (Bickman, 1974 and Bushman, 1988)

Bickman: In this field experiment, a confederate stood in a public place dressed as either a guard, milkman or civilian. The confederate told passers-by to do something, such as pick up a piece of garbage, give 10 cents to a stranger or move away from a bus stop. The results showed that the uniform (authority condition) resulted in the highest levels of compliance.

Bushman: This field experiment was similar to Bickman's, although in this field experiment, the confederate was dressed in professional attire, a uniform or sloppy clothing. The confederate asked passers-by to put money in an expired meter. The highest level of compliance were when the confederate was dressed in uniform.

Bushman and Bickman's studies show how prosocial behaviour can be influenced by having people in positions of authority giving people orders on how to behave. While this might work to promote prosocial behaviour in the short-term, it has limited use for long-term strategies, not to mention the practical and ethical limitations.

Critical Thinking Considerations

- Are there ethical issues in using authority or consensus to gain compliance? What are the practical limitations in using authority to promote compliance?
- These studies were conducted in the USA. Are there any reasons to think that these results might not be generalizable to other cultures?
- Could the empathy-altruism hypothesis be used to create strategies to promote prosocial behaviour?

Research Method #1

Correlational Studies
How and why are correlational studies used in the study of human relationships?

Correlational studies measure how strongly two (or more) variables are related. Unlike experimental methods that include a direction of causality (IV→DV), correlational studies have co-variables.

Key Details

- **Correlational studies on human relationships**: Correlational studies are commonly used when researchers are studying relationships between variables that cannot be manipulated in a laboratory setting. In studies on human relationships, it is often the case that one or more of the co-variables in the study would be difficult (if not impossible) to manipulate in a laboratory setting. For example, manipulating communication between couples or creating a set of cultural values would be almost impossible to create in a true experiment.

- In correlational studies, researchers gather data by first measuring the behaviour in some way. For example, questionnaires, surveys and interviews can be used to measure levels of marital satisfaction, conflict or prosocial behaviour. The co-variables also have to be calculated, and these could be things like communication strategies, cultural values, socioeconomic factors, etc. The correlation co-efficient gives us a value of how strongly the variables are correlated, with 1.0 being a perfect positive correlation and -1.0 a perfect negative correlation (0.0 is no correlation). A 0.4 (or -0.4) correlation is considered moderate and anything around 0.7 (or -0.7) or higher is considered strong.

Key Studies

Personal relationships: Correlational studies on this topic find the strengths of correlation between relationships and factors hypothesized to affect those relationships, like scores on individualism and collectivism. In studies on what people find attractive and the importance of love in a marriage, cultural values associated with individualism and collectivism are correlated with mate preference and the importance of love. Since cultural values would be difficult (if not impossible) to manipulate in a laboratory setting, but can provide evidence for a possible connection, they make for ideal correlational studies.
  - **Buss (1989); Levine et al. (1995);**

Group dynamics: Correlational studies have been used to measure the effects of prejudice and discrimination on attitudes and mental health. There are ethical issues with exposing participants to prejudice and discrimination in a true experiment, so correlational studies are useful for this topic.
  - **Lyons-Padilla et al. (2015); Phelps et al. (2000)**

Social responsibility: Correlational studies are common in the field of social responsibility because variables like population density, cultural values and economic productivity cannot be manipulated in the laboratory, but they're still hypothesized to influence behaviour. Researchers want to calculate correlation coefficients to test these hypotheses.
  - **Levine et al. (1994 and 2001)**

Critical Thinking Considerations

- Correlation does not mean causation. This is the fundamental limitation of correlational studies. One way of making this point is by explaining examples of how other variables might affect the two being correlated in a study. Can you think of examples of this for any of the studies above?
- Another way of critiquing correlational studies is by showing how bidirectional ambiguity may be an issue in the study. Is it variable A affecting B, or vice versa? Can you explain any examples of bidirectional ambiguity in the above studies?

Exam Tips

- For every topic you are preparing to write an essay about, become an expert in one research method and one ethical consideration. Have a second for each as a backup. This will allow you to be fully prepared in case the question asks you to write about only one method or consideration.
- Try to prepare to use the same explanations and studies (where possible) in Paper 2 as well as in Paper 1. For example, if you are explaining the use of correlational studies and one of your co-variables is cultural dimensions, you could also use this material in two of the socio-cultural approach topics.

Ethical Consideration #1

Anonymity in Correlational Studies
How and why is anonymity important in studies on human relationships?

Anonymity *in psychological studies means that the names of participants are not revealed when recording and/or publishing results of studies. This is an especially important consideration when the topics being studied are sensitive.*

Key Details

- In studies about human relationships, the behaviours being investigated are often highly sensitive, including love, attraction, marital satisfaction, prejudice and discrimination, etc. For this reason, anonymity is important because participants probably would not want others to know their results in these studies. Informed consent forms should promise anonymity. If there are exceptions, this should be made clear to the participants before they consent to join the study.

Key Studies

Personal relationships: Mate preference and what someone desires in a partner is an incredibly personal topic. Therefore, anonymity is very important to consider. Also, in Buss and Levine's studies the participants might have had partners already, but they may desire characteristics that are not possessed by their partner and so they wouldn't want them to find out. Also, there may be a stigma attached to marrying for love if you come from a collectivist culture, so participants answers should not be shared with other people (i..e family members) as this could get them into trouble with their family.

    o **Buss (1989); Levine et al. (1995);**

Group dynamics: Anonymity is very important in studies that measure implicit racial bias because people would probably not want others to know their scores on these tests. Similarly, participants in studies on prejudice and discrimination probably wouldn't want people to know their results, as this is a personal subject.

    o **Lyons-Padilla et al. (2015); Phelps et al. (2000)**

Social responsibility: Levine's field experiments have anonymity built into their procedures because people are unaware that they are participating in the study and the researchers don't gather their details – they are simply anonymous citizens walking down the street. However, this adds another issue related to informed consent – if they don't know that they are in the study, how can they give consent? Is it ethical to study people in such a manner without their knowledge?

    o **Levine et al. (1994 and 2001)**

Critical Thinking Considerations

- Are there any limitations in giving anonymity to participants? Can you think of any circumstances or reasons why not giving 100% anonymity might be beneficial?

Exam Tips

- Preparing to use the same studies to support your explanations of research methods and ethical considerations can make your revision more effective.
- An explanation of ethical considerations is most effective when it's linked to common research methodology used to study a particular topic, hence the layout of these review materials (with anonymity being linked to correlational studies). However, you can still write about anonymity in true experiments and/or informed consent in correlational studies.

Experiments
How and why are experiments used in the study of human relationships?

Experiments are used when the researchers measure the effects of an independent variable on a dependent variable. Researchers try to control for extraneous variables as much as possible and measure the effects of the IV on the DV. By carefully controlling the extraneous variables, the researchers can maximize the chances that any differences in the DV can be explained by the IV. This allows for conclusions about causality to be made. Sometimes, natural or quasi-experimental methods are used when the researchers can't directly manipulate the IV.

Key Details

• Experiments on human relationships: In this approach, the focus is on the study of how certain factors can affect human relationships. Therefore, the IV in experiments on human relationships tends to be a factor hypothesized to affect relationships. While true experiments are ideal for making conclusions about causality, it is not always possible for researchers to manipulate the independent variable. For this reason, quasi-experiments become valuable because they can test the effect of a particular independent variable that wasn't manipulated by the researcher. . Another limitation of true experiments is that they are in artificial environments, which is why field experiments can be beneficial as they manipulate an IV in a natural environment.

Key Studies

Personal relationships: Studies on personal relationships have the DV as the factor relevant to personal relationships (e.g. levels of attraction) and the IV is some factor hypothesized to have an effect, e.g. pheromones or testosterone.
    o **Johnston et al. (2001) - quasi-experiment;**
    o **Saxton et al. (2008) - field experiment**

Group dynamics: While it's difficult to measure prejudice and discrimination in a lab, the minimal group paradigm allows for some conclusions to be drawn about in-group bias. The Robber's Cave experiment is a good example of the value of field experiments, although for ethical reasons it probably wouldn't be allowed to be conducted today.

    o **Sherif et al. (1961) – field experiment;**
    o **Tajfel and Turner (1971) – true experiment**

Social responsibility: Social factors hypothesized to have an effect on bystanderism and prosocial behaviour are manipulated either in laboratory or field settings. For example, figures of authority, empathy and social influence are all factors manipulated in the following experiments.
    o **Darley and Latane (1968) and Batson et al. (1981) – true experiments**
    o **Bickman (1974) & Bushman (1988) - field experiments**

Critical Thinking Considerations

• Are true experiments inherently limited in generalizability because of their artificial environments?
• Can you use one type of experiment to highlight the limitations of another? For example, how might the Robber's Cave field experiment be used to highlight the limitations of minimal group true experiments?
• What are the ethical considerations associated with true experiments?

Exam Tips

• Correlational studies are best to write about for human relationships topics. Use the experimental method as a second example only if required or to highlight limitations of correlational studies.

Ethical Consideration #2

Informed Consent in Experiments

Why is informed consent an important consideration in experiments on human relationships?

At the heart of **ethics** in psychological research is considering the impact the research might have on others, especially the participants. **Informed consent** is one consideration that can reduce some of the stress and other negative effects of participating in a study. Informed consent means you get an agreement from participants that they want to be in the study (consent) and they are basing this decision on information you have given them (informed).

Key Details

• In experiments on human relationships, informed consent is an important consideration because the nature of the behaviours being studied are sensitive (e.g. attraction, marital satisfaction, prejudice, conflict, bystanderism). Researchers must also carefully consider how much information to reveal to participants and when. For example, if they reveal too much information too early in the study, this may affect the validity of the study as participants may change their behaviour (e.g. the participant expectancy effect could occur). If they don't reveal enough information for the participants to make an informed decision, they run the risk of their study being deemed unethical.

Key Studies

Personal relationships: In experiments that investigate personal relationships, the effects of biological factors on attraction are measured and the researchers compare conditions. Because these experiments deal with sensitive topics (like menstrual cycles and physical attraction), informed consent is important.
> o **Johnston et al. (2001) - quasi-experiment;**
> o **Saxton et al. (2008) - field experiment**

Group dynamics: In field experiments like Sherif's, informed consent is often sacrificed for the sake of validity (or at least very little information is revealed to participants). As Sherif's experiment was on children, parental consent is also a matter to consider (this experiment was before the times of strict ethical guidelines).

> o **Sherif et al. (1961) – field experiment;**
> o **Tajfel and Turner (1971) – true experiment**

Social responsibility: Studies on social responsibility manipulate a social factor in some way and revealing too much information about what factor is being manipulated may affect the validity of results, so information needs to be withheld. This makes informed consent a difficult task.
> o **Darley and Latane (1968) and Batson et al. (1981) – true experiments**
> o **Bickman (1974) & Bushman (1988) - field experiments**

Critical Thinking Considerations

• How might informed consent affect the validity of a study?
• Should researchers reveal everything in their informed consent forms?
• Are there other ethical considerations relevant to true experiments at the biological approach?

Exam Tips

• You can still write about informed consent in correlational studies, and anonymity in experimental ones. They have been matched with the particular methodologies for ease of revision only.

7 Abnormal Psychology

Abnormal Psychology

Topic	Content
Factors Influencing Diagnosis	• Normality versus abnormality • Classification systems • The role of clinical biases in diagnosis • Validity and reliability of diagnosis
Etiology of Abnormal Psychology	• Explanations for disorders • Prevalence rates and disorders
Treatment of Disorders	• Biological treatments • Psychological treatments • The role of culture in treatment • Assessing the effectiveness of treatment(s)
Ethical considerations and research methods	• Students should also be prepared to discuss one or more of the three approaches (biological, cognitive and sociocultural) in relation to each topic • Students should be able to discuss one or more research methods and ethical considerations related to the relevant studies for one or more of the three topics in this option

Abnormal Psychology

	Content	Key Questions	Key Studies
Factors influencing diagnosis	**Normality versus abnormality**	*How do psychologists try to distinguish abnormality from normality?*	• Rosenhan (1973) • Temerlin (1968) • Bagby et al. (2015)
	Classification systems	*How and why are classification systems used in the diagnosis of disorders?*	• Hafstad et al. (2017) • Bagby et al. (2015) • Kleinman (1982)
	The role of clinical biases in diagnosis	*How can clinical bias influence the diagnosis of disorders?*	• Mendel et al. (2011) • Temerlin (1968) • Bagby et al. (2015) • Rosenhan (1973)
	Validity and reliability of diagnosis	*What factors can influence the validity and reliability of diagnosis?*	• Parker et al. (2001) • Kleinman (1982) • *All studies above*
Etiology of abnormal psychology	**Explanations for disorders**	*What are the explanations for one (or more) psychological disorders?*	• Karl et al. (2006) • Gilbertson et al. (2002) • Urry et al. (2006) • Hitchcock et al. (2015) *See studies below for sociocultural explanations*
	Prevalence rates and disorders	*Why are there differences in prevalence rates for one (or more) disorders?*	• Garrison et al. (1995) • Luby et al. (2013) • Irish et al. (2011)
Treatment of disorders	**Biological treatments**	*How and why can biological treatments be used to treat disorders?*	• Marshall et al. (2001) • Ipser et al. (2006) • MacNamara et al. (2016)
	Psychological treatments	*How and why are psychological treatments used to treat disorders?*	• Rothbaum et al. (2001) • Parsons and Rizzo (2008) • Felmingham et al. (2007) • Roy et al. (2014)
	The role of culture in treatment	*How can culture influence the treatment of disorders?*	• Horne et al. (2004) • Jiminez et al. (2012) • Turvey et al. (2012)
	Assessing the effectiveness of treatment(s)	*How do psychologists assess the effectiveness of treatments for disorders?*	• Marshall et al. (2001) • Ipser et al. (2006) • Rothbaum et al. (2001) • Parsons and Rizzo (2008)

• *All answers should be supported by evidence.*
• *Students should also be prepared to discuss one or more of the three approaches (biological, cognitive and sociocultural) in relation to each topic*
• *Students should be able to discuss one or more research methods and ethical considerations related to the relevant studies for one or more of the three topics in this option*

Normality Versus Abnormality

How do psychologists try to distinguish abnormality from normality?

Psychologists and psychiatrists have long struggled with the concept of what makes someone "abnormal". The distinction between normality and abnormality is an important issue to consider because it can have serious implications for diagnosis and treatment. Classification systems are one way in which psychologists attempt to distinguish abnormality from normality.

Key Details

• **Concepts of normality and abnormality**: The issue of defining normality and abnormality and distinguishing between the two has been a long-standing debate in psychiatry. The reason why psychologists and psychiatrists attempt to distinguish abnormality from normality is because it can facilitate accurate diagnosis. An accurate diagnosis of disorders is important so patients can receive appropriate help and treatment. That being said, how do we define abnormal behaviour? One definition of abnormality is if someone's behaviour is inconsistent with social norms. Another definition is if their behaviour causes themselves (or others) suffering. Yet another definition is whether someone is in a statistical minority. Each of these definitions has problems.

• Rosenhan's famous study demonstrated the difficulties that psychiatrists face in trying to distinguish normality from abnormality.

Key Study

"On being sane in insane places" (Rosenhan, 1973): In this study, Rosenhan and some colleagues pretended to be patients and visited 12 different psychiatric hospitals on the East and West coasts of the United States. The only symptom they gave the hospitals was that they had been hearing a stranger's voice in their head. The voices were unclear, but they told the doctors that they thought they said "thud", "empty" and "hollow". One reason why these words were chosen was that they are signaling some sort of crisis in the individual's life, with their life being "empty" or "hollow." After the pseudo-patients were admitted to hospital, they carried on behaving normally and told the staff their symptoms had stopped. Of the 12 admissions to the hospitals, 11 were diagnosed with schizophrenia and one was diagnosed with manic-depressive psychosis. They remained in the hospitals for a range of 7 to 52 days, with an average of 19 days. They took notes and made other observations, at first hiding this in case the staff found out. After they realized the staff weren't paying much attention to them, they took notes freely. This resulted in other patients in the hospital raising questions about the authenticity of the pseudopatients' illnesses. In fact, during the first 3 admissions to hospitals, 35 of 118 patients expressed some concern regarding whether or not the pseudopatients were really mentally ill. This raises an interesting question: why could the diagnosed "mentally insane" spot normal behaviour, but the trained professionals couldn't? And while the other patients suspected them of being journalists or something similar, some doctors and nurses interpreted the notetaking as symptomatic of their mental illness. This study highlighted the difficulties in distinguishing what is normal from what is abnormal. It also shed light on the dehumanizing treatment of patients in psychiatric hospitals.

Exam Tips

• The textbook *IB Psychology: A Student's Guide* did not go into detail about these topics as it focused more on the other two instead (etiologies and treatments).

• It is technically possible to be asked about the influence of biological factors in diagnosis, which would be a very difficult question to answer. This is why this topic is best as a backup for one of the others (or not covered for exam preparation).

- **Clinical bias**: When determining normal from abnormal behaviour, clinical and confirmation bias can distort this judgement process. *See Mendel's and Temerlin's studies.*
- **Classification systems**: Making an accurate diagnosis is just as important in psychiatry as it is medicine. A misdiagnosis or not offering any diagnosis at all could have negative consequences for patients. That being said, the line between what is normal and abnormal is highly subjective and often difficult to determine. Using classification systems such as the DSM can facilitate the process of diagnosing disorders by providing clear descriptors of symptoms. *See Hafstad et al.'s and Bagby et al.'s studies.*

Further Studies

Rosenhan, continued... After his original study was conducted, one hospital heard of the findings and challenged Rosenhan to send pseudo-patients to their hospital with the belief that they would be able to spot the fake patients from the genuine patients. Over a three-month period, 193 patients were admitted for treatment and received a judgement based on the staffs' beliefs of whether they were an actual patient or not. Of these 193, 41 were judged with high confidence by at least one member of staff of being a pseudo-patient, while 19 were suspected of being a pseudo-patient by a psychiatrist and at least one other member of the staff. In fact, Rosenhan had not sent any pseudo-patients during this time. This is more evidence to show that distinguishing who is "sane" (normal) from "insane" (abnormal) is not easy, even for trained professionals.

Labelling and confirmation bias (Temerlin, 1968): This study shows how the opinions of others can influence our ability to distinguish normal from abnormal behaviour. The study found that when psychiatrists and psychologists were told that a man was quite psychotic, they were far more likely to also consider him psychotic whereas people who were given no prior information were able to make the accurate diagnosis that the individual was healthy and normal (read more in the topic on clinical bias).

Reliability of the DSM in distinguishing normality from abnormality (Bagby et al., 2015): The aim of this study was to test the reliability of the DSM-IV. The results showed that the reliability of diagnosis (i.e. the ability to determine abnormal from normal behaviour) varied depending on how the diagnosis was done. When using an audio recording of an interview between a clinician and a patient, the reliability of diagnosis of the DSM was "good to excellent" with a correlation of 0.80. However, when using a test-retest method (where different clinicians conduct separate interviews), this dropped to "poor to fair" with only 0.47 correlation. The results also suggest that some behaviours may be easier to classify as abnormal compared to others because there was a range in reliability depending on the disorder being diagnosed - major depressive disorder had the highest reliability (0.60), compared with PTSD (0.52) and social phobia (0.25).

Critical Thinking Considerations

- What are the limitations in defining abnormality using the concepts of social norms, statistical abnormality or individual suffering? Can you think of behaviours that may fit these definitions but would clearly not be abnormal?
- Rosenhan's study was from the 1970s. Are these results still valid today? A lot has changed in 50 years of psychiatry.
- What are the ethical issues with Rosenhan's study? Think about how his actions may have led to the lack of care for some people in the follow-up study). That being said, is he to blame for this? Could the long-term benefits outweigh the short-term harm?
- If we use PTSD as an example of trying to distinguish normality from abnormality, how might the symptoms of war actually be explained quite rationally? Is PTSD an example of a disorder (abnormal) or an understandable (and normal) reordering of the brain?

Classification Systems

The DSM and ICD

How and why are classification systems used in the diagnosis of disorders?

The Diagnostic and Statistical Manual of Mental Disorders (DSM) is the primary system used in American psychiatry to diagnose disorders. The International Classification of Diseases (ICD) is an international classification. These manuals are used to help psychologists make valid and accurate diagnoses, but they are not without their limitations.

Key Details

- One way that psychiatrists attempt to clearly distinguish normality from abnormality is with the use of **classification systems**. A classification system is a detailed description of a range of psychological disorders that are categorized (or classified) and accompanied with detailed descriptions of symptoms. The specific disorders are classified by their defining characteristics and symptoms.

- The most common classification system used in Western psychiatry is the **Diagnostic and Statistical Manual of Mental Disorders (DSM)**. The DSM is an extensive manual (print and online) and is currently in its fifth edition because it is regularly reviewed and updated to keep up with developments in the collective understanding of psychological disorders.

- The Word Health Organization's **International Classification of Diseases (ICD)** is similar to the DSM and is now in its eleventh edition. While the DSM is used in American psychiatry, the ICD is the most commonly used classification system internationally.

- While they are similar, there are a few differences. For example, in the DSM, the symptoms of PTSD are listed in groups related to arousal, avoidance and re-experiencing. The ICD, on the other hand, has a more narrow focus. Hafstad et al. found that using the DSM instead of the ICD results in more diagnoses of PTSD.

- While classification systems may help to reduce bias and to improve the validity of diagnosis, studies have found that different rates of diagnosis can be made depending on which system is used. This suggests that they may not be reliable in providing an accurate diagnosis (See Hafstad et al. below).

Key Study

A comparison of PTSD diagnosis with the ICD and DSM (Hafstad et al., 2017): The aim of this study was to compare diagnoses of PTSD using different classification systems. The participants were survivors of the Norway attacks of 2011, when 77 innocent people were killed by a terrorist. For the study, 325 young survivors and their parents were interviewed 4 to 6 months after the attacks and again 15 to 18 months later. The ICD and the DSM were used to diagnose PTSD. The results showed that using the DSM resulted in a higher rate of diagnosis of PTSD. While the difference was quite small when interviewing the survivors (38% prevalence when using the DSM-5 and 35% with the ICD-11), when assessing the parents, the differences in prevalence were much larger (29% with the DSM-5 compared to 17% with the ICD-11). The results also showed that "…the overlap between those meeting the PTSD diagnosis for both ICD-11 and DSM-5 was disturbingly low," which means that the inter-rater reliability of using both systems is low. This could mean that PTSD is over-diagnosed in America or underdiagnosed worldwide.

Exam Tips

- Be prepared to discuss and evaluate the classification systems, which means you need to be able to explain a number of limitations.
- You could be asked about only one classification system, so you need to be prepared to answer a question that requires you to discuss or evaluate just one.

- **Reliability of classification systems**: While the use of classification systems may make the diagnostic process more objective, there is still a lot of subjectivity in the process. The symptoms described in the DSM, for example, are mostly qualitative descriptions because not everyone's symptoms are identical. Maybe having quantitative values would be better, but this could also be problematic. For example, the DSM states that symptoms of PTSD must last for at least 30 days. What happens if someone seeks treatment after three weeks? Would they not meet the criteria and not receive a diagnosis? There are also questions as to how reliable the DSM is for diagnosis. One way of testing this is to have someone receive two diagnoses from different clinicians and to see what percentage of diagnoses match. The reliability of the DSM was tested in such a way by Bagby et al (see below).

- **Classification systems and bias**: One benefit of classification systems is that they can reduce clinical bias because they focus the clinician on the objective summary of symptoms as per the manual. Mendel, Temerlin and Rosenhan's studies can be used to highlight the effects of bias on diagnosis and thus how classification systems might help to reduce bias and improve the validity of diagnosis.

Further Studies

Assessing the reliability of diagnosis using the DSM (Bagby et al., 2015): The aim of this study was to test the reliability of the DSM-IV. They tested 339 psychiatric patients who had a range of disorders. Two different tests of reliability were used. In one type of test, they compared the reliability of diagnosis by listening to an audio recording (it was the same interview but listened to by two different clinicians). The other method was a test-retest method whereby two different clinicians made a diagnosis after a one-to-one in-person interview with a patient one week apart. The results showed that when using an audio recording, the reliability of diagnosis of the DSM was "good to excellent" with a correlation of 0.80. However, when using the test-retest method, this dropped to "poor to fair" with only a 0.47 correlation. There was also a range in reliability depending on the disorder being diagnosed. Major depressive disorder had the highest reliability (0.60), compared with PTSD (0.52) or social phobia (0.25). These results suggest that how reliability is measured can affect diagnosis, as well as which disorder is being diagnosed.

Critical Thinking Considerations

- The DSM has been developed in America, so it might not be useful for people from all cultural backgrounds. How can this affect diagnosis and treatment for some people (e.g. immigrants)?
- The DSM has changed over time and is revised with each edition. For example, homosexuality was considered a disorder in earlier editions. Is this example of a major limitation in the use of classification systems for diagnosis or an example of how our knowledge and understanding of psychiatry is evolving?
- At the moment, psychiatry does not use brain patterns to diagnose disorders. What could be some advantages and disadvantages of using MRI and fMRI scans to diagnose disorders?
- How could the use of a classification system such as the DSM influence clinical bias?

The Role of Clinical Biases in Diagnosis

Clinical and Confirmation Bias
How can clinical bias influence the diagnosis of disorders?

Clinical biases can affect the validity and reliability of diagnosis. One example of a clinical bias that could have an effect is confirmation bias. While the use of classification systems could reduce the influence of clinical bias, it might also lead to it.

Key Details

- **Clinical bias** is a general term that refers to any cognitive bias that can affect the diagnosis made by a clinician (e.g. a psychiatrist or psychologist who is treating a patient). There are many ways that bias can affect diagnosis, but one of the most common is **confirmation bias.**
- Confirmation bias is a cognitive bias in thinking. The term describes how we have a tendency to focus on and remember information that is consistent (i.e. confirms) our existing beliefs and opinions. In the context of making a diagnosis, this can affect the validity (accuracy) of a diagnosis because it can affect how clinicians seek and interpret information. For example, if a clinician has an assumption that a person has a particular disorder, this may affect how they analyze the patient as they may focus on information that is consistent with their original diagnosis.

Key Studies

Effects of confirmation bias on diagnosis (Mendel et al., 2011): The aim of this study was to see if psychiatrists would be affected by confirmation bias when making a diagnosis. They tested 75 psychiatrists by giving them a summary of a case study of an old man. The first summary was written so that the most probable diagnosis was depression, but if all of the information was revealed the actual correct diagnosis was clearly Alzheimer's disease. After an initial diagnosis, participants could then ask to receive additional information related to either diagnosis (depression or Alzheimer's). The researchers measured accuracy of diagnosis and also the correlation between what further information was asked for and correct diagnosis. The results showed that 30% of psychiatrists made an incorrect diagnosis. The results also showed that confirmation bias can affect diagnosis because the psychiatrists who searched for more new information consistent with their original incorrect diagnosis were more likely to keep that incorrect diagnosis. However, if psychiatrists asked for more information that contradicted their original diagnosis (i.e. they asked for information about the Alzheimer's symptoms when they originally diagnosed depression), they were less likely to make an incorrect diagnosis.

Exam Tips

- The IB often uses the phrase "the role of (….x…) in (…y…)" This can be confusing language, so you can just think of any question like this as asking how (….x….) influences (…y…). For this topic, you need to be able to explain how clinical bias can influence diagnosis, using studies to support your answer.
- You may be asked to evaluate one study related to factors influencing diagnosis. Choose a study that you can apply to multiple topics and make sure you can come up with 2-3 good evaluative points about that study.
- A good place to start when evaluating studies is thinking about generalizability and ethical considerations as these are relevant to all studies.
- 'Clinician' is a good term to use because it covers anyone treating a patient, including psychiatrists and psychologists.
- The example of confirmation bias here could be used as one bias in thinking and decision making in the cognitive approach. It would make for an excellent addition to an essay about biases.

- **Labelling theory**: Confirmation bias can also explain some biases in diagnosis related to labelling theory. Labelling theory refers to how a given label can affect the behaviour of an individual. Labels can affect individuals either through how the label affects their own thinking or how others perceive and treat them. Studies have shown that if a patient is given a label (i.e. a diagnosis of a particular disorder) and others are asked to make a diagnosis, they are more likely to make the same diagnosis, possibly because of confirmation bias.

- **Reliability**: One way of reducing clinical bias is to have two separate diagnoses. However, this might still have issues. For example, Temerlin's study shows that judgements can be influenced by a prior judgement. In this case, it was the original diagnosis of the expert psychiatrist that the participants were told about. This means that if one psychiatrist makes an initial incorrect diagnosis, it could affect the second diagnosis.

- **Classification systems**: One way of reducing bias is to use classification systems. This could help clinicians remain objective during the diagnostic process.

Further Studies

Effects of labelling on diagnosis (Temerlin, 1968): In this study, the researchers showed a video tape to their participants (psychiatrists, clinical psychologists and graduate students in clinical psychology). In the video, an actor portrayed a mentally healthy scientist and mathematician. The subject of the video involved the actor discussing a book about psychology he had read and how he wanted to discuss it with a psychologist. In the experimental condition, participants were told that an experienced psychiatrist had said the man was a "very interesting man because he looked neurotic, but actually was quite psychotic" (meaning he had a disorder). In the control groups, however, the participants were either given no prior information or they were told he was mentally healthy. After watching the video, the participants were asked to make a diagnosis. They were given 30 choices that included a range of disorders and general personality types. The correct choice was normal or healthy personality, which was one of the options. However, 60% of the psychiatrists selected a psychotic disorder, as did 28% of the psychologists and 11% of psychology graduate students. By comparison, no one in the control groups chose a diagnosis of a psychotic disorder. These results suggest that any label already given to a patient can affect their follow-up diagnosis, which can be explained by the effects of confirmation bias. This has implications for how clinicians go about using multiple people for accurate diagnosis.

Assessing the reliability of diagnosis using the DSM (Bagby et al., 2015): The aim of this study was to test the reliability of the DSM-IV by getting two diagnoses. They found that there was high reliability (0.80 correlation) when using audio recorded interviews to make the diagnosis. This is one way that bias could be reduced. *See previous section for more details of this study.*

On being sane in insane places (Rosenhan, 1973): When the pseudo-patients were in the hospital, they took lots of notes. The other patients suspected them of being journalists or something similar, whereas some doctors and nurses interpreted the notetaking as symptomatic of their mental illness. This is an example of confirmation bias as they were interpreting the behaviour in a way that confirmed their original beliefs. *See the Normality/Abnormality topic for more details of this study.*

Critical Thinking Considerations

- What are the possible limitations of having two separate diagnoses to test the reliability of the diagnosis?
- What are the limitations of Mendel's research? Think about how they only gave the participants a very limited amount of information. Why is it understandable (and perhaps even desirable) that they would trust the judgement of the initial diagnosis?
- How could the effects of labelling be avoided while still having two diagnoses to test reliability?

Validity and Reliability of Diagnosis

What factors can influence the validity and reliability of diagnosis?

There are multiple factors that can affect the validity and reliability of diagnosis, including clinical bias and the classification system used. Classification systems such as the DSM are an attempt to improve the validity and reliability of diagnosis.

Key Details

- **Validity** of diagnosis refers to how accurate the original diagnosis is.
- **Reliability** refers to the extent to which more than one clinician agrees with the original diagnosis.
- **Clinical bias**: This is one factor that can influence the diagnosis process, as the biases of the clinician can affect their interpretations of a patient's behaviour. This can bias their judgement when making a diagnosis. This can be seen in Mendel et al.'s study.
- **Labelling**: When a patient is given a label, it can affect how they are treated and judged by others. This could be a factor that affects the validity of diagnosis.

Key Studies

Effects of confirmation bias on diagnosis (Mendel et al., 2011): The aim of this study was to see if psychiatrists would be affected by confirmation bias when making a diagnosis. The results also showed that confirmation bias can affect diagnosis because the psychiatrists who searched for more new information consistent with their original incorrect diagnosis were more likely to keep that incorrect diagnosis. However, if psychiatrists asked for more information that contradicted their original diagnosis (i.e. they asked for information about the Alzheimer's symptoms when they originally diagnosed depression), they were less likely to make an incorrect diagnosis. *See the clinical bias topic for more details.*

Effects of labelling on diagnosis (Temerlin, 1968): In this study, the researchers showed a video tape to their participants (psychiatrists, clinical psychologists and graduate students in clinical psychology). In the video, an actor portrayed a mentally healthy scientist and mathematician. The subject of the video involved the actor discussing a book about psychology he had read and how he wanted to discuss it with a psychologist. In the experimental condition, participants were told that an experienced psychiatrist had said the man was a "very interesting man because he looked neurotic, but actually was quite psychotic" (meaning he had a disorder). In the control groups, however, the participants were either given no prior information or they were told he was mentally healthy. After watching the video, the participants were asked to make a diagnosis. They were given 30 choices that included a range of disorders and general personality types. The correct choice was normal or healthy personality, which was one of the options. However, 60% of the psychiatrists selected a psychotic disorder, as did 28% of the psychologists and 11% of psychology graduate students. By comparison, no one in the control groups chose a diagnosis of a psychotic disorder. These results suggest that any label already given to a patient can affect their follow-up diagnosis, which can be explained by the effects of confirmation bias. This has implications for how clinicians go about using multiple people for accurate diagnosis.

Exam Tips

- This is perhaps the most important content point to revise for the topic "Factors influencing diagnosis" as all the content related to this topic is relevant here. Remember to aim to be able to use at least three studies for an essay.

- **Classification systems**: One factor that attempts to improve the validity of diagnosis and to reduce the effects of clinical bias is the use of classification systems. These may help clinicians remain neutral and objective, but this still might not lead to an accurate diagnosis.
- **Culture and "somatization"**: One factor that may affect diagnosis is culture. In particular, people from different cultures may report their symptoms differently. For example, a lot of research has shown that Chinese patients focus less on psychological symptoms and more on somatic (physical) symptoms when meeting with a clinician. One explanation for this is that the symptoms of a disorder may be different for people from different cultures, which was tested by Simon et al. (see below). The way culture affects the presentation of symptoms (i.e. reporting of symptoms to a clinician) is a major factor that can affect diagnosis.

Further Studies

Assessing the reliability of diagnosis using the DSM (Bagby et al., 2015): This study can be used to show that how reliability is measured can affect diagnosis, as well as which disorder is being diagnosed. *See the classification systems section for more details.*

A comparison of PTSD diagnosis with the ICD and DSM (Hafstad et al., 2017): This is another example of how the classification system that is being used (and on whom) could influence the validity and reliability of diagnosis. *See the classification systems section for more details.*

A cross-cultural comparison of reporting symptoms of depression (Parker et al., 2001): This study was conducted in Malaysia and compared how depression was reported in two distinct groups: Malaysian-Chinese and White Australians. The researchers gathered data on the major symptom the patient identified as to why they sought help. The patients also filled out questionnaires about their symptoms. The results showed that even though all patients were diagnosed with depression, 60% of Malaysian-Chinese outpatients identified a somatic (physical) symptom as their major reason for seeking help compared with only 13% of the Australian participants. One conclusion to draw from this study is that culture can affect how symptoms are reported, which in turn can affect the diagnosis of a disorder. More evidence of this can be seen in Kleinman's landmark study below.

The DSM III and somatic symptoms in Chinese patients (Kleinman, 1982): In this study, Kleinman analyzed 100 Chinese patients who had been diagnosed with neurasthenia. This is a disorder that is characterized by somatic symptoms such as fatigue, insomnia, headaches, anxiety and a general low mood. While it is similar to depression, it is a separate diagnosis. As part of the study, Kleinman re-diagnosed the patients using the newly-released DSM-III. As a result, 87% of the patients met the criteria for Major Depressive Disorder (MDD). The initial diagnosis of neurasthenia could be because of differences in how symptoms of depression were reported by the Chinese patients. After taking anti-depressant medication, 70% of patients experienced a major improvement in symptoms. This study highlights a couple of factors: firstly, culture can affect how patients report their symptoms, which can affect the accuracy of diagnosis and secondly, an accurate diagnosis is essential to getting the right treatment.

Critical Thinking Considerations

- What are some limitations in the above studies? What are some reasons why generalizability might be an issue? For example, Kleinman and Parker et al. focus on depression. Can this be generalized to other disorders?
- What are the ethical considerations associated with the above studies?
- One facet of labelling theory is that a label can affect the judgement of the person by others. That being said, it can also affect the behaviour of the individual who has been labelled. Can you think how and why this might happen?
- Are there other reasons why psychiatrists might consciously or unconsciously make a false diagnosis? For example, how might they have an economic incentive to make a diagnosis of a disorder?

Etiologies of Disorders

Biological Explanations of PTSD
What are the biological causes of PTSD?

Abnormalities in the brain are a common explanation for PTSD. In particular, the hippocampus, amygdala and PFC are three parts of the brain that need to explored in order to understand PTSD. However, they are only linked with PTSD due to their role in cognition, and they may also be influenced by sociocultural factors.

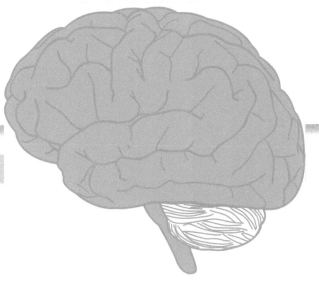

Key Details

Numerous studies have shown that the following brain abnormalities have all been associated with a higher chance of developing PTSD.:
- **The hippocampus**: Low function and volume in the hippocampus is commonly correlated with PTSD symptoms. This could explain symptoms of PTSD associated with loss of memory of the event because the hippocampus is an essential part of the brain that is involved with memory consolidation.
- **The amygdala**: Decreased volume but hyper-responsivity (i.e. increased activity) in the amygdala is a common finding in people with PTSD. This could explain symptoms associated with increased arousal and anxiety, as the amygdala is responsible for triggering the stress response. When the amygdala responds to emotional stimuli, it activates the HPA-axis and stress hormones (e.g. cortisol and adrenaline) are released. This increases feelings of arousal and anxiety, which are symptoms of PTSD.
- **The vmPFC**: Decreased volume and *hypo*-responsivity in the vmPFC have been correlated with symptoms of PTSD *(more details included later in this chapter)*.
- These three areas of the brain are also involved in the process of fear conditioning and fear extinction. The abnormalities may explain why some people are more likely to develop conditioned fears, which can explain symptoms of PTSD associated with increased arousal and anxiety. It may also explain why their symptoms remain (because the fear extinction process does not function properly).

Key Studies

Meta-analysis of MRI studies on patients with PTSD (Karl et al., 2006): This meta-analysis gathered data from 50 different studies that investigated correlations between PTSD and brain regions (23 hippocampal studies and 27 other, including 18 amygdala studies). All studies used MRI and the DSM IV to diagnose symptoms of PTSD. The results showed that the strongest correlation was between reduced hippocampal volume and PTSD (with an effect size of -0.28). There was also a correlation between reduced amygdala volume and PTSD symptoms, although the effect size was smaller. The meta-analysis also included studies on children that found a correlation between reduced frontal lobe volume and PTSD symptoms (but, interestingly, these studies did not find a link between the hippocampus and PTSD).

Case-control study of hippocampal volume and PTSD (Gilbertson et al., 2002): The aim of this study was to see if low volume in the hippocampus is a risk factor for PTSD using 34 sets of identical twins. The study compared the hippocampal volume of veterans with PTSD. All pairs of twins had one twin who did not go to war (trauma-unexposed) while the other did go to war (trauma-exposed). Some trauma-exposed twins developed PTSD, while the others did not. The researchers used MRI to find the volume of their hippocampi and they compared this across the twins. The results showed that veterans with PTSD had an average hippocampal volume 10% smaller than veterans without PTSD. There was also a negative correlation between symptom severity and hippocampal volume. Furthermore, trauma-unexposed twins of veterans with PTSD had smaller hippocampal volume than trauma-unexposed twins of veterans without PTSD. This suggests that the hippocampal volume is a pre-existing risk factor for the development of PTSD symptoms.
See Luby et al. (page 134) for another example of why some people may have smaller hippocampi than others.

Cognitive explanations of PTSD
What are the congnitive causes of PTSD?

Cognitive appraisal is one cognitive factor that is regularly linked with developing PTSD. This is the process of assessing an emotional stimulus. Negative appraisals can explain symptoms of PTSD. However, the brain and social factors are still important to consider.

Key Details

- **Cognitive appraisal**: In the context of PTSD, this refers to how someone thinks about their traumatic experience, its consequences and/or other events following it (e.g. reminders or "triggers"). Appraisal includes a person assessing how threatening something is, how it will affect them and whether or not they have the resources to cope with it. A negative cognitive appraisal, for example, could be a war veteran experiencing "survivor's guilt". Their survival is the consequence of the trauma and they are thinking about it in a negative way – they shouldn't have survived when others died (guilt is a common factor that has been linked with developing PTSD after experiencing trauma). Negative cognitive appraisals can explain symptoms associated with avoidance because the appraisal will increase the person's feelings of stress and negative emotions, so they may want to avoid people and places in an effort to avoid having those negative feelings. This could explain why depression is often diagnosed alongside PTSD.

- **Ehler and Clark's cognitive model of PTSD (2000)**: According to this model, "PTSD becomes persistent when individuals process the trauma in a way that leads to a sense of serious, current threat" (Ehler and Clark, 2000). This sense of threat occurs because of two factors: (1) negative appraisals of the trauma and its effects on the person, and (2) effects on memory, including those related to fear conditioning (associative memory). This is important as it has significant implications in how we can treat PTSD (see more in psychological treatments).

Key Studies

Cognitive appraisal as a predictor of PTSD (Hitchcock et al., 2015): This study is similar to many others in that it investigated correlations between negative appraisals after experiencing a traumatic event and the development of PTSD symptoms. The participants were children aged 7 to 17 years who were admitted to a hospital because they had experienced a one-off traumatic event (e.g. a car accident, injury, house fire). Their symptoms of PTSD were measured within one month of the trauma and again after six months using the "Clinically Administered PTSD Scale" (CAPS) which was modified for children. The kids' negative appraisals

were measured using a 25-item self-report questionnaire called the "Child Post-Traumatic Cognitions Inventory" (CPTCI). The results showed that there was a moderate but statistically significant correlation between negative appraisals and PTSD symptom severity after six months (0.31, $p < 0.001$). This is one example of a study that shows how appraisals can increase the chances of developing PTSD after experiencing trauma.

Cognitive reappraisal and the vmPFC (Urry et al., 2006): *(See next page for more details)*

Etiologies of Disorders

Biology *and* cognition: The brain and appraisals
How do the brain and cognition interact in PTSD?

Key Details

- Cognition and biology are inextricably linked because we cannot have cognitive processes without activity in the brain. Therefore, it is important to look at how brain abnormalities and cognition may interact in the explanation of PTSD symptoms. The ventromedial prefrontal cortex (vmPFC) and the anterior cingulate cortex (ACC) are two areas that are associated with cognitive appraisal and cognitive reappraisal (the ability to readjust an initial appraisal of an emotional stimulus). This could have a top-down effect on the amygdala: positive appraisals can reduce the activity in the amygdala, thus reducing the stress response. However, negative reappraisals can increase activity in the amygdala. Therefore, if someone has low volume or activity in their vmPFC or ACC, it could explain the symptoms of PTSD associated with increased anxiety and arousal because the vmPFC is responsible for cognitive reappraisal and can reduce the activity of the amygdala, helping to reduce the stress response. Without proper activity in this part of the brain, cognitive reappraisal might not be effective (or might not happen), so the activity in the amygdala remains high, which maintains high anxiety and arousal levels.

Key Studies

Cognitive reappraisal and top-down processing of the vmPFC and amygdala activation (Urry et al., 2006): In this study, 19 participants (without PTSD) were exposed to a range of emotional stimuli that were flashed on a screen while they were in an fMRI machine. They were asked to cognitively reappraise the stimuli by either increasing, decreasing or attending. They could "increase" by imagining the scene happening to someone they loved, "decrease" by imagining it wasn't real or "attend" by simply focusing on the details of the image. The results showed a negative correlation between vmPFC and amygdala activation – the higher the vmPFC activity, the lower the amygdala activation. This could explain the common finding of hypofunction and reduced volume in the vmPFC in patients with PTSD.

Critical Thinking Considerations

- This study was conducted on health participants who did not have PTSD. How could this affect the validity of these findings? i.e. are they applicable for people with PTSD?
- The cognitive appraisals performed in this experiment were done in an fMRI. Could this affect generalizability? For example, are there reasons why it might be more difficult to perform these same appraisals in real-life scenarios?
- How could the findings from these studies be applied to help reduce the chances of developing PTSD?

Exam Tips

- When writing about biology or cognition, first establish (and maybe define) the specific factor(s) that you are explaining and the relevant research. Only explain the interaction of factors later in your essay after you have made the basic links first.
- Use the explanations as counter-arguments for one another. This will show your depth of understanding.
- You may be asked about biological, cognitive and/or sociocultural etiologies of one or more disorders.
- The material in the next section can also be used to explain cognitive and biological explanations.
- Drawing diagrams to help represent complex interactions is a good way to clarify and support your explanations in essays.

This QR code will take you to a video with 10 tips for this topic

Critical Thinking Considerations: Biological Etiologies of PTSD

- What factors could be affecting the size of the hippocampus? How do we know (hint: genetics, stress and poverty)?
- How do each of these examples also show that cognition is an important factor?
- What alternative explanations are there for PTSD? For example, how can external factors affect the development of the brain?
- Why is it difficult to know if these are etiologies or symptoms? How might a small hippocampus be a symptom, not an etiology? *Hint: cortisol and the hippocampus*

Critical Thinking Considerations: Cognitive Etiologies of PTSD

- What alternative explanations are there for PTSD? Can you think of any factors that may explain why some people may have different appraisals?
- Hitchcock et al.'s (2015) study is correlational. What are the limitations with this method?

Sociocultural explanations of PSTD
Why are some people more likely to develop PTSD?

Socioeconomic status is one factor that is commonly linked to PTSD. That is to say, the prevalence of PTSD is higher in people who are from poorer communities, including racial minorities. This could be explained by looking at appraisals and the effects of stress on the developing brain.

Key Details

• **Socioeconomic status and appraisals**: A common finding in studies on PTSD is that there is a negative correlation between socioeconomic status and the risk of developing PTSD after a traumatic event. That is to say, the lower your socioeconomic status (e.g. the poorer you are) the more at risk you are for getting PTSD after experiencing a traumatic event. There are two possible explanations for this. One is cognitive (appraisals) and the other is biological (hippocampus), but both involve the interaction of multiple factors.

• The economic resources someone has to deal with trauma may affect their appraisals of the trauma and the situations afterwards. For example, if you are wealthy and you have property damaged in a natural disaster, you may feel like you have the resources to cope with the situation, including replacing damaged possessions

and perhaps even being able to afford therapy. This will lead to positive appraisals. However, if you do not have much money, the impact may be greater and your ability to cope will be less, so you may have more negative cognitive appraisals of the event. This will increase the likelihood of developing PTSD.

• Numerous studies have found that racial minorities are more prone to developing PTSD (especially in the US), which could be linked with socioeconomic status (as in many countries, minority groups tend to have lower socioeconomic status).

Key Studies

• **Correlations between income and PTSD (Irish et al., 2011)**: This study's aim was actually to understand gender differences in the development of PTSD. The study included 356 participants who had all been in car accidents. They found that women were more at risk for developing PTSD. They also found that differences in income between men and women had a significant effect on the risk of developing symptoms of PTSD.

• **Comparison of PTSD after a natural disaster (Garrison et al., 1995)**: The aim of this study was to investigate cross-cultural differences in the US after Hurricane Andrew in Florida. The participants were 350 Black, Hispanic and White teenage participants six months after the hurricane. Structured interviews were used to gather data, including symptoms of PTSD.

The results showed that young women were more than three times as likely to develop PTSD than men (9% and 3%, respectively). The results also showed higher levels of PTSD for Black (8.3%) and Hispanic (6.1%) compared to White participants. The results also showed that the number of stressful events experienced *after* the hurricane had a stronger correlation with PTSD than those experienced during the hurricane itself. This is more evidence to suggest that the role of appraisals following a traumatic event can help in explaining PTSD. This could be due to the differences in economic resources available to different racial groups.

See Hitchcock et al. in the cognitive etiologies section. for more evidence to show the connection between appraisals and PTSD.

Exam Tips

• When explaining a disorder or differences in prevalence rates, is really important that you clearly state that the research has shown that there is a connection between the specific factor(s) you are explaining and the disorder.

• By identifying a social difference in prevalence (e.g. socioeconomic status), you are also giving a sociocultural explanation of the disorder, so the material can be used in both topics.

- Numerous studies have found correlations between poverty and brain development, particularly in the hippocampus, an area of the brain associated with learning, memory and PTSD. The stress caused by poverty could be shrinking the hippocampus because stress releases cortisol and prolonged release of cortisol in the brain has been shown to damage hippocampal neurons (*see Sapolsky et al., 1990 in the emotion and cognition topic in the cognitive approach*). Parenting might be a mediating variable in this relationship. That is to say, parenting styles might explain why poverty is linked with brain development: poverty might increase stress levels, which affects how a parent interacts with their child, which can affect the stress levels of the child, which affects the hippocampus.

Further Studies

Poverty and brain development (Luby et al., 2013): The aim of this study was to see if poverty was correlated with brain development and to see if there were mediating variables related to stress and parenting that could explain this relationship. MRIs were used to see if poverty, stressful events and parenting styles were correlated with hippocampal volume in 145 children over a 10-year period. The results showed a positive correlation between lower socioeconomic status and hippocampal volume (poorer kids had smaller hippocampi). Socioeconomic status was also positively correlated with amygdala volume (lower status = smaller amygdalae). They also found that parenting and stressful life events were mediating variables in this relationship. That is to say, parenting styles might explain why poverty is linked with brain development: poverty might increase stress levels, which affects how a parent interacts with their child, which can affect the stress levels of the child, which affects the hippocampus. The researchers measured the parent-child interactions by giving the child a small gift but telling them they must wait until their parent finishes completing a questionnaire before they can open it. This is designed to test the patience of the parent and to see how they interact with their child. Researchers standing behind a two-way mirror recorded how the parent dealt with the nagging of the child by recording interactions between child and parent. The more positive the parent-child interactions were during the waiting for the gift task, the higher the hippocampal volume of the child. (*Gilbertson et al. and Karl et al. in the biological etiologies section can be used to make the direct link to PTSD*).

This code will take you to a blog post with tips on how to explain prevalence rates and disorders. It also includes details of a study that shows why females may be more likely than males to develop PTSD

Critical Thinking Considerations

- There are some areas of uncertainty and assumptions being made with the above studies. For example, in Garrison's study, they never assessed appraisals or socioeconomic status – we are assuming there is a link. We are also assuming race correlated with socioeconomic status. While statistically this is true in Florida, does this affect the validity of the conclusions that can be made about this study?
- Besides socioeconomic status, what **alternative explanations** are there for differences in the prevalence of PTSD? For example, what other factors might affect the appraisal process or development of the hippocampus?
- The above studies are conducted in the US. Do you think socioeconomic status will be correlated with PTSD across all cultures? Any reasons why this link may not apply to other cultures?

Exam Tips

- Numerous studies in this approach can be used in other topics, including Urry et al.'s study showing the localization of function of the vmPFC in cognitive reappraisal and Luby et al.'s study for neuroplasticity (it shows how environmental factors can influence the development of the hippocampus and amygdala).

Biological Treatments

Drug therapy (SSRIs)
How and why can biological treatments be used to treat disorders?

Drug treatments are a common biological treatment for disorders and they can work to restore chemical imbalances in the brain. They may help PTSD by increasing serotonin transmission and improving function in important areas of the brain, like the PFC.

Key Details

- **Drug therapy (a.k.a. pharmacotherapy)**: The use of medication (e.g. drugs and pills) is a common form of treatment for people suffering from disorders. Of these medications, **selective serotonin reuptake inhibitors (SSRIs)** are one of the most common (examples include Prozac, Zoloft and paroxetine). SSRIs are the only prescribed medication for PTSD in the USA.
- SSRIs increase serotonin levels in the brain by preventing the reuptake of excess serotonin in the synapse. What usually happens is that serotonin in the synapse (the gap between neurons) is reabsorbed into the pre-synaptic neuron. If the reabsorption is blocked, then this will increase the available amount to bind to post-synaptic neurons. The result is an increase in transmission of serotonin. A common finding with people who suffer from depression and anxiety disorders (e.g. PTSD) is that there is dysfunction in their serotonin systems. SSRIs may help reduce symptoms by improving the function of serotonin systems in the brain.

Key Studies

Clinical drug trial of SSRIs for PTSD (Marshall et al., 2001): This clinical drug trial is an example of a random allocation, double-blind, placebo-controlled true experiment on 551 patients with PTSD. They had 12 weeks of treatment with either 20mg per day of the SSRI paroxetine, 40mg per day of the SSRI paroxetine or a placebo. The researchers measured the CAPS scores before and after and found that the paroxetine significantly reduced symptoms more than the placebo group. The percentage of patients who had an improvement was 62% and 54% for the 20mg and 40mg groups, respectively, compared with 37% for the placebo groups. The paroxetine groups also experienced around a 50% reduction in symptoms, compared with about 30% reduction for the placebo group. They also found that there was no difference in effect depending on the type of trauma. However, as with many drugs, there were some side effects reported, including nausea, diarrhea and somnolence (feeling sleepy and drowsy).

Meta-analysis of the effectiveness of medication to treat PTSD (Ipser et al., 2006): This meta-analysis gathered data from 35 short-term studies (less than 15 weeks long) that included a total of nearly 5,000 participants (4,597). They analyzed the results from these clinical trials to assess the effectiveness of using drug therapy to treat PTSD and found that when taking medication, 59.1% of participants had an improvement of symptoms compared to only 38.5% of patients on a placebo. Medication helped to reduce the major symptoms of PTSD, including re-experiencing/intrusion, avoidance/numbing and hyperarousal symptoms. They also found that of the different medications used in the trials, SSRIs were the most effective in reducing symptoms. From this, the researchers concluded that the analysis gives evidence to "support the status of SSRIs as first-line agents in the pharmacotherapy of PTSD, as well as their value in long-term treatment."

Exam Tips

- The material in this topic can also be used for neurotransmitters in the biological approach. I would use MacNamara et al.'s study for an SAQ and a combination of these studies for an essay in Paper 1.
- In any essay about biological or psychological treatments, you may be able to write about one or more. The only time you should be asked specifically to write about two would be if you were asked to contrast one biological with one psychological treatment.
- When explaining why a treatment is effective, the best explanations will make direct links with specific symptoms.
- The same studies can be used for "assessing the effectiveness of treatment" and for research methods and ethics.

- Serotonin receptors are highly concentrated in the prefrontal cortex. Therefore, SSRIs might work by improving activity in this area of the brain. This is important because a common finding in people with PTSD is that they have reduced activity in their PFC.
- The PFC is an area of the brain that enables us to perform **cognitive reappraisal** – an important cognitive task that enables us to regulate our stressful reactions to stimuli. For example, if someone with PTSD is reminded of their trauma, their amygdala is activated and stress hormones are released. They may feel anxious and have increased emotional and physiological arousal, but they could reappraise the situation and assure themselves that they are safe and not in danger. However, if they have low function in their PFC, they may not be able to perform this cognitive process and their amygdala activity (and stress levels) remain high. This explains why they have symptoms related to increased emotional arousal and anxiety.
- Thus, SSRIs may help to reduce symptoms of PTSD by improving the function and activity in areas of the brain that enable cognitive reappraisals and reduce the activation of the amygdala (and the stress response), which may explain why people who take SSRIs experience a reduction in symptoms related to increased emotional arousal.

Further Studies

SSRIs and PFC function (MacNamara et al., 2016): 17 US war veterans were put on a 12-week treatment of paroxetine (an SSRI). The severity of their PTSD symptoms were measured before and after treatment using the Clinician-Administered PTSD Scale (CAPS) in a structured interview for assessing symptoms. The results showed that 12 out of 17 (70%) participants had a 50% or more reduction in symptoms. This is one piece of evidence to show SSRIs can be effective. Another finding from this study was the patients showed improved PFC function during cognitive reappraisal of emotional stimuli. Participants were asked to cognitively reappraise images while in an fMRI machine. Their brain function before and after the SSRI treatment was measured. The results showed that the drug increased function of the dorsolateral PFC (dlPFC) during cognitive reappraisal. This increase in PFC activity might be the reason why their symptoms were reduced – they were able to downregulate their emotion through reappraising stressful events. The results also showed improvement in another part of the brain, the sensory motor area (SMA). This is another part of the brain that is associated with top-down regulation of the amygdala.

Critical Thinking Considerations

- What are the strengths of using drug therapy compared with other options?
- What are the limitations in using drug therapy?
- Can you see any limitations or issues arising from the above studies?

Psychological Treatments

CBT and exposure therapies
How and why are psychological treatments used to treat disorders?

Cognitive behavioural therapies, including exposure therapies, are an important way for psychologists to address the cognitive etiologies and symptoms of disorders such as PTSD.

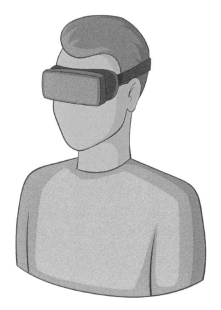

Key Details

- **Cognitive behavioural therapy (CBT)** is one of the most common forms of psychological treatments for psychological disorders. CBT is an umbrella term that refers to treatments designed to improve the relationships between thoughts, emotions and behaviour.
- One type of CBT is **exposure therapy** and there are many types. The goal of any exposure therapy is to reduce anxiety and emotional arousal. It works on the basis of **fear extinction** – removing the conditioned fears of emotional stimuli – by repeatedly exposing someone to their emotional triggers. With repeated exposure, their anxiety and arousal levels decrease.
- One form of exposure therapy that is becoming popular for treating anxiety disorders, including PTSD, is **virtual reality exposure therapy** (VRET). VRET operates to extinguish conditioned fears in PTSD patients by exposing participants to trauma-related stimuli in a virtual world. This can help cause new learning because their brain will automatically respond to the emotional stimuli (e.g. the amygdala activates the stress response) but they know they are safe and not in danger, so their thought processes can reduce their emotional arousal and eventually their brain can create new connections and associations. For this reason, it can also help address negative cognitive appraisals because the person can learn how to cope with emotional triggers and recognize that they are not in danger anymore. This is commonly used in war veterans, who are put in virtual environments that are designed to reflect their war-time experiences.
- VRET may also be able to change the structure and functioning of important parts of the brain, such as the vmPFC and amygdala.

Key Studies

Virtual reality exposure therapy as a treatment of PTSD (Rothbaum et al., 2001): In this study, 10 Vietnam War veterans had virtual reality therapy treatments (eight 90-minute sessions, 2 times per week for 5 to 7 weeks) during which they were exposed to two different environments. In one environment, they were in a Huey Helicopter (the type used to transport troops in Vietnam) flying over a landscape that looked like Vietnam. In the other virtual world, they were in a field surrounded by jungle. Using the Clinically Administered PTSD Scale (CAPs), the results showed that all clients had a reduction of symptoms when they had a check-up six months after the treatment. The reduction in symptoms ranged from 15% to 67%. These results suggest that VRET can be effective in treating PTSD. A meta-analysis of VRET used to treat disorders

(Parsons and Rizzo, 2008): The researchers analyzed data from 21 studies (over 300 total participants) that used VRET to treat anxiety disorders. They found a signifi-cant effect in using VRET to treat a range of anxiety-related disorders, including PTSD and phobias. Their results showed an effect size of 0.87 for PTSD when comparing VRET with other treatments.

Exam Tips

- VRET could be used to support an explanation of how technology can influence the relationship between emotion and cognition. That is to say, VRET can reduce emotional arousal and anxiety, which could help improve working memory (a common finding in people with PTSD is reductions in working memory capacity and executive cognitive control – the ability to control one's thinking).

• VRET is not the only type of exposure therapy used to treat disorders. Another common form is **imagination therapy**. As with VRET and other exposure therapies, imagination therapy involves exposing the patient to reminders of their trauma, but it does so by getting the patients to use their imagination.

• Imagination therapy has also been used in conjunction with **cognitive restructuring** – trying to change a person's negative appraisals of their trauma. For example, during a session, a veteran might recount a traumatic experience involving his friends being killed.

The veteran may feel guilty for surviving, so the therapist would work to restructure and change the veteran's appraisal of the situation so that the veteran is grateful to be alive - perhaps the veteran could thank themselves for being lucky they survived and to not blame themselves for the death of others.

• Exposure therapy may treat disorders by addressing the cognitive etiologies (e.g. conditioned fears and negative appraisals), but they may also help to improve function in important areas of the brain that are correlated with PTSD, such as the PFC and the amygdala.

Further Studies

Imagination therapy and cognitive restructuring for PTSD (Felmingham et al., 2007): This study gathered data on five females and three males who were experiencing PTSD as a result of car accidents or assault. The participants underwent 8 weeks of CBT (imagination therapy and cognitive restructuring). The researchers gathered data on the effectiveness of therapy using a Clinician-Administered PTSD Scale (CAPS) questionnaire. After the eight weeks of sessions, all participants revealed at least a 30% reduction in their CAPS scores. This data alone suggests positive effects of exposure and cognitive therapy. The participants' brain function were also measured before and after the treatments. They were asked to view a range of fearful and neutral facial expressions while in the brain scanner. The results showed a positive correlation between CAPS scores and amygdala activation. That is to say, as CAPS scores decreased, so did the activation of the amygdala. This suggests that the exposure therapy and cognitive restructuring was not only able to reduce symptoms, but it might also have been having an effect on the function of the amygdala. The results also showed a negative correlation between CAPS scores and functioning in the anterior cingulate cortex (ACC), an area of the brain associated with fear extinction and cognitive appraisal. This means that as the activity in the ACC increased, the patients demonstrated fewer symptoms of PTSD.

Exposure therapy and brain function for PTSD (Roy et al., 2014): The aim of this study was to assess the effectiveness of exposure therapy for treating PTSD. The participants were 19 US combat veterans who were randomized to receive virtual reality exposure theory (VRET) or PE (prolonged exposure – a type of imagination therapy). fMRIs were used before and after treatment to assess changes in brain activity and a PTSD questionnaire (CAPS scores) was used to measure PTSD symptoms. The results showed that the VRET group had significant reduction in CAPS scores (20%), while there was no reduction in CAPS in PE group. However, both groups had increased vmPFC and ACC activity as well as reduced amygdala activity. This suggests that VRET may be more effective than imagination therapy for treating PTSD. Also, both types of exposure therapy can reduce PTSD symptoms by improving activity in important areas of the brain associated with PTSD.

Critical Thinking Considerations

• Is VRET equally suitable for all trauma types? Can you think of common causes of PTSD (i.e. trauma types) that might not be suited to VRET?

• What are the limitations of psychotherapies? *Hint: think about practical limitations compared with drugs*

• Why might a combination of treatments be effective?

• Felmingham et al.'s study shows that a 30% reduction was the minimum for all participants, but this is the same as placebo groups in some drug trials (see Marshall et al. for an example of this). What conclusions can be drawn from this?

Assessing the Effectiveness of Treatments

Clinical trials and meta-analyses

How do psychologists assess the effectiveness of treatments for disorders?

Clinical trials are an important way that researchers can assess the effectiveness of treatments. Meta-analyses of clinical trials are another technique used to draw conclusions about these methods.

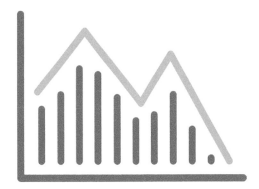

Key Details

- A **clinical trial** is a specific type of study that is conducted on people seeking treatment for a particular disorder. The aim of a clinical trial is to test the effectiveness of a particular treatment. They are used for both psychological and biological treatments.
- **Clinical drug trials as true experiments**: Clinical *drug* trials are the most common for biological treatments and these compare the effects of a drug (e.g. SSRI like paroxetine) with a control group (taking a placebo). The common characteristics of a clinical drug trial are:
    - **Random allocation**: Participants are selected at random to be in the control or treatment group.
    - **Double-blind**: The participant doesn't know which group they are in, and neither does the person gathering data (e.g. the researcher conducting the CAPs interviews)
- **Placebo**: In order to make a comparison by controlling for the placebo effect, some participants are given a placebo.
- **Clinical trials for psychotherapies**: Clinical trials for psychotherapies are still conducted with the aim of assessing the effectiveness of a particular disorder. One limitation, however, is that it is very difficult (if not impossible) to have a placebo-control group (because you either know you are in a virtual reality simulation or not).

Key Studies

Clinical drug trial of SSRIs for PTSD (Marshall et al., 2001): This clinical drug trial is an example of a random allocation, double-blind, placebo-controlled true experiment on 551 patients with PTSD. They had 12 weeks of treatment with either 20mg per day of the SSRI paroxetine, 40mg per day of the SSRI paroxetine or a placebo. The researchers measured the CAPS scores before and after and found that the paroxetine significantly reduced symptoms more than the placebo group. The percentage of patients who had an improvement was 62% and 54% for the 20mg and 40mg groups, respectively, compared with 37% for the placebo groups. The paroxetine groups also experienced around a 50% reduction in symptoms, compared with about 30% reduction for the placebo group.

Clinical trials of VRET - Virtual Reality Exposure Therapy as a treatment of PTSD (Rothbaum et al., 2001): In this study, 10 Vietnam War veterans had virtual reality therapy treatments (eight 90-minute sessions, 2 times per week for 5 to 7 weeks) during which they were exposed to two different environments. Using the Clinically Administered PTSD Scale (CAPs), the results showed that all clients had a reduction of symptoms when they had a check-up six months after the treatment. The reduction in symptoms ranged from 15% to 67%. These results suggest that VRET can be effective in treating PTSD.

Exam Tips

- The material in this topic is the same as for research methods, but be careful not to include Rothbaum et al.'s study as an example of a true experiment. Be sure to also identify the method in meta-analyses as "correlational studies" (the IB does not consider a meta-analysis as a "research method").
- Clinical drug trials can also be used to show the use of true experiments in the biological approach to understanding human behaviour (the brain and behaviour).

Extension

- Clinical trials for various treatments and disorders are conducted all the time around the world. This means there are literally hundreds of studies that have investigated the effects of SSRIs and exposure therapy on PTSD. Some studies show they work, while others have results that show there is no difference between the treatment and control groups. How can we draw firm conclusions? One way is to conduct a **meta-analysis**.
- A meta-analysis gathers the data from many studies and includes all the data in a statistical analysis. The researchers can then find an overall trend in the data and see how strong the relationship is between the treatment and its effect on a particular disorder. This is measured as an **effect size**, which is a statistical measurement of the strength of the effect of the independent variable on the dependent variable. 0.2 is a weak effect size, 0.4 is moderate and 0.8 is considered strong.
- Meta-analyses are valuable when assessing the effectiveness of a treatment because they are drawing on a lot of data from a combination of studies.

Further Studies

A meta-analysis of VRET used to treat disorders (Parsons and Rizzo, 2008): The researchers analyzed data from 21 studies (over 300 total participants) that used VRET to treat anxiety disorders. They found a signifi-cant effect in using VRET to treat a range of anxiety-related disorders, including PTSD and phobias. Their results showed an effect size of 0.87 for PTSD when comparing VRET with other treatments.

Meta-analysis of the effectiveness of medication to treat PTSD (Ipser et al., 2006): This meta-analysis gathered data from 35 short-term studies (less than 15 weeks long) that included a total of nearly 5,000 participants (4,597). They analyzed the results from these clinical trials to assess the effectiveness of using drug therapy to treat PTSD and found that when taking medication, 59.1% of participants had an improvement of symptoms compared to only 38.5% of patients on a placebo. Medication helped to reduce the major symptoms of PTSD, including re-experiencing/intrusion, avoidance/numbing and hyperarousal symptoms. They also found that of the different medications used in the trials, SSRIs were the most effective in reducing symptoms. From this, the researchers concluded that the analysis gives evidence to "support the status of SSRIs as first-line agents in the pharmacotherapy of PTSD, as well as their value in long-term treatment."

Critical Thinking Considerations

- What are the strengths and limitations in using a clinical trial and/or meta-analysis?
- Are there ethical considerations in conducting clinical trials? *See ethics later in this chapter for more guidance.*
- Debriefing could be considered important in a clinical drug trial, but could you see any downsides to this, especially for those in a placebo group?

Exam Tips

- Instead of meta-analyses, you could write about correlational studies using MacNamara et al. and Felmingham et al.'s research.

The Role of Culture in Treatment

Cultural attitudes to etiologies and medication
How can culture influence the treatment of disorders?

The *"role of culture in treatment"* refers to how culture can influence the treatment process. Two ways this can happen is through different cultural attitudes to etiologies of disorders and different cultural attitudes towards specific treatments themselves, like drug therapy (medication).

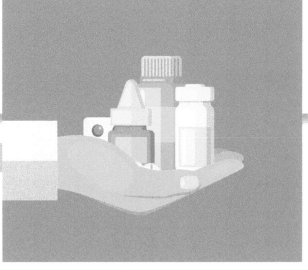

Key Details

• **Cultural attitudes towards drug therapy**: Drug therapy (medication) is a desirable form of treatment because it is relative easy, cheap, can be self-administered, and the effects are experienced in a short period of time (within a couple of weeks). This could be why it is incredibly popular in Western countries, with around half of American and European adults currently on some sort of prescribed medication. Similarly, most drugs are developed in Western countries by Western pharmaceutical companies and treated in clinical trials on Western participants. This cultural bias in the development, testing and administering of drug therapy could affect the treatment process, especially if someone from a non-Western cultural background is seeking treatment for a disorder. For example, some people may be raised in cultures that distrust medication and would prefer natural remedies. If someone has these attitudes towards medication, there is a good chance they would be less likely to follow a prescribed course of drug therapy and it might not be as effective.

• **Cultural competency**: Psychologists need to be culturally competent when administering treatment, which means understanding the cultural backgrounds of their patients. If a clinician adjusts their treatment based on cultural circumstances, this could have a positive effect on the treatment process. For example, clinicians may discuss a range of treatment options with a patient instead of just prescribing one. They may also be more open about the pros and cons of treatments such as drug therapy, so the patient can make an informed decision.

Key Studies

Cultural differences in attitudes towards medication (Horne et al., 2004): This study investigated cultural differences in attitudes towards using medication by gathering data from 500 undergraduate students in the UK who identified as being either from an Asian cultural background or from a European cultural background. They found that the Asian students were more likely to have negative attitudes towards using medication and they were more likely to perceive them as intrinsically harmful and addictive substances. If someone with these culturally-based attitudes was prescribed a course of drug therapy, he or she may not be as willing to follow through with the treatment and this could affect its effectiveness.

Exam Tips

• The material in this topic could potentially be applied to a question on cultural influences on attitudes and behaviour.

- **Cultural attitudes towards etiologies**: One factor that can influence the effectiveness of treatment is whether or not a person believes a treatment will be effective. If they think it will address the root causes (etiologies) of the disorder, it could influence how effective the treatment is. This could be because the placebo effect might occur. It could also be because they may be more likely to maintain the treatment if they think it is working. Studies have found that different cultures have different attitudes towards the origins of psychological disorders.

- **Stigma**: Another factor that may affect the treatment process is the different levels of stigma attached to being diagnosed with a disorder. If a disorder has a stigma attached, this may affect the treatment process as it could have an influence on the patient's behaviour. For example, they may not be as willing to take their medication, especially if there are other people around. Different cultures have different levels of stigma attached to being diagnosed with a disorder.

Further Studies

Comparing cultural attitudes towards etiologies and treatments (Jiminez et al., 2012): This study used questionnaires to gather data on attitudes towards mental health of over 2,000 US participants over 65 years old. They were grouped by ethnicity: non-Latino Whites, African-Americans, Asian-Americans and Latinos. The researchers hypothesized that the minority groups' attitudes towards the origins of mental health problems would be different to White individuals. One of the questions the participants were asked was, "*What do you think causes depression?*" The results revealed a range of different attitudes towards disorders:

  o African-Americans were more likely to believe that depression was caused by stress or worry when compared to other groups.

  o African-Americans were also more likely to say they would seek spiritual advice. Latinos, on the other hand, were more likely to opt for medication.

  o When it came to speaking to someone about their mental health problems, African-Americans were more likely to want to speak to a family member or someone living with them, and non-Latino Whites were more likely to seek help from a psychiatrist. Asian-Americans were less likely to speak to anyone and were more likely to

prefer that their treatment provider belonged to the same racial group as them.

The results supported the researchers' original hypotheses by showing that there were significant differences between racial groups when it came to causes of disorders and the best options for treatment. This could be a challenge for clinicians who are administering treatments because they may need to consider the cultural backgrounds of their participants and provide options for alternative treatments.

A comparison of stigma of depression across cultures (Turvey et al., 2012): This study compared attitudes towards depression in Russian, South Korean and American participants over the age of 60. Only 6% of the American participants viewed depression as a sign of weakness. On the other hand, Russian and Korean participants were far more likely to label those with depression as being weak (61% and 78%, respectively). With this attitude attached to depression in some cultures, individuals may be less likely to seek help for fear that they may be labelled as weak.

See also Kleinman (1982) for an example of how culture can affect diagnosis, which can affect treatment.

Critical Thinking Considerations

- Why is "cultural competency" difficult? Are there any potential limitations in adjusting one's practice depending on the cultural background of their patients?
- Are there methodological or ethical limitations with the above studies?
- Can you hypothesize any other ways culture may influence treatment?

Research Method #1

Correlational studies

How and why are correlational studies used in the study of abnormal psychology?

Correlational studies *measure how strongly two (or more) variables are related. Unlike experimental methods that include a direction of causality (IV→DV), correlational studies have co-variables.*

Key Details

- **Correlational studies on disorders**: Correlational studies are commonly used when researchers are studying relationships between variables that cannot be manipulated in a laboratory setting. In studies on psychological disorders (e.g. PTSD), it is often the case that one or more of the co-variables in the study would be difficult (if not impossible) to manipulate in a laboratory setting.
- In correlational studies, researchers gather data by first measuring the behaviour in some way. For example, questionnaires, surveys and interviews can be used to measure symptom severity. For example, the CAPS interview is used to measure symptom severity of PTSD. The co-variables also have to be calculated, and these could be things like appraisal strategies (using questionnaires) or brain volume (using MRI). The correlation co-efficient gives us a value of how strongly the variables are correlated, with 1.0 being a perfect positive correlation and -1.0 a perfect negative correlation (0.0 is no correlation). A correlation of 0.4 (or -0.4) is considered moderate and anything around 0.8 or higher is considered strong.

Key Studies

Diagnosis: Correlations are calculated in studies that are testing the reliability of diagnosis
- o **Bagby et al., (2015) and Hafstad et al., (2017)**

Etiologies of disorders: Psychological disorders are a naturally-occurring variable and it would be unethical and impractical to try to design an experiment that aimed to see what caused a specific disorder. Correlational studies are valuable because they can measure the naturally-occurring variables that are hypothesized to be linked with the disorder in question. For example, correlational studies are used in the study of etiologies of PTSD by measuring brain volume in an MRI and correlating this with CAPS scores (PTSD symptoms). Socioeconomic status, cognitive appraisals, and stress are all examples of variables that have been correlated with PTSD.
- o **Gilbertson et al., 2002; Karl et al., 2006; Hitchcock et al., 2015; Luby et al., 2013**

Treatment of disorders: Correlational studies on treatments include finding data on the activity in particular areas of the brain (e.g. vmPFC, ACC) and seeing how these are correlated with improvements in symptoms. Seeing how improved function in the brain is correlated with reduced symptoms allows researchers to assess the effectiveness of particular treatments and provides more information as to why they might be effective.
- o **MacNamara et al., 2016; Felmingham et al., 2007**

Critical Thinking Considerations

- How can the experimental method be used to critique correlational studies?
- Correlation does not mean causation. This is the fundamental limitation of correlational studies. One way of making this point is by explaining examples of how other variables might affect the two being correlated in a study. Can you think of examples of this for any of the above studies?
- Another way of critiquing correlational studies is by showing how bidirectional ambiguity may be an issue in the study. Is it variable A affecting B, or vice-versa? Can you explain any examples of bidirectional ambiguity in the above studies?

Exam Tips

- For every topic you are preparing to write an essay about, become an expert in one research method and one ethical consideration. Have a second for each as a backup. This will allow you to be fully prepared in case the question asks you to write about only one method or consideration.
- Try to prepare to use the same explanations and studies (where possible) in Paper 2 as well as in Paper 1. For example, correlational studies using MRIs can be valuable when answering questions about technological techniques to study the brain and/or research methods on the brain and behaviour.

Anonymity in Correlational Studies

How and why is anonymity important in studies in abnormal psychology?

Anonymity in psychological studies means that the names of participants are not revealed when recording and/or publishing results of studies. This is an especially important consideration when the topics being studied are sensitive.

Key Details

- In studies on abnormal psychology, the behaviours being investigated are often highly sensitive, including the causes and effects of particular psychological disorders (like PTSD). For this reason, anonymity is important because participants probably would not want others to know their results in these studies. Informed consent forms should promise anonymity. If there are exceptions, this should be made clear to the participants before they consent to join the study.

Key Studies

Diagnosis: Patients in these studies have been diagnosed with a disorder or are seeking help. They may not want other people to know that they have sought treatment, so their anonymity should be protected.

Etiologies of disorders: Socioeconomic status, cognitive appraisals, and stress are all examples of variables that have been correlated with PTSD using correlational methods. These are very sensitive topics and people should have their anonymity protected. For example, people may not want others to know their level of wealth (socioeconomic status) or their volume in particular areas of the brain. Studies like Luby et al.'s also measure parent-child interactions, which could be a sensitive topic. In this type of study, the parents' right to anonymity should be protected so the participants' psychological well-being is maintained throughout the study.

    o **Gilbertson et al., 2002; Karl et al., 2006; Hitchcock et al., 2015; Luby et al., 2013**

Treatment of disorders: Correlational studies on treatments include finding data on the activity in particular areas of the brain (e.g. vmPFC, ACC) and seeing how these are correlated with improvements in symptoms. This is something that participants may not want other people to know about. For example, they may feel embarrassed or ashamed if they knew that other people would learn about their changes in brain activity (or lack thereof).

    o **MacNamara et al., 2016; Felmingham et al., 2007**

Critical Thinking Considerations

- Are there any limitations in giving anonymity to participants? Can you think of any circumstances or reasons why not giving 100% anonymity might be beneficial?
- Can you think of other ethical considerations associated with these correlational studies?

Exam Tips

- Preparing to use the same studies to support your explanations of research methods and ethical considerations can make your revision more effective.
- An explanation of ethical considerations is most effective when it is linked to common research methodology used to study a particular topic, hence the layout of these review materials. However, you can still write about anonymity in true experiments and/or informed consent in correlational studies.

Experiments

How and why are experiments used in studies in abnormal psychology?

Experiments are used when the researchers measure the effects of an independent variable on a dependent variable. They control for extraneous variables as much as possible and measure the effects of the IV on the DV. By carefully controlling the extraneous variables, the researchers can maximize the chances that any differences in the DV can be explained by the IV. This allows for conclusions about causality to be made.

Key Details

- In abnormal psychology, experiments are conducted when a cause-and-effect relationship wants to be determined. This is not often the case for etiologies of disorders, but it can be done for treatments of disorders.

Key Studies

Diagnosis: Researchers can manipulate factors they think may affect diagnosis, like labels
- **Temerlin, 1968; Bagby et al. 2015**

Etiologies: Experiments on etiologies can be used to help strengthen the explanation for why some parts of the brain are associated with particular disorders. For example, the PFC is one area of the brain that is associated with PTSD. Researchers using an experimental method can investigate the association by seeing what cognitive processes this part of the brain is responsible for. For example, by asking participants to cognitively reappraise stimuli in an fMRI, Urry et al. were able to conclude that this part of the brain is integral in cognitive reappraisal and can also reduce activity in the amygdala.
- **Urry et al. 2006;**

Treatments: Clinical drug trials are the most common form of true experiments on treatments and these compare the effects of a drug (e.g. SSRIs like paroxetine) with a control group (taking a placebo). The common characteristic of a clinical drug trial are they are random, double-blind and placebo-controlled. Meta-analyses of clinical trials can also provide more evidence for the strength of the effect of the treatment on the disorder.
- **Marshall et al., 2001; Ipser et al., 2006**

Critical Thinking Considerations

- Are true experiments inherently limited in generalizability because of their artificial environments?
- Can you use one type of experiment to highlight the limitations of another? For example, how might clinical drug trials be used to highlight the limitations of meta-analyses (correlational studies)?
- What are the ethical considerations associated with true experiments?

Exam Tips

- Research methods and ethics questions will only be asked in relation to topics, not specific content points. You will likely be able to write about "one or more" methods or ethical considerations.
- Research methods and ethics questions are the least likely to appear for any one topic. However, if you are only preparing to write about one topic, you should be prepared to answer a question about methods and ethics for that topic.
- Use one method to evaluate another. This allows you to show deeper understanding of the research and the studies.

Informed consent in experiments
How is informed consent relevant to true experiments in abnormal psychology?

*At the heart of **ethics** in psychological research is considering the impact the research might have on others, especially the participants. **Informed consent** is one consideration that can reduce some of the stress and other negative effects of participating in a study. Informed consent means you get an agreement from participants that they want to be in the study (consent) and they are basing this decision on information you have given them (informed).*

Key Details

• Informed consent requires allowing participants to make informed judgements about participating in a study. In studies in abnormal psychology, there are times when it is obvious which information to reveal. That being said, with clinical drug trials there has to be some information withheld in order to reduce the chances of participant expectancy effects.

Key Studies

Diagnosis: Participants in experiments like Temerlin's might be embarrassed if they have to put their professional reputation on the line to participate in an experiment testing the accuracy of their diagnosis. Informing of them of the procedures beforehand could reduce stress but may affect validity.

   o **Temerlin, 1968**

Etiologies: Experiments on etiologies may require participants to lay in an fMRI and perform cognitive reappraisal while being exposed to emotional images. Because fMRIs are very small, noisy and uncomfortable, this should be told to participants. They should also be given the right to withdraw. Being exposed to emotional images may also be uncomfortable, so they should be aware of this ahead of time.

   o **Urry et al., 2006**

Treatments: Clinical drug trials involve studying individuals who have been diagnosed with a disorder and have sought treatment. However, as part of the methodology, they could be randomly assigned to a placebo group without knowing it. This means that they might be getting a treatment that the researchers are hypothesizing will not have an effect. This should be made known to them before participating as they may end up angry if they find out after a study. However, how much is revealed before the study is also important to consider in order to reduce the chances of participant expectancy effects.

   o **Marshall et al., 2001**

Critical Thinking Considerations

• How might informed consent affect the validity of a study?
• Should researchers reveal everything in their informed consent forms?
• Are there other ethical considerations relevant to true experiments on Abnormal Psychology?

Exam Tips

• You can still write about informed consent in correlational studies, and anonymity in experimental ones. They have been matched with the methodologies for ease of revision only.
• Ethical considerations is the hardest topic to write about. This is why it might be a good idea to have a second topic prepared as a backup, in case a difficult question about ethics shows up on the exam.

8 Developmental Psychology

Bonus Topic!

Developmental Psychology

Some of the topics from this option have been naturally covered in others, like the effect of technology on developing as a learner or the effects of stress on the brain. Because you know there will be one question from each of the three topics, you could be prepared to answer a question from one of these topics without adding to your revision. This chapter will use material from other areas of the course to prepare for the "Developing as a learner" topic.

Topic	Content
Influences on cognitive and social development	• Roles of peers and play • Childhood trauma and resilience • Poverty/socioeconomic status
Developing an identity	• Attachment • Gender identity and social roles • Development of empathy and theory of mind
Developing as a learner	• Cognitive development • Brain development
Ethical considerations and research methods	• Students should also be prepared to discuss one or more of the three approaches (biological, cognitive and sociocultural) in relation to each topic • Students should be able to discuss one or more research methods and ethical considerations related to the relevant studies for one or more of the three topics in this option

Developmental Psychology
Developing as a learner

	Content	Key Questions	Key Studies
Developing as a learner	**Cognitive development**	*What factors can affect cognitive development?*	• Klingberg et al. (2005) • Simons et al. (2016) • Cain et al. (2016) • Christakis et al. (2004) • Lillard and Peterson (2011)
	Brain development	*What factors can influence the development of a child's brain?*	• Luby et al. (2013) • Perry and Pollard (1997) • Kuhn et al. (2014)

• *All answers should be supported by evidence.*

• Students should also be prepared to discuss one or more of the three approaches (biological, cognitive and socio-cultural) in relation to each topic

• Students should be able to discuss one or more research methods and ethical considerations related to the relevant studies for one or more of the three topics in this option

Cognitive Development

Technology and Working Memory
What factors can affect cognitive development?

The use of technology can have both positive and negative effects on our cognitive development. The cognitive processes affected by technology include working memory and attention. Both of these are key in developing as a learner.

Key Details

- **Working memory** is the information that we are conscious of at any one time. More specifically, it is "…the small amount of information that can be held in mind and used in the execution of cognitive tasks" (Cowan, 2013). **Working memory capacity** refers to how much information we can hold in our minds at any one time. This capacity has been linked to many things, including intelligence and academic achievement. Therefore, kids with poor working memory capacity (i.e. unreliable working memory capabilities) struggle in school and often get in trouble. This is a problem for the kids, their parents and teachers. As a result, researchers have been looking for ways to help improve working memory capacity and to understand what factors can affect it.
- One method that has been developed to improve working memory is the use of computer games designed to help the cognitive development of young kids. However, the effectiveness of these games is a source of debate.

Key Studies

Working memory games and improved attention (Klingberg et al., 2005): This study demonstrates the positive applications of understanding working memory processes because it shows we can design computer games to improve the working memory capacity of children and to reduce attention problems. Forty-two kids with ADHD were assigned to two conditions: a computer game designed to improve working memory that gradually got harder (treatment group) or the same game but not designed to stretch their capacity (control group). The kids were expected to play the games for around 40 minutes a day, five days a week. The kids were tested after five weeks of treatment and again after three months. The results showed that the kids in the treatment group had a significant improvement in their working memory capacity. The parents also reported reduced symptoms of inattention and hyperactivity. This is one example of how technology can influence the cognitive development of kids, especially those with cognitive difficulties.

Review of the effects of video games on working memory (Simons et al., 2016): This study was an international collaboration of 133 scientists and practitioners. What they concluded from their review was that the games can help performance on closely-related tasks (e.g. n-back or span board tasks). However, they found that the tasks had limited transfer to other general or related cognitive tasks. What this means, for example, is that the games might improve the kids' scores on the span board task (one task that was used in Klingberg's study), but, if they improved on this task, it doesn't mean that it can be transferred to other cognitive skills such as reading comprehension, the ability to inhibit impulsive thoughts and actions, or improving long-term memory. They also found numerous flaws in many of the studies that claimed to demonstrate the positive effects of these programmes.

Exam Tips

- Studies on the brain can also be used to explain cognitive development. For example, if we have small hippocampi, then we may have memory problems. This could affect our developing as a learner.
- Please note that this bonus material does not cover research methods and ethics. If you are planning on answering a question from this option, you need to make sure you are prepared for those questions, too.

• While computer game training designed specifically to help cognitive development could have positive effects, ordinary everyday use of technology might have detrimental effects on the cognitive development of young kids. With the massive rise in the use of smartphones and tablets, this is a particularly concerning issue.

Further Studies

Effects of media use on working memory capacity (Cain et al., 2016): The aim of this study was to see if there was a correlation between use of media (TV, cellphones, etc.) and working memory capacity (among other things). Seventy-four eighth graders from Boston, USA participated in the study. Data was gathered on their media use through questionnaires. The amount of time using media was correlated with the students' test scores of their working memory capacity (e.g. on n-back and digit span tasks). The results showed a statistically significant (yet moderate) negative correlation between working memory capacity and media usage, with -0.27 for digit span tasks and -0.38 for n-back tasks. This is evidence to suggest that too much cell phone use can have a negative impact on working memory capacity, which is a key aspect to developing as a learner because it is correlated with many other things including intelligence, reading comprehension and general academic abilities.

Longitudinal study of TV watching and attention problems (Christakis et al., 2004): This longitudinal study was conducted on over 1,000 American children with the aim of seeing if watching TV as a young child (ages one and three) would increase the chances of having attentional problems when they got older (at age seven). After conducting their correlational analyses, the results showed that the main predictor for attentional problems at age seven was hours spent watching TV at ages one and three. One finding from the study was that for every hour on average they watched TV at age three, children were 10% more likely to have attentional problems at age seven.

Different types of TV and working memory (Lillard and Peterson, 2011): In this study, the researchers randomly allocated 60 four-year-old children to one of three conditions. In the fast-paced TV condition, the children watched SpongeBob SquarePants (which has an average scene length of 11 seconds). In the slow-paced TV condition, children watched another cartoon, Caillou (which has an average scene length of 34 seconds). The third group watched no TV and did drawing activities, instead. The kids watched TV (or drew) for nine minutes before completing a range of tests on their working memory, including a digit span task. The results showed that the kids who watched nine minutes of SpongeBob (the fast-paced TV condition) scored significantly less on the digit span and other tests of executive function compared to the group in the drawing and slow-paced TV conditions. It seems that it might not just about how much TV a child watches, but also the type of TV a child watches.

Critical Thinking Considerations

• The examples provided in this topic show the effects of technology on cognitive development. What other factors could be influential? How might development of the brain be connected to cognitive development?
• These samples come from developed, Western cultures. Can we generalize these results to other cultures?
• How could the findings from these studies be used to help improve the cognitive development of children? For example, what are the possible applications of these findings?
• Are there any ethical issues or other limitations with the above studies?

Brain Development

Neuroplasticity
What factors can influence the development of a child's brain?

We used to think that our brain's development was fixed, but we now know that our brains continue to grow and develop (or shrink) as a result of our experiences. If the development of important parts of the brain is impeded, this could have detrimental effects on our development as a learner.

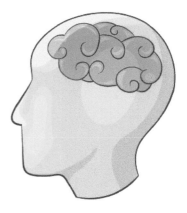

Key Details

- Numerous studies have found correlations between poverty and brain development, particularly in the hippocampus (an area of the brain associated with learning and memory). This correlation could be explained by a lack of stimulation. Our neurons connect to one another and create neural networks as we learn new things; if we are deprived of stimulation, then our brains are not developing the neural networks we need to learn, so some areas of the brain like the hippocampus might not develop fully.

- Parenting styles and stressful life events might also be mediating variables in the relationship between poverty and brain development. That is to say, poverty might affect parenting and stress which, in turn, affects the hippocampus. This could be because stress releases cortisol, and prolonged release of cortisol in the brain has been shown to damage hippocampal neurons (see Sapolsky et al., 1990 in the Neuroplasticity topic).

Key Studies

Poverty and brain development (Luby et al., 2013): The aim of this study was to see if poverty was correlated with brain development and to see if there were mediating variables related to stress and parenting that could explain this relationship. MRIs were used to measure correlations of poverty, stressful events and parenting styles with hippocampal volume in 145 children over a 10-year period. The results showed a negative correlation between poverty and hippocampal volume. They also found that parenting and stressful life events were mediating variables in this relationship, so while poverty corelates with brain development, the parenting styles and stressful life events affected by poverty explain this correlation. If kids have smaller hippocampi, it might affect their learning because this is an important part of the brain that is responsible for turning short-term memories into long-term memories.

Neglect and brain development (Perry and Pollard, 1997): Using MRI scans, this study used naturally-occurring neglect in human children as a variable that was correlated with brain development. They found that kids who suffered from multiple types of neglect (including emotional, physical and social) had reduced volume in their cerebral cortices. This is similar to rat studies that have found that putting rats in cages with no stimulation reduced brain volume compared to rats in cages with other rats and lots of stimulation (see Rosenzweig and Bennett's study in the Biological extension). Neglect could result in a lack of learning, so neural connections are not made and the brain does not develop normally.

Exam Tips

- When you are writing about studies like these ones that can apply to multiple topics, your ability to write clear conclusions becomes very important. The conclusion to any of the studies that you use should be linked directly to the question you are answering. For example, if I was writing about Luby et al. in relation to etiologies of PTSD, my conclusion would be different if I was using it in a question about developing as a learner. These 1-2 sentence conclusions can make a huge difference in your final marks because they show understanding.

- If you are planning on writing about this topic in the exam, it is important that you are also prepared to answer questions about research methods and ethics. A common method includes correlational studies while ethical considerations could be related to informed consent or anonymity (just to name two).

- We know from many MRI studies that our brain changes as a result of experience – this is called neuroplasticity. Therefore, it is not unrealistic to think that hours spent playing video games could have significant effects on important parts of the brain, like the hippocampus (associated with memory) and the prefrontal cortex. In particular, the dorsolateral prefrontal cortex is important because it has been linked with working memory and cognitive control. It might be that playing video games can improve brain function, which can improve cognition.
- Understanding the effects of video gaming on the brain and cognition is important because video game addiction is a growing concern, especially for young people.

Further Studies

Video game playing and the brain – a correlational study (Kuhn et al., 2014): This study gathered data on 152 teenagers (14 year olds). They measured how much time they spend playing video games and used MRI to measure their cortical thickness in various parts of the brain, including the dlPFC. The results showed a "robust positive association between cortical thickness and video gaming duration," meaning that those kids that played more video games tended to have thicker dlPFCs (correlation = 0.30). The researchers conclude that these differences could explain findings in studies like Klingberg et al.'s that show computer gaming can have a positive effect on working memory. An interesting (but maybe not surprising) finding from the study was that boys played video games more than girls and there were no boys who said they did not play video games. However, even after the researchers controlled for gender, age and parents' education levels, the correlation remained.

Critical Thinking Considerations

- Kuhn et al.'s study is correlational. One way of explaining a limitation of a study like this is to give an example of bidirectional ambiguity – it is logical to conclude that video gaming increased dlPFC volume, but could this be explained in the other direction?
- What are the potential negative effects of computer gaming on cognition?
- These studies are done on Western kids. Are there reasons why these results might not be applicable to other cultures or countries?
- Are there any ethical issues with these studies? For example, whenever studies are measuring sensitive things like brain development, why is anonymity important?

9 Paper Three
Research Methods

- **HL students only**
- **1 hour**
- **24 marks total**
- **5 questions answered (from a possible 9 static questions)**

Question 1 (actually three separate questions): (9 marks total)
You will need to answer *all* three of the following questions in relation to the stimulus provided.
   a) Identify the research method used and outline two characteristics of the method.
   b) Describe the sampling method used in the study.
   c) Suggest an alternative or additional research method giving one reason for your choice.

Question 2: (6 marks)
You will be given *one* of these questions (i.e. you don't choose – only one will appear).
   • Describe the ethical considerations that were applied in the study and explain if further ethical considerations could be applied.
   • Describe the ethical considerations in reporting the results and explain ethical considerations that could be taken into account when applying the findings of the study.

Question 3: (9 marks)
As with Question 2, you will be given *one* of the following questions:
   • Discuss the possibility of generalizing/transferring[1] the findings of the study.
   • Discuss how a researcher could ensure that the results of the study are credible.
   • Discuss how the researcher in the study could avoid bias.

You will be given a one-page summary of a study, so your revision needs to be based on methodology, *not* on existing studies. Having said that, an effective way to prepare for Paper Three *and* Paper One and/or Two at the same time is to choose a range of different studies (qualitative and quantitative) that you might use in Paper One and/or Two and practice writing Paper Three answers about those studies.

---

[1] Generalizing is a term used for quantitative studies, whereas transferring is used for qualitative studies. In essence, they mean the same thing – the extent to which we would expect the same results with a different group of participants.

Question 1a: Research Method

1a. Identify the research method used and outline two characteristics of the method.

You need to be able to state the research method used in the stimulus (1 mark) and outline two characteristics of the method (2 marks). Therefore, make sure you know at least <u>two</u> characteristics of the method.

Quantitative Research Methods

Method	*Key characteristics*
True experiment (a.k.a. laboratory experiment) *(Experimental Method)*	a) Examines the effects of an IV on a DV b) The researcher manipulates the IV, so random allocation to the treatment or control condition is possible c) Takes place in a controlled environment and extraneous variables are controlled
Field experiment *(Experimental Method)*	a) Examines the effects of an IV on a DV b) Takes place in a naturalistic setting c) Control of extraneous variables is not always possible
Quasi-experiment *(Experimental Method)*	a) Examines the effects of an IV on a DV b) One or more conditions of a true experiment can't be met, e.g. no random allocation is possible c) "In quasi-experiments, participants are grouped based on a characteristic of interest, such as gender, ethnicity, or scores on a depression scale" (IB Psychology Guide, p. 37)
Natural experiment *(Experimental Method)*	a) Examines the effects of an IV on a DV b) The IV is naturally occurring c) Extraneous variables may not always be controlled Note: there is often not a clear distinction between a quasi-experiment and a natural experiment.
Correlational study *(Non-experimental method)*	a) Does not have an IV or DV, but has co-variables b) Tests the strength of relationships of co-variables by calculating a correlation coefficient c) Values of coefficients range from -1.0 to 1.0
Case study *(Non-experimental method)*	a) An in-depth investigation of an individual, small group or organization b) Multiple methods are used to gather data (which is what makes them "in-depth") c) They often use a combination of quantitative and qualitative methods
Survey[2]	a) Gathers data on a large number of participants b) Uses data gathering techniques such as questionnaires c) Often calculates correlations between co-variables

---

[2] This is unlikely to be a research method used in the stimulus material, but it is mentioned in the guide.

Qualitative Research Methods

Method	Key characteristics
Naturalistic observations	a) Subjects' behaviour is observed in a naturalistic environment b) Field notes and other data gathering techniques are used c) Observations may be followed by interviews
Covert and overt observations	a) Covert = subjects are not aware they are being observed b) Overt = subjects are aware they are being observed c) Usually take place in naturalistic environments in qualitative research
Participant and non-participant observations	a) Participant = the researcher becomes a member of the group they are observing b) Non-participant = the researcher stays removed from the group they are observing
Qualitative interviews	a) Face-to-face discussion involving the researcher asking questions to the participants b) The researcher gathers qualitative data c) There are many different types of qualitative interviews (see below)
Semi-structured interviews	a) An interview that follows an interview schedule – it includes an outline of topics to be covered, but allows for deviation and elaboration b) Can include a combination of open and closed questions c) It resembles a conversation
Unstructured interviews	a) The interviewer has topics to cover, but there is a lot of freedom and the precise questions and order are not fixed b) Can include open and closed questions c) The interview evolves as a result of the interactions between the researcher and the interviewee
Focus group interviews	a) A group interview (about 6-10 participants) b) Focus groups rely on group processes and the interaction of individuals to help reveal information that might not be revealed in individual interviews c) The interviewer acts as a moderator and, if done well, the interview will resemble a group discussion

1b. Describe the sampling method used in the study.

You need to be able to state the sampling method used in the stimulus (1 mark) and describe the method (2 marks). Therefore, make sure you know at least <u>two</u> characteristics of the method.

Sampling Techniques	
Random sampling	<ul><li>When every member of the target population has an equal chance of being selected</li><li>The aim is to obtain a sample that is representative of the target population</li><li>It can reduce the chance of sampling bias</li></ul>
Convenience/opportunity sampling	<ul><li>Gathers participants who happen to be available for study at a convenient time or place.</li><li>It is based on convenience, for both researcher and participant</li><li>Depending on the nature of the study, it may lead to sampling and/or researcher bias.</li></ul>
Volunteer/self-selected sampling	<ul><li>Participants are the ones that approach the researchers and volunteer to participate in the study</li><li>There is typically some form of marketing that calls for volunteers</li><li>Participants may have more commitment to the study due to the fact that they volunteered.</li></ul>
Purposive sampling	<ul><li>Participants who share characteristics that are relevant and of interest to researchers are asked to participate in the study</li><li>It may use snowballing methods to gather the sample</li><li>They may be recruited through a range of methods, including direct contact or referral from someone else</li></ul>
Snowball sampling	<ul><li>A group of initial participants (called "seeds") invite others to participate in the study</li><li>The sample keeps growing in size until the desired size has been reached</li><li>It is particularly useful when studying "hidden populations" (people who do not want others to know about them or who are hard to find).</li></ul>

Question 1c: Alternative (or Additional) Research Method

1c. Suggest an alternative or additional research method giving one reason for your choice.

You need to state the alternative or additional research method (1 mark) and explain how and/or why the method could be used (2 marks). If possible, apply details from the stimulus to support your answer.

Tip: It will probably be easier to explain an *additional* method, rather than an *alternative* one. Explaining how an additional qualitative method (e.g. interview) is often much easier than explaining an aternative quantitative method.

Points to consider for additional research methods

Triangulation	• The use of an additional method is methodological triangulation. This could increase the credibility (qualitative) or reliability (quantitative) of the study if similar findings are reported • If using this explanation, consider if there is a reason to think that the study would benefit from triangulation
Experimental research	**Effects of an IV on a DV** • An experiment may be conducted if there is a reason why researchers may want to study the effect(s) of one or more variables on a particular behavior • Perhaps a different type of experiment could be conducted (e.g. a field experiment) to test the effects in a naturalistic setting. Alternatively, a laboratory environment could be proposed to control for extraneous variables. A natural experiment could be used if a naturally-occurring IV could be identified • An experimental method could test hypotheses generated from a qualitative study
Correlational study	**Relationships between co-variables** • This could be a suitable method if there are two co-variables that can be identified in the study and researchers can see how strongly they are connected • The correlational method could deduce the strength of the relationship. This could lead to further development of hypotheses
Naturalistic observations	**Observing behavior in a naturalistic environment** • This could be a suitable method if prior studies have been conducted in artificial environments and/or they have gathered behavioral data using questionnaires, interviews or other non-observational methods
Interviews	**Gathering qualitative data on specific experiences** • Interviews can make for valuable follow-ups to observations as they allow researchers to gain an understanding of what they have observed • Focus group interviews could be conducted to triangulate research from individual interviews, or vice-versa

You will be asked one of two possible questions on ethics (6 marks):
Q1: *Describe the ethical considerations that were applied in the study and explain if further ethical considerations could be applied.*

This question requires you to explain a minimum of *six* ethical considerations because your examiner will award a maximum of one mark per relevant point and you need to explain at least three considerations for each part of the question.

For the first part "ethical considerations that were applied," these should be stated in the stimulus, so re-state these in your answer, define them and give one reason why they were applied.
For the second part, you should state three considerations that were *not* mentioned in the stimulus, define these and explain how and/or why they could have been applied to the study.

Conside-rations	Definition	Explanation
1. Informed consent	When participants agree to participate in a study and have been given enough information to make an informed decision.	Can reduce stress and discomfort from participants because they know what to expect. It also allows them the chance not to participate, which is relevant if there could be any negative effects from participating in the study. *Tip: Look for a reason in the study why people might not want to participate.*
2. Anonymity	Removing participants' names from their data during the gathering, analyzing and publication process.	Can avoid the invasion of participants' privacy and saves participants from possible embarrassment from participating in the study. *Tip: Look at the results and think of a reason why people might not want their results known.*
3. Debriefing	This happens at the end of a study and is when the researchers reveal the full nature of the study, including aims and results.	Can reduce the possibility of any long-term negative effects of the study. This is also important when not all information is given in the consent process. *Tip: See if there was any information that was withheld from participants or if deception was used.*
4. The right to withdraw	Before the study begins, participants are assured that they can leave at any time.	Allows participants to avoid harm or stress by assuring them they can end their participation at any time. *Tip: Look for any reason why someone might want to withdraw from the study.*
5. Approval from an ethics review committee	Before a study can take place, in most countries it needs to be approved by a group of people who make sure it meets the standards of ethical research.	This simply makes sure that the study is judged as being ethical by an appropriate committee. *Tip: Look for any way the study might cause harm for participants. This helps explain the need for approval from a review committee.*
6. Justification for any stress or harm	If harm or stress is expected to occur, this should be reasonable and minimized as much as possible. Ethics review committees usually make the final decision about whether a study's methodology is justified.	Sometimes there is the potential for participants to experience stress or harm during an experiment, but the long-term benefits should outweigh these short-term costs. This is also relevant in animal studies. *Tip: Look for a way that the study might cause harm, but also why it might be justified.*

Reminder: An "ethical consideration" is anything the researchers can do to ensure their study doesn't cause long-term negative effects for participants. All participants should finish the study in the same (or better) mental and physical health than when they began. If you search "Belmont Report" on our blog you'll find some more possible points to make about ethics.

You will be asked one of two possible questions on ethics (6 marks):

Q2: *Describe the ethical considerations in reporting the results and explain additional ethical considerations that could be taken into account when applying the findings of the study.*

Make sure you write about three considerations for each part of the question (six in total). For each point, make sure you state the relevant consideration and explain how it is relevant to the question. You can select any of the following if they are relevant to the stimulus.

To answer the second part of the question, you can explain how anyone applying the findings needs to consider how this application could have a negative effect on others – a specific ethical guideline does not necessarily need to be stated (remember: "guideline" and "consideration" don't need to be the same).

Ethical Considerations

	Reporting the results…	Applying the findings…
Anonymity	Participants' names should be removed from the data when the results are reported. This can save participants from potential embarrassment. *Tip: Explain why participants in the study might want to remain anonymous.*	
Debriefing	In qualitative studies, participants may be asked follow-up questions and have additional sessions to make sure the researcher's recording of their data is accurate. This can happen during the debriefing stage and before results are reported. *Tip: Look for any reason why participants may want to learn more about the study before results are reported.*	If the study is being conducted with a particular application in mind, this may be revealed to participants either during the informed consent phase or during the debriefing phase of the study. *Tip: If this question is asked, applications of findings will probably be mentioned in the stimulus. Use this information. If it's not, you are free to make hypotheses (or guesses) about how the results could be applied and answer accordingly.*
Informed consent	It may be relevant for researchers to inform participants before the study how the results are intended to be reported.	
The right to withdraw	In some cases, participants may wish to have their data removed from the study before the results are reported. *Tip: Look for any reason why participants may want to have their data withdrawn from the final report.*	If participants hear about how the study may be applied, they should be given the right to end their participation in the study if they have issues with the proposed applications. This may also be relevant after the study is conducted, whereby participants have the right to withdraw any data.
Disclosing conflicts of interest	If researchers have a possible conflict of interest, this should be disclosed when reporting the results (e.g. who is funding the study or a researcher's personal link to the topic/participants).	

Other Considerations:
- **Validity / Credibility**: It could be considered unethical to apply findings from studies that have not been replicated to ensure that they are reliable.
- **Fair reporting by the media**: Results of studies are not just reported by the researchers, but also by others (including the media and other psychologists). Anyone reporting the results of a study has an ethical obligation to be truthful in how they are reporting those results (this does not always happen in the media).

General Tip: Writing in bullet points is acceptable for some Paper 3 answers.

You will be asked one of the following questions:
- *Discuss how a researcher could ensure that the results of the study are credible.*
- *Discuss how the researcher in the study could avoid bias.*
- *Discuss the possibility of generalizing/transferring the findings of the study.*

These questions can be answered by looking at similar factors, including triangulation, sampling, controls and replication. Remember that to score full marks you must "make effective use of the stimulus material" (e.g. by selecting quotes and details to support your answer) and you must describe strengths and limitations of the approaches to research relevant to the question.

Credibility (Validity)

- Discuss how a researcher could ensure that the results of the study are credible.

Definitions

Credibility: *General speaking, credibility refers to the extent to which something or someone can be believed and trusted. In a research context, it refers to the extent to which the results of a study accurately represent what was being studied. If a study is credible, it means they truthfully report what really happened.*

Validity: *The quantitative research equivalent of credibility, validity refers to the accuracy of the methods in achieving the desired aims. See internal and external, as well as construct, population, and ecological validity.*

Factors Affecting Credibility

Triangulation
- The use of triangulation can reduce the effects of researcher bias, which increases credibility (or validity) and the possibility of generalizing or transferring the findings to other contexts.
- Researcher triangulation: This could help reduce researcher bias, which will improve credibility/validity of the study. Researcher triangulation can be used to assess inter-rater reliability, which, if reported, can help the credibility/validity of the findings. It can occur during the recording, analysis and/or reporting of the data.
- Methodological triangulation: Using more than one method to gather data can also improve the credibility/validity of the findings because it allows the phenomenon being studied to be viewed from multiple perspectives.
- Data triangulation: Gathering data at more than one time can improve the credibility/validity of the findings because it increases the chances that the data is an accurate reflection of reality and that the results weren't by chance.

Sampling
- Using a large sample can improve the credibility/validity of the findings. The larger the sample, the more likely it is that findings are representative of a population and can be generalized. That being said, this is difficult in some studies, especially qualitative ones.

Controls
- Any control used in a study can help ensure credibility/validity of the findings. Researchers can use any of the following to control for extraneous variables in their studies: using a single- or double-blind design, having a control condition (e.g. placebo group), counterbalancing, random allocation, or design type (e.g. repeated measures, independent samples, matched pairs).

Replication
- If a study is replicated (reproduced) and similar results are obtained, this can increase the credibility/validity of the findings of the original. A study is said to have test-retest reliability if more than one researcher has conducted the study and achieved the same (or similar) results. Psychology is going through a "credibility crisis" at the moment because of the reproducibility project.

---

[3] The term credibility is not often used in quantitative studies. If you are asked about credibility in an experiment or correlational study, you can use the concepts of validity and reliability to assess credibility.
[4] This is a large-scale project that have involved 100s of famous studies being replicated but an alarming amount of the replications are not getting the same results as the originals.

Avoiding Bias

- *Discuss how the researcher in the study could avoid bias.*

Definition

Bias: *When an individual's existing thoughts, beliefs or ideas influence their thinking or behaviour. Researcher bias is when the thoughts, beliefs or ideas of the researcher are negatively influencing the results of the study in some way.*

Ways to Avoid Bias

Triangulation
- The use of triangulation can reduce the effects of researcher bias.
  - **Researcher triangulation** could help reduce researcher bias. By using more than one researcher in the process, it reduces the chances that one researcher's beliefs or opinions can affect the study. Researcher bias could happen at multiple different times in a study, including during designing the study, gathering data, analyzing data and writing the report.
  - **Methodological triangulation**: If gathering data using a qualitative method (e.g. interviews or observations), using an additional quantitative method (e.g. questionnaires) can help avoid the effects of researcher bias because quantitative data is less susceptible to bias compared to qualitative methods. By comparing the data for consistency (and making this comparison transparent in the report), it can be made clear that the chances for researcher bias were reduced.

Sampling
- Some sampling methods are more prone to being influenced by researcher bias than others. For example, purposive sampling involves the researchers selecting participants for the study – they may select participants whom they think will provide them with the best results. One way bias could be avoided is to use a sampling method that doesn't involve researcher selection, such as random, self-selected or opportunity sampling.

Controls
- Using a double-blind design in experimental research can be used to avoid researcher bias. By not having researchers aware of which participants are in which condition, it reduces the chances that they will have a biased interpretation of the results of the study.

Replication
- Having a different group of researchers try to replicate a study is one way of avoiding researcher bias from influencing the validity of the findings. If a study is replicated (reproduced) and similar results are obtained, it suggests that researcher bias was not a factor in the original, because different researchers are getting the same results.

Reflexivity
- This is a process in qualitative research that involves the researcher constantly reflecting on their role in the researcher process, and how the research might be affecting them. By practicing being reflexive, the researcher can be aware of their own potential for biases affecting the results and take steps towards reducing and avoiding these potential effects.

Tips:
- **Limitations** - Don't forget to write about strengths and limitations of the approaches to research in your answer. A good time to do this is after you explain what a researcher could have done to avoid bias or ensure credibility – after the explanation you can follow this with a limitation. For example, if explaining how they could have used triangulation to reduce bias this could be followed with practical limitations of using triangulation (e.g. it's time consuming and requires more people).
- You have one hour for Paper 3. Therefore, you should spend roughly 20 minutes on each of the three questions (you will have 5 minutes of reading time to read the stimulus). This means your answer to question 3 will be similar in length to a short answer response (i.e. about 300-400 words) rather than a regular discussion essay.

Generalizability / Transferability

- *Discuss the possibility of generalizing/transferring the findings of the study.*

Definitions

Generalizability: The extent to which conclusions from a study can be applied to (generalized) contexts beyond the study itself. This is another term for external validity.

Transferability: The extent to which we can transfer the findings from one study to another context. It is the qualitative research equivalent of generalizability and means the same thing. The reason we do not use the term generalizability in qualitative research is because the sampling methods are not representational and so the findings are never meant to be generalized.

Factors Influencing Generalizability/Transferability

When assessing generalizability or transferability, you need to try to explain reasons why it might (or might not) be possible to apply the findings to another context. In other words, whether we could expect the same results if the study was conducted on a different group of people or in a different place.

Sampling
- When discussing generalizability based on the sample, we are assessing "population validity."
- In quantitative studies, using representative sampling measures (e.g. random sampling) increases the chances of generalizability. The goal of representative sampling is to get a sample that is representative of the wider population being studied. If this is achieved, there is a high chance that the results are generalizable.
- Similarly, the larger the sample size, the more likely it is to accurately represent the target population, which also helps to increase generalizability.
- In qualitative studies, non-representative sampling methods are used (e.g. snowball and purposive sampling). These samples are often small in size and are not gathered with the purpose of generalizability or transferability.

Procedures
- When discussing generalizability or transferability, it is important to consider the procedures used in the study. This is especially true for experimental research. For example, a study might lack ecological validity (a type of generalizability) if it can be clearly explained why we might not expect the same results in a different environment.
- A study could be said to lack mundane realism if the procedures do not accurately reflect real-life situations. This is another important consideration when assessing generalizability.

Replication
- If a study has been replicated in a different context, it could increase the possibility of generalizing/transferring the findings.

Tip – Limitations: When you are writing about a specific research or sampling method for this question, don't forget to add the limitations of using that sampling method to make sure you're meeting all the demands of the rubric.

Tip: Try to identify specific characteristics of the study and explain why we might not expect the same results in a different context. Relevant characteristics include the nature of the sample (age, gender, nationality, culture, education, background, language, religion, etc.) or the nature of the procedures (location, situation, etc.)

Practice Paper Three

The stimulus material below is based on a research article.

Physical displays of power are common in the animal kingdom and amongst humans. These displays of power are often the result of our physiology. For example, people with high testosterone and low cortisol are more likely to have high status in society (testosterone is a hormone associated with power and status and cortisol is a stress hormone). However, Carney, Cuddy and Yap wanted to see if the opposite could be true - could displaying power cause changes in our physiology?

The researchers hypothesized that that "...high-power poses (compared with low-power poses) would cause individuals to experience elevated testosterone, decreased cortisol, increased feelings of power, and higher risk tolerance." To test their hypotheses, they gathered 42 students as participants and randomly allocated them to one of two conditions: high power pose (HPP) or low power pose (LPP). Participants signed up for the study by replying to a recruitment flyer advertised in an online college magazine.* In the HPP, the participants made themselves big and expansive (e.g. by sitting with their legs apart and shoulders spread). In the LPP, participants made themselves small and hunched.

A number of dependent variables were measured, including changes in hormone levels (testosterone and cortisol), their willingness to take risks and their feelings of power (recorded using self-report forms). Results showed that those in the HPP condition increased confidence in gambling and those in the HPP condition reported feeling more "powerful" and "in-charge." Finally, testosterone increased and cortisol decreased in the HPP condition, whereas the opposite was true for the LPP condition. These results supported the researchers' hypotheses and Cuddy later remarked that she felt very happy that "everything went in the direction it was supposed to."
The researchers concluded that "...a person can, by assuming two simple 1-minute poses, embody power and instantly become more powerful" and that this "has real-world, actionable implications." For example, they suggest that power posing could help people in situations like job interviews, public speaking, taking risks or disagreeing with someone higher in rank (e.g. a boss or teacher).

After this study was published, Amy Cuddy gave a very popular TED Talk and began giving motivational talks to companies and organizations so people could use power posing to help in their personal and professional lives. The study was also widely reported in the media as it seemed to have real-life applications for many people, especially those who are low in confidence. However, the study has come under scrutiny after 11 other studies have failed to replicate the same effects of power posing on behaviour.

This sentence has been added to explain how the sample was gathered, as this was omitted from the original report.
Carney, Dana R., et al. "Power Posing." *Psychological Science*, vol. 21, no. 10, 2010, pp. 1363–1368., doi:10.1177/0956797610383437
Dominus, Susan. "When the Revolution Came for Amy Cuddy." *The New York Times*, The New York Times, 18 Oct. 2017, www.nytimes.com/2017/10/18/magazine/when-the-revolution-came-for-amy-cuddy.html.

Answer all of the following three questions, referring to the stimulus material in your answers. Marks will be awarded for demonstration of knowledge and understanding of research methodology.

1. (a) Identify the research method used and outline two characteristics of the method. (3 marks)
(b) Describe the sampling method used in the study. (3 marks)
(c) Suggest an alternative or additional research method giving one reason for your choice. (3 marks)

2. Describe the ethical considerations in reporting the results and explain additional ethical considerations that could be taken into account when applying the findings of the study. (6 marks)

3. Discuss how the researcher in the study could avoid bias. (9 marks)

10 Writing Guide and Example Answers

General Writing Tips

1. Remember the two key questions that are central to the study of IB Psychology:
   a. How and why do humans think and act the way they do?
   b. How do we know?

Almost every IB Psychology exam question is directly related to these two questions.

2. There are 5 types of common questions in IB Psychology exams, so in Papers 1 and 2 expect questions about:
   a. Variables and behaviour
   b. Models and theories
   c. Research methods (and techniques)
   d. Ethical considerations
   e. Research related to a topic or phenomenon

3. Make sure you understand how to show the following in your exam answers:
   a. Knowledge and understanding of psychology (cognition, behaviour, research methods and ethics)
   b. Understanding of research (studies)
   c. Critical thinking skills (in essay answers only)

4. All SAQs can be answered using the same structure, so the command terms are irrelevant.

5. Discuss and evaluate questions can be answered in a similar way (I would argue they are almost identical). To what extent questions can be answered using a similar structure to discuss and evaluate questions. Contrast means to highlight the differences.

6. Use the writing frameworks in this chapter as a guide. You should adjust your writing and structure to suit the question.

Writing Guide and Example Answers

By the numbers:
- 250 - 400 words
- Mostly require one central argument and at least one supporting study
- 2 - 5 minutes planning
- 15 - 20 minutes writing
- Brief introduction and conclusion

This code will take you to a video about how to answer any SAQ

Example questions
- Explain the effects of one hormone on human behaviour.
- Describe social cognitive theory.
- Explain the use of one research method used to study cognitive processes.
- Outline one or more ethical considerations related to studies on cultural origins of behaviour.
- Describe one study related to schema theory.

Some tips to remember
- At the heart of IB psychology are two questions:
  - Why do people think and act the way they do?
  - How do we know?
    - Use these to guide revision for Paper One, Part A.

Suggested Short Answer Response Structure

Introduction
(State your argument(s) and evidence)

Central Argument
(State your argument(s) and evidence)

Supporting Evidence
(Describe the study, then explain how it supports the central argument of the topic)

Conclusion

What is a central argument in a topic?
The SAQ will ask you to explain a topic, research methods or ethics. Your central argument is your explanation of the topic in the question. This is then demonstrated by your evidence (one or more studies).

Example SAQ

	Comments
Explain the use of one technique used to study the brain and behaviour.	
FMRIs are one technique used to study the brain and behaviour. They are often used in experimental research to see how chemical messengers can influence brain activity, which can provide deeper understanding of how those messengers can affect behaviour. This can be seen in Passamonti et al.'s study on serotonin and the brain.	The introduction clearly states the argument being presented and the supporting evidence.
FMRI machines measure the activity of areas of the brain when the participant is performing a task or cognitive process and are often used in experimental research where the level of a chemical messenger is the IV (e.g. serotonin or testosterone levels). The effect on brain activity is studied using the fMRI. *Participants receive a treatment (e.g. injection with a treatment or placebo) and then lay in the fMRI. They are then asked to perform a task (like viewing different types of faces). The task they perform is related to the behaviour being studied. For instance, viewing different types of emotional faces is designed to represent experiencing a social threat. Their brain activity is measured by the fMRI detecting changes in blood flow while they are performing this task – the more blood flowing in a particular region the higher the activity. By doing this, the researchers can see how chemical messengers can affect activity in certain parts of the brain during certain tasks, which could provide deeper explanations of behaviour.*	Before explaining the study, the answer explains how and why the technique is used to study the brain and behaviour – this shows conceptual understanding relating to the topic.
For example, in Passamonti et al.'s study, participants had their serotonin levels manipulated and they were placed in an fMRI machine and exposed to different types of faces. The results showed that reduced serotonin levels reduced activity in the prefrontal cortex (PFC) and reduced connectivity between the amygdala and the PFC when viewing images of angry faces. This could provide an explanation for the connection between serotonin and antisocial (e.g. aggressive) behaviour since the PFC is important in regulating impulsive aggressive reactions. The use of fMRI to show this is valuable in being able to make the connection between serotonin, brain activity and behaviour.	Relevant details of the study are described and its relevance to the question is clearly explained.
Studies like Passamonti et al.'s provide greater insight into how chemical messengers like neurotransmitters (e.g. serotonin) and hormones (e.g. testosterone) may influence behaviour because of their influence on brain function (e.g. the amygdala and prefrontal cortex). The use of fMRIs in this way could help understand origins of behaviours such as violence. (approximately 350 words)	The conclusion of the study is directly related to the question. The conclusion is clear and concise.

IB Paper 1 Section A: Short Answer Rubric (from the IB)

Mark	Level Descriptor
7-9	The response is fully focused on the question and meets the command term requirements. Knowledge and understanding is accurate and addresses the main topics/problems identified in the question. The response is supported by appropriate research which is described and explicitly linked to the question.
4-6	The response is relevant to the question, but does not meet the command term requirements. Knowledge and understanding is accurate but limited. The response is supported by appropriate research which is described.
1-3	The response is of limited relevance to or only rephrases the question. Knowledge and understanding is mostly inaccurate or not relevant to the question. The research supporting the response is mostly not relevant to the question and, if relevant, only listed.
0	The answer does not reach a standard described by the descriptors above.

Paper One: Section B and Paper Two Essays

Overview
- Approximately 800 - 1,000 words
- 5 - 10 minutes planning
- 50 - 55 minutes writing
- 3 - 5 sentence introduction and brief conclusion
- Paper 1 (Part B) and Paper 2
- 3 x questions, answer only one
- Four possible command terms: evaluate, discuss, to what extent and contrast
- HL students will have one, two or three essay questions in Paper 1 based on the extensions

Three Rules of Three
1. Three studies (guideline only)
2. Three sections:
   a. Central argument(s)
   b. Evidence (studies)
   c. Counter-argument(s) (critical thinking)
3. Three counter-arguments (examples of critical thinking)

Example Questions
- Evaluate one or more research methods used to study cognitive processes.
- Discuss one or more effects of neurotransmitters on behaviour.
- To what extent do genes influence human behaviour?
- Contrast two explanations for one disorder.

"Critical Thinking"

There are two major differences between SARs and essays:
1) More studies in an essay (aim for 3 studies in an essay and one in a SAR)
2) Essays need to show evidence of your critical thinking

The IB has identified some areas of critical thinking that you could use in your essay. They are:
- **research design and methodologies**
- **contradictory evidence or alternative theories or explanations**
- **areas of uncertainty**
- **triangulation**
- **assumptions and biases**

Applications of studies, theories and findings are also a good way to show critical thinking.

Tip: Aim to include 2-3 different counter-arguments in your essay so you are showing your range of critical thinking skills (see example essay).

Introduction

One major requirement for your essays in Paper One and Two is that you show your "critical thinking." So, what is "critical thinking"? The IB has identified a number of ways you can think critically. The first two in the list below are the most commonly used. For every topic you are preparing to write an essay about, you should aim to be able to make three critical thinking points.

a)   **Research design and methodologies**: Explain strengths and limitations of the research methods used in the studies you have explained in your essay. For example, you could explain why the results of one study might not be generalizable and/or a strength of the study was how they controlled for confounding variables (see next page).

b)   **Contradictory evidence or alternative theories or explanations**: You can show critical thinking by arguing against your central argument and/or providing an alternative argument. For example, in a discussion of social identity theory, you could provide realistic group conflict theory as an alternative theory of prejudice and discrimination.

c)   **Areas of uncertainty**: This will require you to look carefully at your central argument(s) and evidence to find things we still don't know. For example, if you're writing about how the MAOA gene affects behaviour, an area of uncertainty is that we're not sure why low expression of this gene reduces the activity in important areas of the brain.

d)   **Triangulation**: This is really a sub-branch of research design and methodologies – it refers to gathering and/or analysing data using more than one perspective (e.g. method, researcher, etc.) You could also write about the similar concept of test-retest reliability. Has the study been successfully replicated, or is there contradictory evidence, or is it a relatively new study with no replications yet?

e)   **Assumptions and biases**: It's unlikely that researcher bias will be a relevant consideration to any of the studies you're writing about. However, you can look for your own assumptions in your answers. For example, a limitation of the multi-store model might be that it assumes that all information is processed the same way, which we now know is not the case.

f)   **Applications**: This is not in the IB list but it is generally accepted by examiners that explaining applications of studies and theories is a valuable way of showing critical thinking. For example, one strength of schema theory is that it has been applied in schools to help students improve their reading comprehension.

The key to remember with critical thinking is that it's a critical reflection on your knowledge and understanding and the evidence (studies) upon which that is based; this is why they are counter-arguments. In your essay, you put forward a central thesis in response to the topic, support it with evidence but then you must critically reflect (i.e. think critically) upon the validity of your arguments and evidence – your counter-argument(s) is where you show your critical thinking.

Exam Tips:
- Use the terms in bold above when you are writing your counter-arguments to highlight that you are showing critical thinking.
- Use the "critical thinking consideration" boxes in each topic to guide your planning and revising.
- Search "population validity" or "ecological validity" for detailed posts about how to evaluate studies based on these concepts.

Most students will offer alternative explanations and evaluate studies as their way of showing critical thinking, so here are a few more tips.

Alternative Explanations
- The best alternative explanations will be those that are linked to the central argument in some way. This is especially true for "discuss" essay questions. If the question is "to what extent…" then the direct link with the central argument is not essential, but it's still preferable. See the box below for an example.

Central Argument	Weak Alternative Explanation	Strong Alternative Explanation
One explanation of PTSD is that it is caused by abnormalities in the brain.	Another explanation is that it might be because of cognitive appraisals.	Another explanation is that the damage to the brain might affect the ability to make effective appraisals, so the combination of factors must be considered. *This is better because the cognitive explanation in the counter-argument is linked with the biological explanation in the central argument.*

Research Methodologies
- It is unlikely that you are going to be able to explain a limitation of a peer-reviewed study without regurgitating what someone else has already said about the study (which is not critical thinking). Therefore, if you are evaluating an experiment[1], I recommend explaining strengths of a study by looking at its internal validity and the limitations in external validity.

External Validity (Generalizability) *Can we apply these results to other people, situations or places?*	The key question to ask is, "would we expect the same results with a…" • …different group of people (population validity) • …real-life setting or location (ecological validity) • …real-life set of procedures (mundane realism)	Exam Tip: If you're not sure which type of validity you're writing about, just refer to "generalizability" and explain how or why you think the results might not be applicable to another group of people, situation or setting. The best explanations will be 3-5 sentences and will give reasons why we might not expect the same results.

Internal Validity *How well-controlled was the study? Is it possible that other factors (other than the IV) may have affected the results?*	• Exam Tip: Choose one study per topic that you are planning on writing an essay about and try to find one or two controls that were used in the study so you can explain these as strengths of the study. For example, in Bandura's Bobo Doll study they used a matched pairs design to control for existing levels of aggressiveness.

---

[1] For correlational studies, explain possible examples of bidirectional ambiguity.

Example Essay

To what extent do genes influence human behaviour?	Comments
One gene that has been linked with behaviour is the MAOA gene, which the media has called the "warrior" gene because of its connections with antisocial behaviour and aggression. The effects of the MAOA gene could be explained by its influence on brain activity, as shown in Meyer-Lindenberg's study. However, Caspi et al.'s study shows that the gene alone doesn't influence behaviour and childhood abuse is also important to consider. Other factors such as culture and social learning could also be important factors to consider, as well.	The introduction begins by restating the question (this guarantees one mark). The intro also outlines the essay by stating the central argument, the studies and the counter-arguments.
To begin with, expression of the MAOA gene could affect brain activity, which is why it might be linked with aggressive behaviour. Genes are sequences of DNA that are found in chromosomes in cells. When a gene is expressed, it sends messages from the cells that trigger other reactions in the body, including neurotransmission activity in the brain. The effects of gene expression on brain activity could be how genes, such as the MAOA gene, can influence human behaviours like aggression.	Relevant details of genetics are described and their relevance to the question is made very clear. This explanation shows knowledge and understanding.
Gene expression of the MAOA gene produces an enzyme (monoamine oxidase A) that affects neurotransmission. Some variants of the MAOA gene have less gene expression. These variants are collectively known as MAOA-L. The reduced expression could explain why studies have shown that people with the reduced MAOA gene variation have differences in brain activity when perceiving emotional stimuli. This could explain increases in impulsive-reactive aggression.	The explanation of the link between genes and behaviour is further elaborated.
For example, Meyer-Lindenberg (2008) studied MAOA gene variants and brain function. This study compared the brain function of two groups of healthy participants. One group had high expressing MAOA gene (MAOA-H), whereas another group had the variant that has low expression of the MAOA gene, which is the type correlated with aggressive behaviour (MAOA-L). When viewing angry and fearful faces in an fMRI, the MAOA-L group had significantly increased activity in their amygdala and reduced activity in their prefrontal cortex.	Relevant details of the supporting study are described. This scores points for use of research.
This could explain the link with aggression since negative emotions (such as anger, which is closely tied with aggression) are generated in the amygdala, so perhaps increased amygdala activity could increase negative emotions and aggression. This, coupled with the reduced activity in the PFC (which can top-down regulate the emotion generated in the amygdala and inhibit impulsive behaviour), could lessen an individual's potential to reduce their anger and ability to control their behaviour, resulting in reactive aggression when they are in confrontational situations. So, with an increased emotional arousal and inability to regulate emotion or impulsive actions, MAOA-L carriers may be prone to impulsive-reactive aggression.	The significance of the study is clearly explained and linked back to the question.
However, one limitation of the research methodology of this study is that it took place in an fMRI and they did not actually directly measure aggression. There is an assumption being made that a person with reduced PFC activity would react aggressively, but this might not necessarily be true.	Critical thinking is shown by explaining a limitation of the study (counter-points don't have to come at the very end).
Furthermore, there are alternative explanations as other studies have shown that people with the MAOA-L variation who have experienced trauma or abuse as a child are more prone to being aggressive and antisocial adults (compared with those who have the MAOA-L gene without experiencing childhood abuse). This suggests it is not just genetics that influence this behavior.	
For example, Caspi et al.'s longitudinal study of MAOA-L variants, childhood abuse and antisocial behaviour (a.k.a. "The Dunedin Study") followed over 1,000 children in New Zealand across 25 years and took measures every few years. They found that the	The studies are used effectively in supporting the argument and meeting the demands of the command

MAOA-L gene moderated the effects of experiencing child abuse on adult aggression – that is to say, those participants with the MAOA-L gene variant and who were abused were more likely to be antisocial and aggressive adults.

However, aggression is not only affected by genetics and other biological factors; another alternative explanation is that our social and cultural environment could be influential, as well. For example, according to Bandura's social cognitive theory, aggression can be a learned behaviour caused by observing others' violent actions and being motivated to copy them. Similarly, if an individual is born into a cultural environment with a "culture of honour," you may be more likely to value defending yourself when you are threatened and less likely to "turn the other cheek," which is another factor to consider when explaining aggression, especially impulsive-reactive aggression.

In his famous study, Bandura showed that young children (aged 4-6) could be influenced by social learning and this could affect their aggressive behaviour. Kids in the first condition watched an adult model behaving aggressively towards an inflatable clown doll while in the control group the kids did not watch any model. They were then placed in the same room as the doll and their aggressive behaviour was recorded. The results showed that those kids who watched the aggressive model were more likely to react aggressively. This suggests that aggression is not just genetic but that it can be influenced by what we see in our environment, as well.

These results might provide an alternative explanation for Caspi et al's findings that child abuse was more likely to lead to aggression; perhaps participants in Caspi's study observed violence when they were children and were more likely to copy it when they got older. Therefore, it might not have been the genes or the abuse but instead it may have been about social learning.

One final factor to consider is the area of uncertainty about the extent to which genetic explanations can explain all types of aggression. This answer has mostly focused on one type of aggression: reactive aggression, as this is what Cohen studied and is also what is measured in fMRI studies like Meyer-Lindenberg's. These explanations do not necessarily cover other types of aggression and anti-social behaviour such as unprovoked aggression (when the aggression comes from a person who has not been threatened).

In conclusion, while the MAOA gene has been linked with aggression and this link could be explained by looking at its effects on brain activity, it is not the only factor that we need to consider when explaining behaviour. (approximately 1,000 words)

term (to what extent…)

Critical thinking is shown in the counter-arguments by explaining a range of points that address the "to what extent" command term.

The counter-arguments demonstrate an ability to evaluate research and provide alternative explanations.

A third study is used and it's relevant to the question.

The conclusion to this study explains its relevance to genetics.

An alternative explanation is given for previous results. This links both studies together nicely.

A third counter-argument is provided, which is showing a range of critical thinking.

The conclusion is clear and

IB Psychology Essay Rubric

Criterion A: Focus on the Question	Criterion B: Knowledge and Understanding	Criterion C: Use of Research to Support Answer	Criterion D: Critical Thinking	Criterion E: Clarity and Organisation
2 Explains the problem/issue raised in the question.	**5-6** The response demonstrates relevant, detailed knowledge and understanding. Psychological terminology is used appropriately.	**5-6** Relevant psychological research is used in support of the response and is thoroughly explained. Research selected is effectively used to develop the argument.	**5-6** The response consistently demonstrates well-developed critical thinking. Evaluation or discussion of relevant areas is consistently well developed.	**2** The answer demonstrates organization and clarity throughout the response.
1 Identifies the problem/issue raised in the question.	**3-4** The response demonstrates relevant knowledge and understanding but lacks detail. Psychological terminology is used but with errors that do not hamper understanding.	**3-4** Relevant psychological research is used in support of the response and is partly explained. Research selected partially develops the argument.	**3-4** The response contains critical thinking, but lacks development. Evaluation or discussion of most relevant areas is attempted but is not developed.	**1** The answer demonstrates some organization and clarity, but this is not sustained throughout the response.
0 Does not reach the standard described by the descriptors above.	**1-2** The response demonstrates limited relevant knowledge and understanding. Psychological terminology is used but with errors that hamper understanding.	**1-2** Limited relevant psychological research is used in the response. Research selected serves to repeat points already made.	**1-2** There is limited critical thinking and the response is mainly descriptive. Evaluation or discussion, if present, is superficial.	**0** Does not reach the standard described by the descriptors above.
	0 Does not reach the standard described by the descriptors above.	**0** Does not reach the standard described by the descriptors above.	**0** Does not reach the standard described by the descriptors above.	

Practice Paper Three Answers

These answers are in response to the practice paper on pg 164

1. (a) Identify the research method used and outline two characteristics of the method. (3 marks)

- *Method – true (laboratory) experiment*
- *A true experiment tests causal relationships between and IV and a DV (the IV in this study was the type of posing and there were three DVs, including sense of power, hormone levels and confidence)*
- *Often take place in controlled environments*
- *Random allocation is possible (random allocation was used in this study)*

(b) Describe the sampling method used in the study. (3 marks)

- *Sampling method = self-selected (volunteer) sampling*
- *Participants are the ones that approach the researchers to volunteer to participate in the study*
- *There is typically some form of marketing that calls for volunteers. In this case, they were responding to an advertisement in a school magazine*

(c) Suggest an alternative or additional research method giving one reason for your choice. (3 marks)
Additional method = interview

- *A semi-structured interview could be used to follow-up the experimental results. Researchers could ask questions about how powerful and confident they felt before and after doing the posing.*
- *This helps to triangulate findings and gathering qualitative data might help get a deeper understanding of the psychological effects of power posing.*

2. Describe the ethical considerations in reporting the results and explain additional ethical considerations that could be taken into account when applying the findings of the study. (6 marks)

Reporting the results: One consideration is anonymity. The researcher should keep the names of the participants anonymous. This protects their privacy and dignity. For example, people might not want others to know that they participated. This story also made big news, so if their names were published, they might get hassled by media.

Another consideration is how these results are reported in the media. Cuddy gave a popular TED Talk, so she has an ethical responsibility to genuinely report the results, including if she was aware of any replication issues that the study was facing (e.g. not being replicated). Not reporting all results could be deemed unethical. Similarly, journalists reporting the results need to be ethical in how they are writing about the study, which would include its failure to be replicated.

It can be argued that reporting the possible applications of the results (e.g. for job interviews) could be unethical if the experiment has not had rigorous replications.

Applying the findings: One consideration related to applying the findings is informed consent. The researcher hypothesized that power posing would have an effect and were probably aware of the potential applications before they conducted the study; they would need to consider whether or not to disclose this information during the informed consent phase or the debriefing phase of the study.

Cuddy began applying these findings in her motivational talks to "…companies and organizations so people could use power posing to help in their personal and professional lives." However, the study has failed numerous replications and the validity of the findings are in doubt. It would be highly unethical to continue to deliver these talks with this knowledge.

There could be ethical issues in applying these findings in different cultures. For example, the researchers conclude that this has applications for people wanting to challenge someone with a higher rank (e.g. a boss). This is not always a desirable quality in cultures (for example, in some cultures it is considered disrespectful to challenge people who have higher status than you do) so it could be considered unethical to use these findings to promote this type of behaviour.

3. Discuss how the researcher in the study could avoid bias. (9 marks)

Bias is when an individual's existing thoughts, beliefs or ideas influence their thinking or behaviour. Researcher bias is when the thoughts, beliefs or ideas of the researcher are negatively influencing the results of the study in some way. In this study, there were a few ways the researchers could have avoided bias, including triangulation, sampling, controls and replication.

To begin with, researcher bias is a real issue that could have affected this study because the researchers had a preconceived idea about what might happen as they hypothesized that "…high-power poses (compared with low-power poses) would cause individuals to experience elevated testosterone, decreased cortisol, increased feelings of power, and higher risk tolerance." Also, we can see the bias from the response by Cuddy when she said "everything went in the direction it was supposed to."

Triangulation is one way to reduce bias. For example, having more than one researcher gather and analyze the data (researcher triangulation) could help to reduce bias. This could have been done with the questionnaires and assessing the hormone samples. However, one limitation of this is that it requires more people and more work. Researchers could not conduct a study themselves and would need to find others to help.

Using a double-blind design is another way bias could have been avoided. For example, the researchers who analyzed the hormone samples or analyzed the questionnaire data should have been blind and not known which participant was in which condition. One limitation of this is that it requires someone who is neutral to the experiment to oversee the procedures (because at least one person needs to know who is in which condition so that the analysis can be conducted.

The study used a self-selected sample, which could result in a biased sample because not everyone had an equal chance of being in the study. It may have led to sampling bias. For example, the effects might only be noticeable for young people. One way to avoid this would have been to use a more representative sampling method, like random sampling. However, a limitation with this is that random sampling is often not practical because it's difficult to make sure that every person in the target population has an equal chance of participating in the study.

One last way that researcher bias could been avoided is through having other researchers replicate the study to see if they get the same results. If different researchers get the same results, it suggests that bias is not a factor. However, this study has been replicated 11 times and all have failed to get the same results, which means that there is a chance that researcher bias was a factor in the initial study.

In conclusion, while this study's findings are interesting, it is clear that researcher bias could have been an issue and there are a few ways the researchers could avoid this.

Paper 3, Question 3 Rubric

Mark	Level Descriptor
7-9	The question is understood and answered in a focused and effective manner with an accurate argument that addresses the requirements of the question. The response contains accurate references to approaches to research with regard to the question, describing their strengths and limitations. The response makes effective use of the stimulus material.
4-6	The question is understood, but only partially answered, resulting in an argument of limited scope. The response contains mostly accurate references to approaches to research which are linked explicitly to the question. The response makes appropriate but limited use of the stimulus material.
1-3	The question is misunderstood and the central issue is not identified correctly, resulting in a mostly irrelevant argument. The response contains mostly inaccurate references to the approaches to research or these are irrelevant to the question. The reference to the stimulus material relies heavily on direct quotations from the text.
0	The answer does not reach a standard described by the descriptors below.

Study Smarter

Take the time to plan your approach to each topic and see how you can maximize the overlaps between the approaches and the options.

Work Hard

Try to create your own revision materials based on the information in this book. For example, making flashcards is an excellent way to review key terms and studies. If you make Quizlet flashcards you can easily print these so you have a hard copy set (instructions on our blog).

Be Brave

Do not be afraid to use different examples to the ones I have listed in this textbook for each topic. For example, just because Passamonti's study and the example of serotonin being linked with antisocial behaviour is in the neurotransmitters topic in the biological approach, it doesn't mean you can't ignore that and use the materials from the Abnormal option on SSRIs and serotonins connection with PTSD when writing an answer for the neurotransmitters topic.

Many a little makes a mickle!

This means that a little bit of work very frequently will amount to a large amount of work. Do not leave your revision until the last minute – set yourself a goal of studying 10 minutes every night for at least 8 weeks leading up to your exams.

Ask Questions

If you're not sure, ask! Your teacher is your first person you should ask and you can always post questions to our Facebook Group (ThemEd's IB Psychology Students – QR code is at the front of this book).

Think like a psychologist

Think about the key questions you're expected to understand for each topic and think how these relate to psychology as a subject. For example, try not just to look at the biological approach as a collection of complex terms and studies – keep thinking that each topic is just an example of how we're understanding behaviour by looking at biology. Similarly, when you're studying theories like social identity theory, think first about what the theory is trying to explain and then revise the theory so that you can provide that explanation.

GOOD LUCK!

Lightning Source UK Ltd.
Milton Keynes UK
UKHW051949010323
417861UK00010B/45